T0192600

Architecting and Operating OpenShift Clusters

OpenShift for Infrastructure and Operations Teams

William Caban

Apress®

Architecting and Operating OpenShift Clusters

William Caban
Columbia, MD, USA

ISBN-13 (pbk): 978-1-4842-4984-0
https://doi.org/10.1007/978-1-4842-4985-7

ISBN-13 (electronic): 978-1-4842-4985-7

Copyright © 2019 by William Caban

This work is subject to copyright. All rights are reserved by the Publisher, whether the whole or part of the material is concerned, specifically the rights of translation, reprinting, reuse of illustrations, recitation, broadcasting, reproduction on microfilms or in any other physical way, and transmission or information storage and retrieval, electronic adaptation, computer software, or by similar or dissimilar methodology now known or hereafter developed.

Trademarked names, logos, and images may appear in this book. Rather than use a trademark symbol with every occurrence of a trademarked name, logo, or image we use the names, logos, and images only in an editorial fashion and to the benefit of the trademark owner, with no intention of infringement of the trademark.

The use in this publication of trade names, trademarks, service marks, and similar terms, even if they are not identified as such, is not to be taken as an expression of opinion as to whether or not they are subject to proprietary rights.

While the advice and information in this book are believed to be true and accurate at the date of publication, neither the authors nor the editors nor the publisher can accept any legal responsibility for any errors or omissions that may be made. The publisher makes no warranty, express or implied, with respect to the material contained herein.

Managing Director, Apress Media LLC: Welmoed Spahr
Acquisitions Editor: Louise Corrigan
Development Editor: James Markham
Coordinating Editor: Nancy Chen

Cover designed by eStudioCalamar

Cover image designed by Freepik (www.freepik.com)

Distributed to the book trade worldwide by Springer Science+Business Media New York, 233 Spring Street, 6th Floor, New York, NY 10013. Phone 1-800-SPRINGER, fax (201) 348-4505, e-mail orders-ny@springer-sbm.com, or visit www.springeronline.com. Apress Media, LLC is a California LLC and the sole member (owner) is Springer Science + Business Media Finance Inc (SSBM Finance Inc). SSBM Finance Inc is a **Delaware** corporation.

For information on translations, please e-mail rights@apress.com, or visit http://www.apress.com/rights-permissions.

Apress titles may be purchased in bulk for academic, corporate, or promotional use. eBook versions and licenses are also available for most titles. For more information, reference our Print and eBook Bulk Sales web page at http://www.apress.com/bulk-sales.

Any source code or other supplementary material referenced by the author in this book is available to readers on GitHub via the book's product page, located at www.apress.com/9781484249840. For more detailed information, please visit http://www.apress.com/source-code.

Printed on acid-free paper

To my wife, Maria, who has always supported my constantly traveling job and my urge to drive technical excellence. You are, and always will be, my perfect wife and the supermom to our wonderful children.

To my son Seth and to my daughter Juliette for their patience with the many days and weekends I had to unplug from everything to stay home writing. Thank you for your understanding and support. You two are the greatest son and the greatest daughter a father can have.

To my parents, Willie and Annie, without whom none of my success would be possible.

Table of Contents

About the Author

William Caban has more than 25 years of experience in IT and has been consulting and designing large-scale datacenter solutions in multiple vertical markets. He has worked for diverse customers ranging from financial institutions, healthcare institutions, and service providers. His personal motto is "Changing the world one 'bit' at a time." He has written several courses and training guides in the past. This is his first book with Apress.

About the Technical Reviewer

James Cryer is a Lead Principal Engineer with over 8 years of experience working with Cloud-native solutions on AWS, GCP, and Azure. James has a passion for architecting and developing highly available, fault-tolerant, and secure systems. James' experience is broad; he has worked in a variety of sectors with companies such as the BBC, Investec Asset Management, and, more recently, Sophos. When away from his laptop, James loves to travel with his wife and child, get outdoors, and read.

Acknowledgments

This book is the result of my quest to find a way to provide additional technical information about *OpenShift Container Platform (OCP)* and *OKD* to answer the type of questions I see from the operations teams in our customers today. The same questions my former self had many years ago when I started migrating from upstream Kubernetes into a supported Kubernetes distribution.

This book has been possible thanks to the support from a brilliant Red Hat OpenShift-SME community, the Red Hat OpenShift Business Unit, and each one of the product managers and their teams which are the ones that make the OpenShift magic happen. From these, I would like to give a special thank you to Marc Curry, Ben Breard, Brian Harrington, Paul Morie, and William Oliveira. Thank you for the times you took to reply an e-mail or hop in a call to answer my many questions trying to understand the behind-the-scenes plumbing of the many features.

Also, some of the information in this book has been possible thanks to the extended community from which I would like to give a special thank you to Salah Chaou and Alpika Singh (DriveScale Inc.), Christopher Kurka (HPE), and Bin Zhou (Lenovo).

Introduction

The rapid evolution of the Kubernetes platform and the ecosystem around it represents an excellent opportunity to drive modernization inside an organization while defining new operational paradigms.

This book is for the architects and operations teams of those organizations using OpenShift as one of their tools in their transformation. This is for the organization's hidden heroes that need to have a good understanding of how different elements interact in such a platform to be able to optimize it for their organization's specific workloads. This is not a book listing all the existing commands for every possible option, but a book explaining how the platform comes together to understand the possible locations in features into where to apply fine-tunings for their optimization.

CHAPTER 1

The OpenShift Architecture

To properly architect an OpenShift cluster, we need to understand the different components of the platform, their roles, and how they interact with each other. This base knowledge is important to be able to fine-tune OpenShift cluster design to your organization's need beyond what is covered in this book.

Before going into each main component of OpenShift, it is important to understand how it relates to *Linux Containers* and *Kubernetes*.

Linux Containers

Nowadays, when we see the term *Linux Containers,* it is easy to think it only refers to *Docker,* but that is not the case. The term *Linux Containers* denotes a group of technologies used to package and isolate applications, their dependencies, and their runtimes, in a portable way so it can be moved between environments while retaining full functionality.

A source of confusion is because the term *Docker* refers to various elements of a technology that popularized the *Linux Containers*.

First, there is *Docker Inc.*, the name of the company that popularized the Linux Containers technology with the *Docker* platform. The *Docker* platform was originally built as a series of enhancements on top of the LXC technology to bring better isolation and portability to the containers.

Second, there is *Docker Daemon* which is the daemon or service that serves the Docker API, handles the API requests, and manages images, containers, networks, and volumes.

1

© William Caban 2019
W. Caban, *Architecting and Operating OpenShift Clusters*, https://doi.org/10.1007/978-1-4842-4985-7_1

Finally, there are *Images* and *Containers* respectively referred to as the *Docker Images* and *Docker Containers*. The *Image* is the read-only template containing the application, the application dependencies, and the required runtime environment. All this packaged in a standard format used by the *Docker Daemon*. The *Container* refers to a runnable instance of an *Image*.

As it can be seen in Figure 1-1, *Docker* is a client-server application to build and run containers following a standardized container format. The *docker* client is the tool used to interact with the docker server over the API exposed by the *Docker Daemon*.

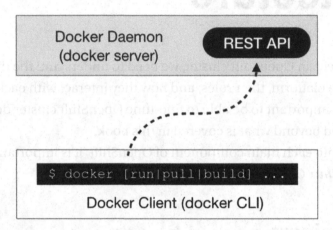

Figure 1-1. *The Docker client-server architecture*

Note   The terms *Docker Daemon* and *Docker Engine* are used interchangeably to refer to the docker server.

Linux Container: Under the Hood

Beyond the conceptual definitions of containers as an artifact containing an application and all its dependencies, or as an artifact that is built once and deployed "anywhere," what is a Linux Container?

To understand containers and how they work, we must explore some important building blocks at the Linux Kernel: *namespaces* and *cgroups*.

Linux *namespaces* provide process isolation. There are seven[1] kinds of Kernel namespaces:

- **Mount**: The mount namespace isolates the set of filesystem mount points. This enables the creation of different views of the filesystem hierarchy or making certain mount points read-only for processes in different mount namespaces.

- **UTC**: This namespace enables for each container to have its own *hostname* and NIS domain name.

- **IPC**: This isolates interprocess communication (IPC) resources between namespaces. This enables more than one container to create shared memory segments and semaphores with the same name but is not able to interact with other containers' memory segments or shared memory.

- **PID**: Each process receives PID namespace provided. The container only sees the processes within the container and not any processes on the host or other containers.

- **Network**: This allows the container to only communicate with internal or external networks. This provides a loopback interface as the initial network interface. Additional physical or virtual network interfaces can be added to the namespace. Each namespace maintains a set of IP addresses and its own routing table.

- **User**: This isolates the *user* IDs between namespaces providing privilege isolation and *user* ID segregation.

- **Control Group (cgroup)** (the namespace): This virtualizes the view of *cgroups* for a set of processes enabling better confinement of containerized processes.

The namespaces are Kernel-level capabilities. As such, each namespace has visibility about all the host capabilities and system resources. Namespaces isolate system

---

[1]In some documentation, you may find a statement about the existence of six namespaces, and in other documentations, you will find seven namespaces listed. Those lists do not count the *cgroup namespace* which virtualizes the *cgroup* capabilities as a namespace. For details about the namespace vs. the capability, refer to the Linux man page *cgroup_namespaces,* the Linux man page for *cgroups,* and the Linux man page for *namespaces.*

resources by providing an abstraction layer for the processes inside the namespaces. It does this by creating a view where it appears as the processes have the global resources.

A way to think about *namespaces* is going back to our science fiction world of *parallel universes*. Each *namespace* is a parallel reality or a parallel universe inside the universe represented by the host. These parallel universes do not know of the existence of any other universe and cannot interfere with them.

Now, if each namespace has a full view of the host system resources, by default, it could assume it can consume all the resources it detects, for example, all the memory and all the CPU resources. To limit the access to the system resources is the functionality of the next building block: *Control Groups* or *cgroups*.

Control Groups (cgroups), the Kernel feature, are used for limiting, accounting, and controlling resources (i.e., memory, CPU, I/O, check pointing) of a collection of processes. A container is a collection of processes under a PID namespace. To control and limit resources for a container, we use *cgroups*.

Bringing all these concepts together, we can visualize containers as illustrated in Figure 1-2.

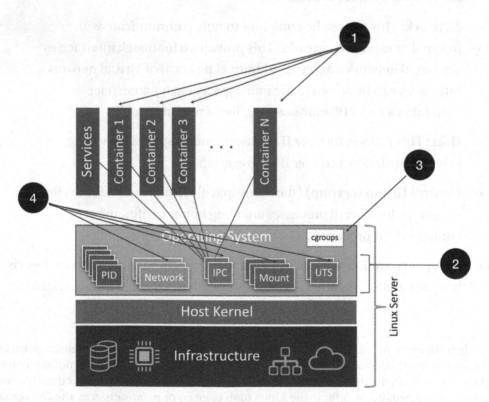

Figure 1-2. *Linux namespaces and Containers*

To explain the details of Figure 1-2, follow the numbers from the illustration with the numbers of this list:

1. Each *Container* has a unique PID namespace running its group of process. Inside the Container, the first process is seen as PID 1. From the host perspective, the *Container PID* is a regular process ID.

2. The *Namespaces* exist at the Kernel level. Namespaces provide the isolation for the system resource but are part of the same Kernel.

3. *Control Groups* or *cgroups*, the feature, are used to limit the access to system resources by a group of processes.

4. In addition to the PID namespace, *Containers* will have other dedicated namespaces which provide their view of system resources or they can use the *default namespace* which is shared with the host.

Container Specifications

As can be seen from the previous section, from the technical perspective, in its core, Linux containers are a group of Linux processes existing in *namespaces* using *cgroups* to control and limit the access to system resources.

The core building blocks for Linux Containers are simple but powerful. Following the popularity of *Docker* containers, the industry recognized the need for a set of specifications (Figure 1-3) supported by open communities to maintain compatibility while enabling innovation and creation of solutions on top of the capabilities provided by Linux Containers.

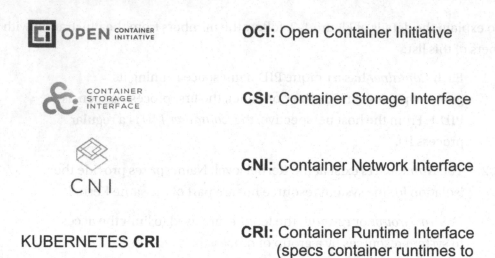

OCI: Open Container Initiative

CSI: Container Storage Interface

CNI: Container Network Interface

CRI: Container Runtime Interface (specs container runtimes to integrate with kubelet)

Figure 1-3. *The Container specifications*

Today, the widely recognized container specifications are

1. **Open Container Initiative (OCI)**: The OCI specification defines a *standard* container format. This is what is usually referred as the *Docker format* (Figure 1-4).

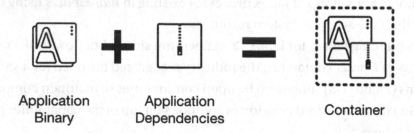

Application Binary   Application Dependencies   Container

Figure 1-4. *The OCI-compliant container image*

Note   Demystifying containers—An OCI-compliant image, or an image following the *Docker format*, can be seen as a TAR file of a filesystem layout containing the application binaries, its dependencies, and some XML formatted files with metadata describing the container namespaces. A container with multiple layers is a TAR file of TAR files, each representing a particular layer of the container.

---

2. **Container Storage Interface (CSI)**: The CSI specification
   describes a standardized interface to present storage resources to
   a container. Prior to this specification, each storage vendor had
   to create, certify, and maintain their own storage plugin for every
   container solution. With CSI, vendors maintain a single plugin
   which can be used by any container solution supporting the
   specification.

3. **Container Network Interface (CNI)**: The CNI specification
   standardizes an interface to provide networking services
   to containers. This helped in reducing the proliferation of
   networking plugins which were incompatible among themselves.

Container Runtime and Kubernetes

The creation of the OCI specification also provided the freedom to replace the container
runtime beyond the *Docker Daemon*. A *container runtime* only needs to understand the
OCI format to be able to run the container.

Traditionally, by default, container runtime like the *Docker Daemon* handles
containers in a single host. Over time, some of these tools evolved into fat daemons or
services trying to include container orchestration and to solve and handle too many
things (resource consumptions, scheduling, control, etc.).

Note   For the remaining of this book, we use the term Linux Container,
Containers, and Container Images to refer to a Linux Container following the OCI
specification.

With Kubernetes, Google provided a way to orchestrate, manage, and operate
containers at scale across thousands of nodes. Kubernetes abstracted the management
of individual containers with the notion of managing *Pods* and *Services*. Kubernetes,
as the container orchestration platform, requires minimal actions to be handled by the
container runtimes: create Pod, start Pod, stop Pod, and remove Pod.

With this new understanding, the Kubernetes community explored ways to replace
traditional fat daemons with purpose built container runtimes. The community defined

7

the **Container Runtime Interface (CRI). CRI**[2] provides a specification for integrating container runtimes with the *kubelet* service at each Kubernetes worker node. Since then, there has been a proliferation of CRI-compliant container runtimes for Kubernetes optimizing for speed, isolation, and breaking dependencies to a runtime daemon. Among these new options, we can find containerd, Kata Containers, and CRI-O.

Note   OpenShift 3.x supports the *Docker Daemon* as the default container runtime. Starting with OpenShift 3.10, it also supports CRI-O as the container runtime. With OpenShift 4.0, CRI-O will be the default container runtime.

Introduction to OpenShift Architecture Components

OpenShift is built on top of Kubernetes. While Kubernetes provides the container orchestration capabilities, *Pod* resiliency, *Services* definitions, and *Deployment* constructs to describe the desire state of a microservice-based application, there are many other components required to make it work. For example, Kubernetes does not provide a default Software-Defined Networking (*SDN*) or a default method to steer traffic into the applications running on Kubernetes clusters. It is up to the cluster admin to bring additional tools and projects to operate and manage the Kubernetes cluster and any application running on it. For the developers it also means they need to learn a new CLI or YAML specification to be able to deploy and test their applications. For the security teams, it means figuring out ways to map the organization's policies into new constructs and identifying additional projects to enforce additional ones not provided by the default capabilities of Kubernetes.

These additional capabilities are part of what is provided out of the box with OpenShift Container Platform or OKD (the upstream community project) (see Figure 1-5). In fact, at the time of this writing, OpenShift is a Kubernetes superset combining over 200 open source projects into a fully integrated solution with strong focus on a developer experience, operational capabilities, monitoring, and management with strong and secure defaults. All these while being pluggable so platform admins

---

[2]The CRI specification defines four actions: CreatePod, StartPod, StopPod, and RemovePod.

can replace out of the box components and services with their own. For example, using third-party SDN to provide the networking capabilities or third-party storage solutions to provide persistent storage for the applications running in the environment.

The *OKD* based commercial distribution productized and supported by Red Hat.	The *Origin* community distribution of Kubernetes that powers Red Hat OpenShift.
http://openshift.com	http://okd.io

Figure 1-5. *OpenShift Container Platform (OCP) vs. OKD (formerly OpenShift Origin)*

Note   In this book the term OpenShift is used to denote both the OpenShift Container Platform (OCP), which is the Red Hat–supported product, and OKD, the upstream community project. Unless otherwise specified, everything in this book applies to OCP and OKD.

Kubernetes Constructs

Having Kubernetes as its foundation, OpenShift inherits all the base constructs for the *Containers'* orchestration from Kubernetes and, in addition, extends them. A great deal of these extensions come from adding the capabilities or functionalities that are not part of the base of Kubernetes but that are required to successfully operate the platform. Other extensions come from enforcing prescriptive best practices designed to comply with the stability and regulations required on enterprise environments (i.e., RBAC, CI/CD Pipelines, etc.).

Some of the important Kubernetes constructs inherited by OpenShift (not an exhaustive list) are

- **Pods**: A *Pod* is a group of one or more tightly coupled *Containers* sharing a set of Linux namespaces and cgroups (Figure 1-6). Among those, the *Containers* inside the Pod share the same *Mount* and *Network* namespace (i.e., same IP address and TCP/UDP ports) (see per-Pod IP addresses in Figure 1-6). Within a *Pod* each *Container* may have further sub-isolations (i.e., different UTC namespaces). *Pods* communicate with each other using *localhost*.

IP: 10.5.1.20   IP: 10.5.1.73   IP: 10.5.1.42

Pod with single App Container. This is the most common and preferred type of Pod.

Pod with primary App Container and helper sidecar Container (i.e. using helper as data change watcher)

Pod with App Container and Sidecar Container (i.e. when using Envoy Proxy)

 Container Volumes: The *Volumes* can be shared among *Containers* in the same *Pod*

Figure 1-6. *Example of Pod configurations*

- **Services**: A *Service* is a Kubernetes object that maps one or more incoming ports to *targetPorts* at a selected set of target of *Pods*. These represent a microservice or an application running on the cluster. The *Services* are discoverable by *Pods* running on the cluster. Generally, *Pods* interact with other applications or microservice on the cluster through the *Service* object (Figure 1-7).

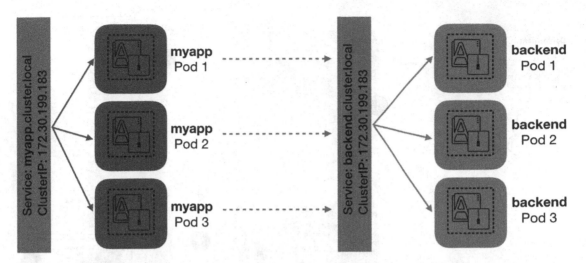

Figure 1-7. *The Kubernetes Service object abstracts one or more Pods running an application or microservice*

- ***ReplicationController (RC)***: The *ReplicationController* (the object) ensures the requested number of *Pods* are running at any given time. If there are too many *Pods*, the *ReplicationController* terminates any number of *Pods* in excess of the specified amount. If there are too few, the *ReplicationController* starts additional *Pods* until the specified amount. In case of a *Pod* failure, or if *Pods* are deleted or terminated, the *ReplicationController* takes care of re-creating the failed, deleted, or terminated *Pods* to match the requested number of *Pods*.

- ***ReplicaSets***: The *ReplicaSets* are considered the next generation of *ReplicationControllers*. From the high-level perspective, *ReplicaSets* provide the same functionalities as the *ReplicationControllers* with the difference being these are intended to be managed by *Deployments*.

- ***Deployment*** *(the object)*: The *Deployment* object is a declarative configuration describing the desired state, quantity, and version of Pods to deploy. The *Deployment controller* defines a *ReplicaSet* that creates new *Pods* or executes a rolling upgrade with the new version of the *Pods*. The *Deployment Controller* changes and maintains the state of the *Pod* and *ReplicaSet* to match the desire state (Figure 1-8).

11

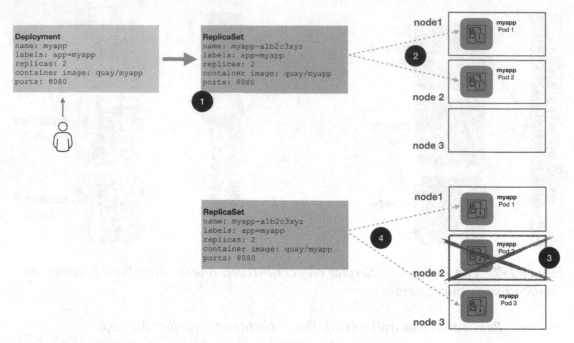

Figure 1-8. *Deployment and ReplicaSet*

- The steps illustrated by the pseudocode in Figure 1-8 are as follows:

  1. The *Deployment* object creates a *ReplicaSet* with the information of the desired state.

  2. The *ReplicaSet* deploys the requested version and total number of *Pods*.

  3. In case of *Pod* failure (i.e., because of node failure), the total number of *Pods* will be less than the desired amount.

  4. The *ReplicaSet* will deploy additional Pods until the number of desired replicas specified by the *Deployment*.

- **Volumes**: The *Volumes* provide persistent storage for the Containers inside a *Pod*. Data in a *Volume* is preserved across Container restarts. *Volumes* outlive *Containers* and remain in existence for the lifetime of a *Pod*.

- **PersistentVolume (PV)**: The *PersistentVolume* represents the actual storage resource provisioned for the cluster. *PVs* are *Volume* plugins with a lifecycle independent of any *Pod* that uses the *PV*.

- *PersistentVolumeClaim (PVC)*: The *PersistentVolumeClaim* is the storage request for the PV storage resources. A *PVC* is bind to a *PV* matching the requested storage characteristics and access mode. Refer to Figure 1-9.

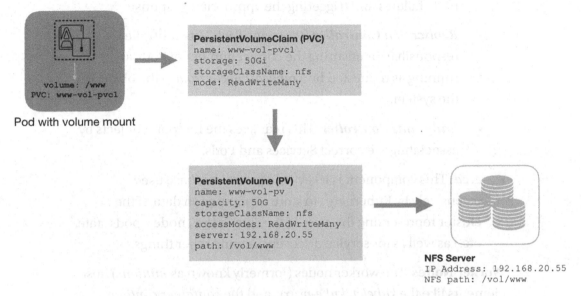

Figure 1-9. *Relationship between Volume, PersistentVolumeClaim, and PersistentVolume*

The Kubernetes architecture is comprised of the following core elements (not an exhaustive list):

- **Master Nodes**: The master nodes are the nodes hosting core elements of the control plane like (not an exhaustive list) the *kube-api-server, kube-scheduler, kube-controller-manager,* and in many instances the *etcd* database.

  - *kube-api-server*: This component is what is commonly referred as the Kubernetes API. This is the frontend API to the control plane of the Kubernetes cluster.

  - *kube-scheduler*: This component takes care of handling the scheduling of Pods into nodes, taking into account resource requirements, policy constraints, affinity or anti-affinity rules, and other filters.

13

- *kube-controller-manager*: This component runs multiple controller services at the master. Among these controllers, we can find (not an exhaustive list)

  - *Node Controller*: This controller is responsible for detecting node failures and triggering the appropriate response.

  - *Replication Controller* (*the controller*): This controller is responsible for ensuring the correct number of Pods are running as requested by a *replication controller* (the object) in the system.

  - *Endpoints Controller*: This manages the Endpoint objects by associating the correct Services and Pods.

- *etcd*: This component is a key-value store database used extensively by Kubernetes to store configuration data of the cluster representing the state of the cluster (i.e., nodes, pods state, etc.) as well as for service discovery, among other things.

- **Worker Nodes**: The worker nodes (formerly known as *minions*) host elements like the *kubelet*, *kube-proxy,* and the *container runtime*.

- *kubelet*: Also known as the *node agent*, is the Kubernetes agent that runs on each node. The *kubelet* ensures containers are started and continue to run as specified by the *container manifest* (a YAML file describing a Pod) and updates the node accordingly.

- *kube-proxy*: A simple Kubernetes network proxy agent running on each node. The *kube-proxy* abstracts network services defined on the host, forwards traffic to the appropriate *Service,* and provides traffic load balancing. It does this by managing *iptables* rules of the host.

- *A Container Runtime*: Any CRI-compliant runtime capable of running OCI-compliant *Containers* (i.e., Docker Daemon, CRI-O, containerd, etc.).

- **Ancillary Services**: Services required for the proper operation of the Kubernetes cluster but that are not technically considered to be part of the Kubernetes components. These services may be running as part of the *Master Nodes, Worker Nodes,* or dedicated *Nodes,* or even be services external to the cluster. Among these services, we can find DNS (i.e., SkyDNS or KubeDNS), Web UI Dashboards, container resource monitoring services, and cluster-level monitoring and logging services.

Figure 1-10 illustrates how all these elements integrate and interact to form the Kubernetes architecture.

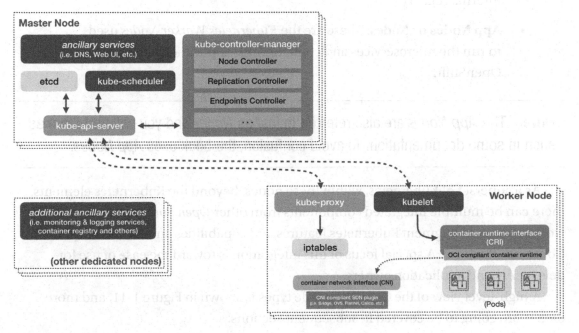

Figure 1-10. *The elements of the Kubernetes architecture*

OpenShift Constructs

The OpenShift architecture builds on top of Kubernetes and is comprised of three types of nodes:

- **Master Nodes**: These nodes are *Kubernetes Master Nodes* which may be providing additional functionalities like the web console with the self-service portal as well as the developers and operations-focused dashboards.

- **Infrastructure Nodes**: These are *Kubernetes Worker Nodes* dedicated to host functionalities like the *OpenShift Routes* and the OpenShift internal registry.

- **App Nodes or Nodes**: These are the *Kubernetes Worker Nodes* used to run the microservices and containerized applications deployed on OpenShift.

Note   The *App Nodes* are also referred to just as *Nodes* and you will find them as such in some documentation. To avoid confusion, the book uses *App Nodes.*

As a superset of Kubernetes, within these nodes, beyond the Kubernetes elements, there can be multiple integrated components from other *Open Source* projects that work together to augment Kubernetes features and capabilities and form the OpenShift Container Platform. A special focus of this integration is toward the ease of use for developers and application owners.

A high-level view of the OpenShift node types is shown in Figure 1-11, and more details are going to be covered in subsequent sections.

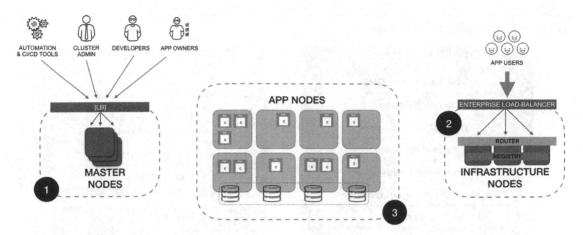

Figure 1-11. *The OpenShift node types*

Master Nodes

The *Master Nodes* are the main control elements of the OpenShift control plane.
These are Kubernetes Master Nodes and they provide the services expected from any
Kubernetes Master and additionally provide a series of functionalities built on top of
Kubernetes which create OpenShift. See Figure 1-12 for reference.

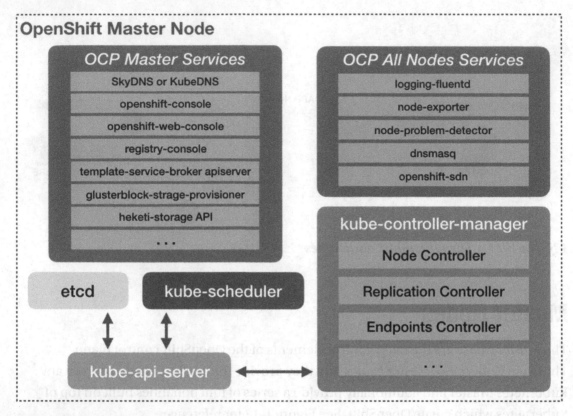

Figure 1-12. *OpenShift Master Node details*

From Figure 1-12 we can see the *Kubernetes Master Node* elements are present in the *OpenShift Master Nodes.* The actual list of these will be dependent on the services enabled for the cluster as many are optional services.

- **Kubernetes DNS**: The OpenShift 3.x releases are using SkyDNS as part of Kube-DNS. As of the writing of this book, this is transitioning to CoreDNS. By default, this DNS service listens on port 8053.

- **OpenShift Web Console**: This is the microservice providing the self-service portal or developer console.

- **OpenShift Console**: This is the microservice providing the operations console (former Tectonic console).

- **Registry Console**: This is the microservice providing a basic web UI to interact with the internal container registry.

- Additional **APIs** and **Consoles**: Many optional cluster services
  have their own API interfaces and web frontends. These APIs and
  frontends are provided as containers which, by default, will be hosted
  in the *Master Nodes*. Some examples are Template Service Brokers
  and the OpenShift Container Storage (glusterfs).

In addition, in Figure 1-12 we can see a partial list of services that may be present in every OpenShift Node. Their presence depends on the services enabled for the cluster. Let's go into the details of some of them (the actual service names may have slightly variations from the containers or Pods name):

- *Fluentd*: The Fluentd service runs in every node. It aggregates logs
  from the host Node, including logs from *Pods* and *Projects*, and sends
  them to the *Elasticsearch (ES)* database running on the *Infrastructure
  Nodes.*

- *node-exporter and kube-state-metrics*: These services are part of
  the OpenShift cluster monitoring solution based on Prometheus.
  The *node-exporter*[3] agent collects node hardware and OS metrics and
  makes them available for Prometheus. The *kube-state-metrics* agent
  converts metrics from Kubernetes objects (i.e., from the *kubelet*) into
  metrics consumable by Prometheus.

- *node-problem-detector*: This is a service that runs in each node to
  detect multiple problems[4] on the node and reports them to the API
  Server.

- *dnsmasq*: As part of the Kube-DNS service, this service is
  automatically configured on all nodes. Pods use the node hosting
  them as their default DNS. When receiving a name resolution
  request, dnsmasq will send the query to the *Kubernetes DNS* at the
  Master Nodes, and if not a resolution, it will try recursive DNS to the
  upstream DNS server originally configured on the node.

---

[3]For more details, visit https://github.com/prometheus/node_exporter
[4]For more details, visit https://github.com/kubernetes/node-problem-detector

Note   Every node is running *dnsmasq* listening on port 53. For this reason, nodes cannot run any other type of DNS application.

- ***openshift-sdn***: This consists of a series of privileged containers providing the Software-Defined Network (SDN) of the OpenShift cluster using Open vSwitch (OVS).

Infrastructure Nodes

These are dedicated *Kubernetes Worker Nodes* hosting important elements for the proper operation of the OpenShift Cluster. Among these, we have the *Container Registry* and the *OpenShift Router*. Figure 1-13 illustrates some additional services running on the *Infrastructure Nodes*.

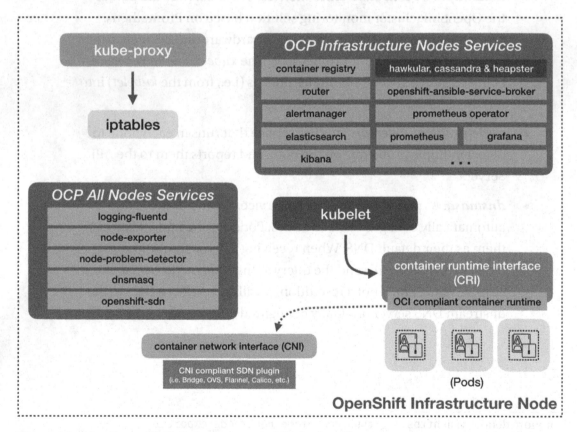

Figure 1-13. *OpenShift Infrastructure Node details*

From the diagram in Figure 1-13, we can deduce on *Infrastructure Nodes* there are some services which seem to overlap in functionalities. This is the case with services like *Hawkular, Cassandra, and Heapster* which are being deprecated in OpenShift 3.11 and being replaced by the Prometheus-based monitoring solution which is deployed and managed by the Prometheus Operator.

As with the *Master Nodes*, the exact list of services running on the *Infrastructure Nodes* is completely dependent on the services enabled for the cluster. Out of the services shown in the illustration, only few deserve mention at this point:

- **OpenShift Container Registry (OCR)**: The *OpenShift Container Registry* is a containerized *Docker Registry* service used internally by the cluster. Additional details are covered in the corresponding section.

- **OpenShift Router**: The *OpenShift Router* is used to expose a *Kubernetes Service* to external clients by a *FQDN*. Additional details are covered in the corresponding section.

- **Elasticsearch (ES) and Kibana**: *Elasticsearch* is used to collect all the logs sent by the *Fluentd* service running in every node. The *Kibana Web UI* is used to interact with the data and create visualization and dashboards of the aggregated data.

- **Prometheus**, **Grafana**, and the **Prometheus Operator**: These are the components of the new *OpenShift Monitoring* and *Metrics* solution. These are used to collect information about the health of the cluster and all the services and components running on it. The *Grafana Web UI* is used to create dashboards visualizing the status of the elements being monitored.

App Nodes

The OpenShift App Nodes, or simply *OpenShift Nodes*, are *Kubernetes Worker Nodes* dedicated to running the workloads deployed to an OpenShift cluster. These include applications, microservices, or containerized applications.

As it can be seen in Figure 1-14, the OpenShift App Nodes are dedicated to running the applications deployed on the OpenShift cluster. Beyond the elements of the

Kubernetes Nodes, it contains the common OpenShift Services to provide the network connectivity for the Pods, the DNS resolution, node monitoring, and log aggregation.

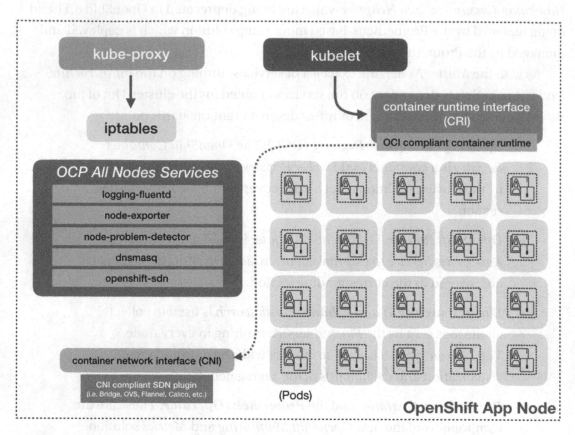

Figure 1-14. *OpenShift App Node details*

OpenShift Consoles

OpenShift provides developer-centric consoles and operations-centric consoles. The first console a user of the platforms receives is the *Service Catalog console* (see Figure 1-15) which contains the self-service catalog of pre-approved container images and templates (see #2 of Figure 1-15) available for the particular user. These catalogs can be cluster-wide catalogs or project-specific catalogs. From this initial console, the user can choose from a drop-down menu (see #1 of Figure 1-15) to switch to the operations *Cluster Console*.

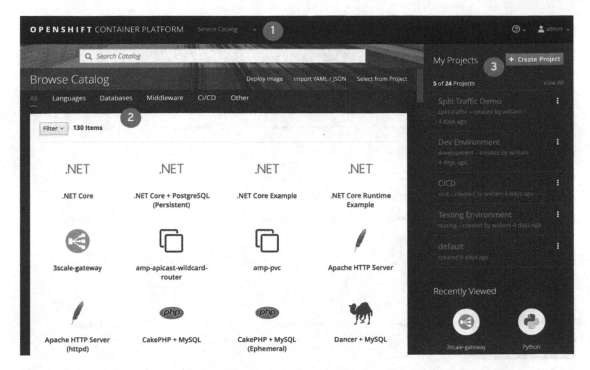

Figure 1-15. *The OpenShift self-service portal also known as the developer console*

The *Cluster Console* (Figure 1-16), sometimes referred to as the *Cluster Administrator Console,* provides access to cluster operations and functions. At first glance it provides a cluster health and status view (see #1 and #2 of Figure 1-16).

Figure 1-16. *The OpenShift Cluster Console also known as the cluster admin console*

For users with deep understanding of the Kubernetes, this console also exposes the Kubernetes objects with a more traditional *Container as a Service (CaaS)* experience (see #1 of Figure 1-17). From here, a cluster admin has an aggregated view into the Kubernetes and OpenShift objects like *Namespaces, Pods, Deployments, Secrets, Deployment Configs,* and *ConfigMaps.*

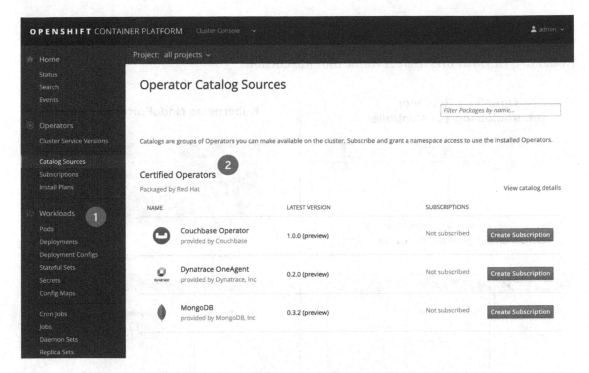

Figure 1-17. *The OpenShift Cluster Console managing subscriptions to Kubernetes Operators*

In addition, the *Cluster Console* provides a graphical interface for interacting with *Kubernetes Operators* (see #2 of Figure 1-17).

OpenShift Routers

Steering traffic to applications running on a Kubernetes cluster, until this day with Kubernetes 1.13, it is still highly dependent on where the Kubernetes cluster is running (i.e., on-premise vs. at a Cloud provider). When using a Kubernetes offering from a Cloud provider, they will provide a network service that maps to the *LoadBalancer* object in Kubernetes. Those load balancers provided by the Cloud infrastructure are what is used to steer traffic to the *Service* objects or *Pods* in the cluster.

Outside these options, it is up to the cluster operator to combine Kubernetes constructs with third-party solutions or other Open Source projects to bring the traffic into the cluster. Until now, the options are limited to *NodePort*, *HostPort*, and *Ingress* with an *Ingress Controllers*. The particular implementation details for each one of these objects are beyond the scope of this book, but it's worth having a general overview of

25

these concepts to properly understand the *OpenShift Router*. Figure 1-18 showcases the main difference between using *OpenShift Routes* or *Kubernetes Ingress* and using *NodePorts* or *HostPorts* to steer traffic into the cluster.

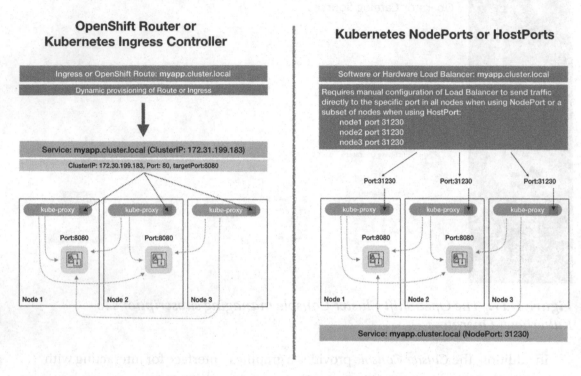

Figure 1-18. *OpenShift Routes, Kubernetes Ingress, NodePorts, and HostPorts*

Note   OpenShift supports *OpenShift Routes* and the native Kubernetes *Ingress*, *NodePort*, and *HostPort* resources.

The main difference to keep in mind is that when using *NodePorts*[5] or *HostPorts*,[6] the user is responsible for the configuration and updates to the configuration of the

---

[5]When using NodePorts, the requested or dynamically assigned port is allocated in all the nodes of the particular cluster. Additional details are available at https://kubernetes.io/docs/concepts/services-networking/service/#nodeport

[6]In general the use of *HostPort* is discouraged. Acceptable use cases are DaemonSets or some networking services. Upstream *HostPort* documentation is scarce, but functionality is similar to NodePorts but for a subset of *Nodes*.

external load balancer or proxy used to steer the traffic toward all the *Nodes* or subset of *Nodes* when using *HostPorts.*

The *OpenShift Router* and the *OpenShift Routes* are a predecessor of the *Ingress Controller* and the *Ingress* object. Even when *Ingress* and *Ingress Controllers* are still available since Kubernetes 1.1, they are still considered Beta in Kubernetes 1.13.[7] There is still no feature parity between *Routes*[8] and *Ingress* objects as it can be seen from Table 1-1.

Table 1-1. *OpenShift Routes vs. Kubernetes Ingress*[9]

Feature	Ingress	Route
Standard Kubernetes object	X	
External access to services	X	X
Persistent (sticky) sessions	X	X
Load-balancing strategies	X	X
Rate-limit and throttling	X	X
IP whitelisting	X	X
TLS edge termination	X	X
TLS re-encryption		X
TLS passthrough		X
Multiple weighted backends (split traffic)		X
Pattern-based hostname		X
Wildcard domains		X

When using the *Ingress* object in OpenShift, internally, the *Ingress Controller* creates one or more *Route* objects to satisfy the conditions specified by the *Ingress* configuration file. Listing 1-1 represents the *Ingress* configuration file, and Listing 1-2 is the resulting *Route* configuration.

---

[7]Kubernetes Ingress feature state: https://kubernetes.io/docs/concepts/ services-networking/ingress/#prerequisites

[8]OpenShift Routes: https://docs.openshift.com/container-platform/3.11/architecture/ networking/routes.html

[9]Reference https://blog.openshift.com/kubernetes-ingress-vs-openshift-route/

Listing 1-1. Define an Ingress object for example.com

```
kind: Ingress
apiVersion: extensions/v1beta1
metadata:
  name: example
spec:
  rules:
  - host: example.com
    http:
      paths:
      - path: /example
        backend:
          serviceName: example-svc
          servicePort: 80
```

Listing 1-2. Resulting Route object for example.com

```
kind: Route
apiVersion: route.openshift.io/v1
metadata:
  # Note: The Route name is auto generated by route object
  # using the Ingress name as prefix
  name: example-a24dc
  ownerReferences:
  - apiVersion: extensions/v1beta1
    kind: Ingress
    name: example
    controller: true
spec:
  host: example.com
  path: /example
  to:
    name: example-svc
  port:
    targetPort: 80
```

OpenShift Registry

One of the ancillary services required by Kubernetes is a container registry where the OCI-compliant container runtime can pull the container images. OpenShift provides an integrated container registry known as the *OpenShift Container Registry (OCR)*. This is not a replacement to the organization's enterprise container registries. The purpose of the *OCR* is to provide a built-in location to store images that are deployed into the cluster or images build by the cluster using the native build strategies[10] like Source-to-Image (S2I).[11]

The *OpenShift Container Registry* is hosted on the *Infrastructure Nodes* (refer to Figure 1-13). Among the additional capabilities available with the OCR is the ability to trigger redeployments if a new version of the container image becomes available in the registry.

Summary

In this chapter we provided a map between the Kubernetes architecture and constructs and the OpenShift architecture. We saw how OpenShift is built on top of the Kubernetes primitives and then augment its capabilities by integrating additional Open Source projects. The result is an integrated multitenant Kubernetes platform which enables developers to deploy applications into a Kubernetes cluster without understanding or learning the specifics of Kubernetes while providing the operations teams the ability to manage Kubernetes with a low learning curve. All of this while being a pluggable architecture in which any of the components can be swapped by other projects or software providing the specific capabilities.

Chapter 2 goes into the details on how high availability is achieved for the OpenShift platform and in each one of the core components.

---

[10]For information about build strategies, visit `https://docs.openshift.com/container-platform/3.11/architecture/core_concepts/builds_and_image_streams.html`

[11]Source-to-Image (S2I) is an Open Source project (`https://github.com/openshift/source-to-image`) to create container images from source code. For information on how to use S2I in OpenShift, refer to `https://docs.openshift.com/container-platform/3.11/creating_images/s2i.html`

CHAPTER 2

High Availability

As we saw from Chapter 1, OpenShift Container Platform is comprised of multiple
elements build on top of Kubernetes. When designing production environments, we
should understand the high availability (HA) built into the different elements of the
platform. Each one of the HA elements can be scaled independently.

The desired level of HA for each platform element and how a cluster will be scaled
out over time may have a direct influence in the initial design considerations.

In this chapter, we will cover the HA configurations, what may be considered the
most relevant elements of the OCP architecture, but the reader should keep in mind
there might be many other components which are not covered here.

Control Plane and Data Plane

From the OpenShift and Kubernetes perspective, there is a clear definition of the Control
Plane, but, when it comes to the Data Plane, it is loosely defined and its definition is
normally based on the context it is being used. To avoid confusion, this is the way we use
the terms here:

- **OpenShift Control Plane**: The *OCP Control Plane* is comprised
  of the Kubernetes Control Plane[1] (Kubernetes Master[2] and the
  kubelet process in each node). For the purpose of this book, we are
  considering the OpenShift consoles, logging, metrics, and cluster
  monitoring services as part of this plane.

---

[1]See official definition here: `https://kubernetes.io/docs/concepts/#kubernetes-control-plane`

[2]API Server, Controllers, Scheduler, and etcd database

© William Caban 2019
W. Caban, *Architecting and Operating OpenShift Clusters*, https://doi.org/10.1007/978-1-4842-4985-7_2

- **OpenShift Data Plane**: The term *OCP Data Plane*, even when not officially defined in the OKD and OCP documentation, is normally used to describe the traffic forwarding plane of the SDN layer.

Note   The terms *Control Plane*, *Management Plane*, and *Data Plane* have a clear separation of concerns when used in computing, networking, and telecommunications systems. There is no direct mapping of the Kubernetes constructs into these concepts. Kubernetes, as a project, does not provide a clear separation of concerns between the functions that would normally go into the *Control Plane* and those that go into the *Management Plane*. When considering the OpenShift architecture, we could clearly map OpenShift components for each one of these planes. For example, the *OpenShift Cluster Console* is what would normally be considered part of the *Management Plane*. Unfortunately, for those of us used to architecting solutions with these differentiations, the terms *Management Plane* and *Data Plane* have not been officially adopted by the OKD and OpenShift community.

HA for Control Plane

The elements of the OpenShift Control Plane are protected in different ways, and as such, to achieve high availability differs for each one.

HA for ETCD

The *etcd* database is one of the critical components of the Kubernetes. It is used to store status and details of the Kubernetes objects, store information and status of the *Nodes*, scheduler results, and much more.

From the technical point of view, *etcd* is a distributed *key-value* store using the *RAFT* consensus algorithm.

Because of the *consensus* required by the *RAFT algorithm* (see details in section "*RAFT Consensus Algorithm*"), the *etcd* service must be deployed in odd numbers to maintain *quorum*. For this reason, the minimum number of *etcd* instances for production environments is three.

Note   Using one instance is considered a testing or demo environment as it is a single point of failure.

From the operational aspects of *etcd*, the *etcd* service is considered an *active-active* cluster. Meaning, an *etcd Client* can write to any of the *etcd* nodes and the cluster will replicate the data and maintain consistency of the data across the instances.

Failures of the etcd database can be classified under one of the following scenarios:

1. **Losing the *etcd Leader* or losing less than (N-1)/2 nodes of an N size etcd cluster**: These are considered temporary failures from which the cluster recovers automatically.

2. **Losing *etcd* quorum**: This failure happens when the cluster loses more than (N-1)/2 nodes of the etcd cluster. This is a major failure as once the quorum is lost, the cluster is incapable of reaching consensus and cannot accept any additional update. When this failure happens, applications already running on OCP are unaffected. However, the platform functionality is limited to read-only operations. Under this failure scenario, it is not possible to take actions such as scaling an application up or down, changing deployment objects, and running or modifying builds.

3. **Losing the data of *etcd* cluster**: Losing the data from the *etcd* cluster will render the Kubernetes and OCP cluster unusable. The only way to recover from this failure scenario is by restoring the *etcd* data from backup.

From the deployment aspect, the *etcd* service can be colocated in the *Master Nodes* with other master services. It is a common practice to colocate the *etcd* service in the *Master Nodes*. In this case, a minimum of three Master nodes is required. The minimum of three Masters is because the *etcd* deployment must guarantee quorum so the *etcd* *RAFT* protocol can reach consensus in the case of a Node failure.

Note   Up to OpenShift 3.11, there is the option to have external dedicated etcd Nodes. Starting with OpenShift 4.0, the etcd service will always be on the cluster.

From the implementation perspective, in OpenShift 3.11 the etcd instances are deployed as a series of privileged Pods running in the *kube-system* project[3] or namespace.[4] Additional details are covered in "HA for Masters Services" section.

RAFT Consensus Algorithm

The basis of the RAFT algorithm states that for any action (add, remove, update, etc.) to be accepted, there needs to be quorum. Quorum is decided by having a number of voting members greater than 50% of the total number of *etcd* instances or *Nodes*. For example, with three etcd Nodes, a minimum of two etcd Nodes are required to have quorum and achieve consensus.

The RAFT Consensus Algorithm consists of three states:

1. Follower

2. Candidate

3. Leader

There are two timeout settings which control the process of the election of a Leader node in the RAFT algorithm:

1. **Election Timeout**: The time a Follower waits before becoming a Candidate. This is a random number between 150ms and 300ms.

2. **Heartbeat Timeout**: Regular interval of time a Leader sends *Append Entries* messages to *Followers* to replicate logs.

All nodes start in the *Follower* state (see Step 1 of Figure 2-1). The nodes wait for *Election Timeout*. If a *Follower* doesn't hear from a *Leader* in *Election Timeout,* they can become *Candidate* (see Step 2 of Figure 2-1) and initiate new *Election Term*. The *Candidate* node votes for itself and *Request Votes* from the other nodes. If the receiving node hasn't voted yet in this *Election Term*, then it votes for the candidate and resets its

---

[3]OpenShift Projects are Kubernetes Namespaces used to organize and manage content in isolation for a community of users. https://docs.openshift.com/container-platform/3.11/dev_guide/projects.html

[4]Kubernetes Namespaces are used to divide cluster resources among multiple projects and users. https://kubernetes.io/docs/concepts/overview/working-with-objects/namespaces/

Election Timeout. A *Candidate* becomes *Leader* if it gets the majority of the votes from the nodes (see Step 3 of Figure 2-1).

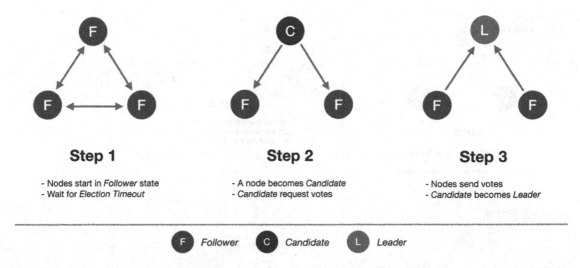

Step 1

- Nodes start in *Follower* state
- Wait for *Election Timeout*

Step 2

- A node becomes *Candidate*
- *Candidate* request votes

Step 3

- Nodes send votes
- *Candidate* becomes *Leader*

F Follower   C Candidate   L Leader

Figure 2-1. *The RAFT algorithm Leader election process*

Once a *Leader* is elected, all changes to the system go through the *Leader*. A client sends a change to the *Leader*. The *Leader* appends this to the *Replication Log* (see Step 1 of Figure 2-2). The change is sent to the *Followers* on the next *Heartbeat* (see Step 2 of Figure 2-2). Once an entry is committed and acknowledged by the majority of the *Followers* (see Step 3 of Figure 2-2), the cluster has reached *Consensus*. A response is sent to the client (see Step 4 of Figure 2-2).

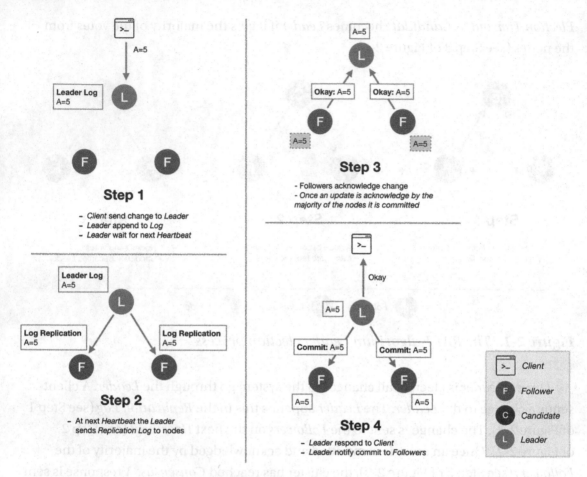

Figure 2-2. *Update value in RAFT algorithm*

HA for Master Services

When we talk about Master services, we are referring mainly to the API Server, the Controllers, and the etcd service. In OpenShift these services are deployed as privileged containers and pods (see Figure 2-3).

```
1
2    [root@bastion ~]# kubectl get pods -n kube-system -o wide   1
3    NAME                                     READY    STATUS    RESTARTS    AGE    IP              NODE
4    master-api-master1.demo.internal        1/1      Running   1           22h    192.168.0.93    master1.demo.internal
5    master-api-master2.demo.internal   2    1/1      Running   1           21h    192.168.0.230   master2.demo.internal
6    master-api-master3.demo.internal        1/1      Running   1           22h    192.168.0.63    master3.demo.internal
7    master-controllers-master1.demo.internal   1/1   Running   1           22h    192.168.0.93    master1.demo.internal
8    master-controllers-master2.demo.interna  3 1/1   Running   1           22h    192.168.0.230   master2.demo.internal
9    master-controllers-master3.demo.internal   1/1   Running   1           22h    192.168.0.63    master3.demo.internal
10   master-etcd-master1.demo.internal       1/1      Running   1           22h    192.168.0.93    master1.demo.internal
11   master-etcd-master2.demo.internal   4   1/1      Running   1           21h    192.168.0.230   master2.demo.internal
12   master-etcd-master3.demo.internal       1/1      Running   1           21h    192.168.0.63    master3.demo.internal
13
14   [root@bastion ~]# oc get pods -n kube-system -o wide   1
15   NAME                                     READY    STATUS    RESTARTS    AGE    IP              NODE
16   master-api-master1.demo.internal        1/1      Running   1           22h    192.168.0.93    master1.demo.internal
17   master-api-master2.demo.internal   2    1/1      Running   1           22h    192.168.0.230   master2.demo.internal
18   master-api-master3.demo.internal        1/1      Running   1           22h    192.168.0.63    master3.demo.internal
19   master-controllers-master1.demo.internal   1/1   Running   1           22h    192.168.0.93    master1.demo.internal
20   master-controllers-master2.demo.interna  3 1/1   Running   1           22h    192.168.0.230   master2.demo.internal
21   master-controllers-master3.demo.internal   1/1   Running   1           22h    192.168.0.63    master3.demo.internal
22   master-etcd-master1.demo.internal       1/1      Running   1           22h    192.168.0.93    master1.demo.internal
23   master-etcd-master2.demo.internal   4   1/1      Running   1           22h    192.168.0.230   master2.demo.internal
24   master-etcd-master3.demo.internal       1/1      Running   1           22h    192.168.0.63    master3.demo.internal
25   [root@bastion ~]#
26
```

Figure 2-3. *The kube-system namespace or project*

From what can be seen in Figure 2-3, the *kube-system* namespace or project host the containers Pods for the *API Server* (see #2 of Figure 2-3), the *Controllers* (see #3 of Figure 2-3), and the *etcd* (see #4 of Figure 2-3) instances. Each *Master Node* contains an *API Server Pod*, a *Controller Pods* and an *etcd Pods*.

Note   The reader may notice the output in Figure 2-3 is the same when using the *kubectl* or the *oc[5]* command-line interfaces. The *kubectl* is the official Kubernetes CLI and *oc* is the OpenShift CLI. The oc CLI includes the *kubectl* and shares the same syntax. In addition to the standard features, the *oc* CLI extends capabilities and brings native support to OCP features like authentication, routes, DeploymentConfigs, ImageStreams, and others.

Looking into the details of one of these Pods, the *etcd Pods*, we can clearly see they are running as privileged containers (see #3 of Figure 2-4), and they are running in the *kube-system* (see #2 of Figure 2-4) namespace or project.

---

[5]For details about the differences between *oc* and *kubectl*, visit https://docs.openshift.com/container-platform/3.11/cli_reference/differences_oc_kubectl.html

```
1    [root@bastion ~]# oc get pod master-etcd-master1.demo.internal -n kube-system -o yaml
2    apiVersion: v1
3    kind: Pod  1
4    metadata:
5      ...
6      labels:
7        openshift.io/component: etcd
8        openshift.io/control-plane: "true"
9      name: master-etcd-master1.demo.internal
10     namespace: kube-system  2
11     ...
12   spec:
13     containers:
14     ...
15       name: etcd
16       resources: {}
17       securityContext:
18         privileged: true  3
19
```

Figure 2-4. *Details of the etcd Pod definition highlighting the privileged mode*

One of the reasons these Pods need the privileged access is because they access host resources. As we can see in Figures 2-5, 2-6, and 2-7, some host resources are mapped as volumes to the containers.

The details of the *etcd Pod* in Figure 2-5 highlight how paths from the Master Node (see #1 and #3) are mapped as volumes for the container (see #1).

```
1   [root@bastion ~]# oc get pod master-etcd-master1.demo.internal -n kube-system -o yaml
2   ...
3      volumeMounts:  1
4      - mountPath: /etc/etcd/
5        name: master-config
6        readOnly: true
7      - mountPath: /var/lib/etcd/
8        name: master-data
9      workingDir: /var/lib/etcd
10  dnsPolicy: ClusterFirst
11  hostNetwork: true
12  nodeName: master1.demo.internal  2
13  ...
14  volumes:
15  - hostPath:  3
16      path: /etc/etcd/
17      type: ""
18    name: master-config
19  - hostPath:
20      path: /var/lib/etcd
21      type: ""
22    name: master-data
23  ...
```

Figure 2-5. *Details of etcd Pod highlighting host path mounts as volumes*

Figure 2-6 (see #4 and #5) provides the detail of the host paths mounted by the *API server Pod* from the *Master Nodes.*

```
1   apiVersion: v1                                30  ...
2   kind: Pod                                     31  volumes:
3   metadata:                                     32  - hostPath:  5
4   ...                                           33      path: /etc/origin/master/
5     labels:                                     34      type: ""
6       openshift.io/component: api               35    name: master-config
7       openshift.io/control-plane: "true"        36  - hostPath:
8     name: master-api-master1.demo.internal      37      path: /etc/origin/cloudprovider
9     namespace: kube-system                      38      type: ""
10  ...                          1                39    name: master-cloud-provider
11  spec:                                         40  - hostPath:
12    containers:                                 41      path: /var/lib/origin
13  ...                                           42      type: ""
14      name: api   2                             43    name: master-data
15  ...                                           44  - hostPath:
16      resources: {}                             45      path: /etc/pki
17      securityContext:                          46      type: ""
18        privileged: true  3                     47    name: master-pki
19      terminationMessagePath: /dev/termination-log   48  ...
20      terminationMessagePolicy: File            49
21      volumeMounts:                             50
22      - mountPath: /etc/origin/master/  4       51
23        name: master-config                     52
24      - mountPath: /etc/origin/cloudprovider/   53
25        name: master-cloud-provider             54
26        mountPath: /var/lib/origin/             55
27        name: master-data                       56
28      - mountPath: /etc/pki                     57
29        name: master-pki                        58
30  ...                                           59
```

Figure 2-6. *Details of API server Pod highlighting host path mounts as volumes*

Similarly, Figure 2-7 highlights the host paths from the Master Node (see #4 and #5) mounted by the *Controllers Pod*.

```
1   apiVersion: v1                                     32   ...
2   kind: Pod                                          33     volumes:              5
3   metadata:                                          34     - hostPath:
4   ...                                                35         path: /etc/origin/master/
5     labels:                                          36         type: ""
6       openshift.io/component: controllers            37       name: master-config
7       openshift.io/control-plane: "true"      1      38     - hostPath:
8     name: master-controllers-master1.demo.internal  39         path: /etc/origin/cloudprovider
9     namespace: kube-system                           40         type: ""
10  ...                                                41       name: master-cloud-provider
11  spec:                                              42     - hostPath:
12    containers:                                      43         path: /etc/containers/registries.d
13  ...                              2                  44         type: ""
14      name: controllers                              45       name: signature-import
15      resources: {}                                  46     - hostPath:
16      securityContext:                               47         path: /usr/libexec/kubernetes/kubelet-plugins
17        privileged: true         3                   48         type: ""
18      terminationMessagePath: /dev/termination-log   49       name: kubelet-plugins
19      terminationMessagePolicy: File                 50     - hostPath:
20      volumeMounts:                                  51         path: /etc/pki
21      - mountPath: /etc/origin/master/    4          52         type: ""
22        name: master-config                          53       name: master-pki
23      - mountPath: /etc/origin/cloudprovider/        54   ...
24        name: master-cloud-provider                  55
25      - mountPath: /etc/containers/registries.d/     56
26        name: signature-import                       57
27      - mountPath: /usr/libexec/kubernetes/kubelet-plugins  58
28        mountPropagation: HostToContainer            59
29        name: kubelet-plugins                        60
30      - mountPath: /etc/pki                          61
31        name: master-pki                             62
32  ...                                                63
```

Figure 2-7. *Details of Controllers Pod highlighting host path mounts as volumes*

In all these cases, the configuration files, certificates, and other information reside on the Master Node but are consumed directly by these privileged *Pods* which are core components of the *Control Plane*.

One of the missing elements of the *Control Plane* not running as a *Pod* or as privileged *Container* is the *kubelet* service. The *kubelet* service runs as a traditional privileged process on the *Master Node* (see Figure 2-8).

Note   The reader may notice the *hyperkube* binary used to invoke the *kubelet* service (see #1 of Figure 2-8). The *hyperkube*[6] is the all-in-one binary with all the Kubernetes server components: *kube-apiproxy, kubelet, kube-scheduler, kube-controller-manager, kube-proxy.*

---

[6]Refer to the GitHub project for additional details: `https://github.com/kubernetes/kubernetes/tree/master/cluster/images/hyperkube`

```
root      6353 5.4  0.7 1459828 126880 ?      Ssl 12:00    2:26 /usr/bin/hyperkube kubelet --v=2 --address=0.0.0.0
--allow-privileged=true --anonymous-auth=true --authentication-token-webhook=true --authenti    .tion-token-webhook-cache-ttl=5m
--authorization-mode=Webhook --authorization-webhook-cache-a     orized-ttl=5m --authorization-webhook-cache-unauthorized-ttl=5m
--bootstrap-kubeconfig=/etc/origin/node/bootstrap.kubeconfig  -cadvisor-port=0 --cert-dir=/etc/origin/node/certificates
--cgroup-driver=systemd --client-ca-file=/etc/origin/node/client-ca.crt  -cluster-dns=192.168.0.93
--cluster-domain=cluster.local --container-runtime-endpoint=/var/run/do  .rshim.sock --containerized=false
--enable-controller-attach-detach=true --experimental-dockershim-root-directory=/var/lib/dockershim --fail-swap-on=false
--feature-gates=RotateKubeletClientCertificate=true,RotateKubeletServerCertificate=true --healthz-bind-address=
--healthz-port=0 --host-ipc-sources=api --host-ipc-sources=file --host-network-sources=api --host-network-sources=file
--host-pid-sources=api --host-pid-sources=file --hostname-override= --http-check-frequency=0s
--image-service-endpoint=/var/run/dockershim.sock --iptables-masquerade-bit=0 --kubeconfig=/etc/origin/node/node.kubeconfig
--max-pods=250 --network-plugin=cni --node-ip= --node-labels=node-role.kubernetes.io/master=true,runtime=docker
--pod-infra-container-image=registry.redhat.io/openshift3/ose-pod:v3.11.51 --pod-manifest-path=/etc/origin/node/pods
--port=10250 --read-only-port=0 --register-node=true --root-dir=/var/lib/origin/openshift.local.volumes
--rotate-certificates=true --rotate-server-certificates=true --tls-cert-file=
--tls-cipher-suites=TLS_ECDHE_ECDSA_WITH_CHACHA20_POLY1305 --tls-cipher-suites=TLS_ECDHE_RSA_WITH_CHACHA20_POLY1305
--tls-cipher-suites=TLS_ECDHE_ECDSA_WITH_AES_128_GCM_SHA256 --tls-cipher-suites=TLS_ECDHE_RSA_WITH_AES_128_GCM_SHA256
--tls-cipher-suites=TLS_ECDHE_ECDSA_WITH_AES_256_GCM_SHA384 --tls-cipher-suites=TLS_ECDHE_RSA_WITH_AES_256_GCM_SHA384
--tls-cipher-suites=TLS_ECDHE_ECDSA_WITH_AES_128_CBC_SHA256 --tls-cipher-suites=TLS_ECDHE_RSA_WITH_AES_128_CBC_SHA256
--tls-cipher-suites=TLS_ECDHE_ECDSA_WITH_AES_128_CBC_SHA --tls-cipher-suites=TLS_ECDHE_ECDSA_WITH_AES_256_CBC_SHA
--tls-cipher-suites=TLS_ECDHE_RSA_WITH_AES_128_CBC_SHA --tls-cipher-suites=TLS_ECDHE_RSA_WITH_AES_256_CBC_SHA
--tls-cipher-suites=TLS_RSA_WITH_AES_128_GCM_SHA256 --tls-cipher-suites=TLS_RSA_WITH_AES_256_GCM_SHA384
--tls-cipher-suites=TLS_RSA_WITH_AES_128_CBC_SHA --tls-cipher-suites=TLS_RSA_WITH_AES_256_CBC_SHA
--tls-min-version=VersionTLS12 --tls-private-key-file=
```

Figure 2-8. *Details of the kubelet process running in a node*

In a multimaster deployment, the default is to use *native* high availability (HA) to determine how to load balance the API requests across the *Master Nodes*. This *native* HA method takes advantage of the built-in native HA master capabilities in OCP and can be used with any load balancing solution.

Each Master Node runs all the master server components. Accessing the API server at Master Nodes does not require session awareness or stickiness. Each Master Node answers to the cluster internal name, the cluster external name, and its own hostname.

The OpenShift advanced installation using *openshift-ansible* supports the definition of an *[lb]* section in the inventory file which automatically installs and configures an HAProxy to act as the load balancing solution for the *Master Nodes*.

Note   The *[lb]* definition ONLY manages or load balances traffic toward the *Master Nodes*. It does NOT load balance traffic toward the *Infrastructure Nodes* or applications running on the OpenShift cluster.

To better illustrate this configuration, refer to Figure 2-9. As seen in Figure 2-9, there is the concept of an *External Cluster Name* and *Internal Cluster Name,* and each *Master Node* has their own assigned *FQDN*.

The *External Cluster Name* is defined in the advanced installation *inventory* file by the *openshift_master_cluster_public_hostname* variable. Similarly, the internal cluster name is specified by the *openshift_master_cluster_hostname* variable.

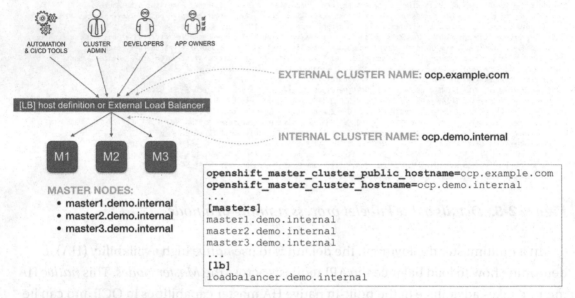

Figure 2-9. *The native HA and load balancing for Master Nodes*

Any external load balancer can be used to load balance the traffic among the *Master Nodes*. The requirements for using external load balancer are simple:

1. Define a virtual IP or VIP to represent the cluster.

2. Configure the VIP for SSL passthrough.

3. Configure the VIP to listen to the port specified by the openshift_ master_api_port variable of the inventory file. If no port is specified, the API server will listen in port 8443 in every Master Node.

Note   In some load balancer might require a different *external VIP* and an *internal VIP*. Other load balancers will handle both external and internal cluster names with a single VIP.

---

4.   Configure the DNS to resolve the *External Cluster Name* to the *external VIP* and the *Internal Cluster Name* to the *internal VIP.*

The HA styles for each of the master services can be summarized as in Table 2-1. Some services handle their internal HA, while others are completely active-active HA.

Table 2-1. *The Native HA of Master Services*

Role	HA Style	Notes
etcd	Active-Active	The *etcd* service is highly redundant and using the RAFT algorithm to maintain data replication and consistency. By default, in OpenShift, this is only accessible from within the cluster. There is no external access or exposure to the *etcd* service.
API Server	Active-Active	Any *Master Node* can handle requests to the API Server. The external load balancer can choose the preferred method to distributing the load.
		When using the *[lb]* host, the *HAProxy* distributes the traffic using the *source* balancing mode which is based on the hash of the source IP address making the request.
Controllers and Schedulers	Active-Passive	One *Controller* instance is elected as the cluster leader at a time.
		Each API Server handling a request interacts with their local *Controller* instance. The local *Controller* instance is aware and communicates with the leader *Controller* which is the only instance scheduling and controlling Pods in the cluster at any given time.

The specific configuration for the *[lb]* hosts is shown in Figure 2-10. As it can be seen, the HAProxy is deployed to listen on *openshift_master_api_port*, in this example port 443 (#2 of Figure 2-10). The load balancing is a simple TCP passthrough (#3 of Figure 2-10) toward the *Master Nodes*. The load balancing mode is a *source* (#4 of Figure 2-10) which balances based on the resulting hash of the source IP address making the request.

```
37    listen stats ①
38        bind :9000
39        mode http
40        stats enable
41        stats uri /
42
43    frontend  atomic-openshift-api ②
44        bind *:443
45        default_backend atomic-openshift-api
46        mode tcp
47        option tcplog
48
49    backend atomic-openshift-api ③
50        balance source ④
51        mode tcp
52        server      master0 192.168.0.93:443 check
53        server      master1 192.168.0.230:443 check
54        server      master2 192.168.0.63:443 check
```

Figure 2-10. *Relevant HAProxy configuration for the [lb] host*

Beyond what can be achieved by the load balancers, the system takes care of restarting any of the *Containers* and *Pods* providing the master services just like it will do to remediate deviations from the desired configuration or state for any other *Pod* running an application in Kubernetes.

HA for OpenShift Consoles

The OpenShift consoles are deployed as Kubernetes objects and use *Services*, *ReplicationController,* or *Deployment* objects to maintain HA. Consider the output shown in Figure 2-11. #1 of Figure 2-11 lists the *Pods* corresponding to each of the *Consoles*: *registry-console, openshift-web-console,* and *openshift-console.*

The HA for the *Container Registry Console* is achieved by the Service named *registry-console* and the ReplicationController named registry-console-1 (see #2 of Figure 2-11). The HA for the developer console (openshift-web-console) is achieved by a *Service* named *webconsole* and a *Deployment* object named *webconsole* with its corresponding *ReplicaSet* (see #3 of Figure 2-11). Finally, the HA for the OpenShift operations console (openshift-console) is achieved by a Service named *console* and a Deployment object named *console* with its corresponding ReplicaSet (see #4 of Figure 2-11).

```
1   NAMESPACE              ①        NAME                          READY  STATUS            NODE
2   default                         registry-console-1-qhmz8      1/1    Running    ...    master1.demo.internal
3   openshift-console               console-6f5f4bd585-hrpf6      1/1    Running    ...    master3.demo.internal
4   openshift-console               console-6f5f4bd585-lmq64      1/1    Running    ...    master2.demo.internal
5   openshift-console               console-6f5f4bd585-zd5v6      1/1    Running    ...    master1.demo.internal
6   openshift-web-console           webconsole-7d6bd48dcd-l9scb   1/1    Running    ...    master3.demo.internal
7   openshift-web-console           webconsole-7d6bd48dcd-rqz9k   1/1    Running    ...    master2.demo.internal
8   openshift-web-console           webconsole-7d6bd48dcd-whl62   1/1    Running    ...    master1.demo.internal
9
10
11  [root@bastion ~]# oc get rc registry-console-1 -n default    ②
12  NAME                 DESIRED    CURRENT    READY      AGE
13  registry-console-1   1          1          1          1d
14
15
16  [root@bastion ~]# oc get deployment,rs -n openshift-web-console    ③
17  NAME                                  DESIRED   CURRENT   UP-TO-DATE   AVAILABLE   AGE
18  deployment.extensions/webconsole      3         3         3            3           1d
19
20  NAME                                           DESIRED   CURRENT   READY   AGE
21  replicaset.extensions/webconsole-7d6bd48dcd    3         3         3       1d
22  [root@bastion ~]#
23
24
25  [root@bastion ~]# oc get deployment,rs -n openshift-console    ④
26  NAME                               DESIRED   CURRENT   UP-TO-DATE   AVAILABLE   AGE
27  deployment.extensions/console      3         3         3            3           1d
28
29  NAME                                         DESIRED   CURRENT   READY   AGE
30  replicaset.extensions/console-6f5f4bd585     3         3         3       1d
31  [root@bastion ~]#
```

Figure 2-11. OpenShift Console Pods, ReplicationControllers, and Deployments

With the use of the native Kubernetes constructs to protect these Consoles, there is no additional configuration required for its HA.

HA for Logging, Metrics, and Monitoring

The OpenShift Monitoring, Logging, and Metrics services are comprised of multiple elements, all of which are deployed and managed as Kubernetes objects: *Service, DaemonSet, Deployment, ReplicationController,* and *DeploymentConfig.* As such, these mechanisms take care of maintaining the high availability for each one of these services. The *OpenShift Monitoring* components are deployed on the *openshift-monitoring Namespace* or *Project.*

Note   A *DeploymentConfig* or *OpenShift Deployment Configuration*[7] is an OpenShift-specific object that predates *Kubernetes Deployment*. The *DeploymentConfig* was built on *ReplicationController* to support the development and deployment lifecycle of an application. In addition to the capabilities of the *Deployment*, the *DeploymentConfig* provides the ability to specify deployment strategies (i.e., rolling strategy, recreate strategy, etc.) to change or upgrade an application; ability to set up triggers to automatically change, redeploy, or upgrade an application and the deployment strategy to use during the transition; and the ability to define hooks to be run before or after creating the *ReplicationController*.

Even when the system takes care of maintaining the availability of these services, it is good to understand how these services are deployed should there be a need for troubleshooting.

OpenShift Monitoring

The *OpenShift Monitoring* is a cluster monitoring solution comprised of *Prometheus*[8] with its plugin ecosystem and *Grafana* for the dashboards. OpenShift uses the *Cluster Monitoring Operator*[9] to configure, deploy, and maintain the *OpenShift Monitoring* stack.

The elements of OpenShift Monitoring are illustrated in Figure 2-12. The details of each component are described in the following list:

- **Prometheus**: Prometheus itself is an Open Source project for monitoring and alerting.

---

[7]For more information about *Deployments* and deployment strategies, visit `https://docs.openshift.com/container-platform/3.11/dev_guide/deployments/how_deployments_work.html`

[8]Prometheus is an Open Source project for monitoring and alerting. Additional information can be found at `https://prometheus.io/docs/introduction/overview/`

[9]The Cluster Monitoring Operator is an Open Source Kubernetes Operator to manage a Prometheus-based cluster monitoring stack. More information can be found here: `https://github.com/openshift/cluster-monitoring-operator`

- **Prometheus Operator**: A *Kubernetes Operator* to create, configure, and manage *Prometheus* and *Alertmanager* instances. In *OpenShift Monitoring*, this component is deployed as a *Deployment* which creates a *ReplicaSet (RC)*. The RC maintains one *prometheus-operator Pod* running in any of the *Infrastructure Nodes*.

- **Cluster Monitoring Operator**: Watches the deployed monitoring components and resources of the OpenShift Monitoring and ensures they are up to date. This element is deployed as a Deployment which creates the ReplicaSet *(RC)*. The RC maintains one *cluster-monitoring-operator Pod* running in any of the *Infrastructure Nodes*.

- ***prometheus-k8s***: The actual Prometheus instances responsible for monitoring and alerting on cluster and OpenShift components. This component is deployed as a *StatefulSet* and maintains a copy in every *Infrastructure Node*.

- **Alertmanager**: A global cluster component for handling alerts generated by all the *Prometheus* instances in the particular cluster. This element is deployed as a *StatefulSet* and maintains two prometheus-k8s Pods across any of the *Infrastructure Nodes*.

- **node-exporter**: Prometheus exporter or agent deployed on every Node to collect metrics from its hardware and Operating System. This element is deployed as a *DaemonSet*. There is one *node-exporter Pod* in every *Node* of the cluster.

- **kube-state-metrics**[10]: Prometheus exporter or plugin to convert metrics from Kubernetes objects into metrics consumable by *Prometheus*. This is deployed as a *Deployment* which creates a *ReplicaSet* and runs a *kube-state-metric Pod* in any of the *Infrastructure Nodes*.

---

[10]Additional details about the metrics collected by this agent can be found at `https://github.com/prometheus/node_exporter`

- **Grafana**[11]: An extensible Open Source metrics analytics and visualization suite. This element is deployed as a *Deployment* which creates a *ReplicaSet* and runs a *Grafana Pod* in any of the *Infrastructure Nodes*.

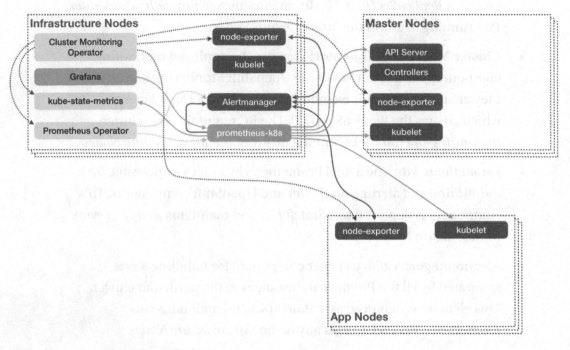

Figure 2-12. *The OpenShift Monitoring architecture*

Metrics

What is considered *OpenShift Metrics* are the original OpenShift components used to collect metrics information from *Containers, Pods,* and *Nodes* across the entire OpenShift cluster. These collected metrics are then available over the OpenShift Console or can be exported to an external system. These metrics can also be used for the *Horizontal Pod Autoscaler (HPA)*[12] to scale the number of *Pods* in a *ReplicationController* or *ReplicaSet* based.

---

[11]Additional information can be found at `https://grafana.com/grafana`

[12]Kubernetes Horizontal Pod Autoscaler (HPA) automatically scales the number of Pods. For more information, visit `https://kubernetes.io/docs/tasks/run-application/horizontal-pod-autoscale/`

Note   OpenShift 3.11 is the last version supporting the traditional *OpenShift Metrics* service.[13] These are being deprecated in OpenShift 4.0. Most of the functionalities are replaced by the *OpenShift Monitoring* solution based on the Prometheus project, and the remaining functionality is superseded by the *Kubernetes Metrics Server.*

All the components of the traditional OpenShift Metrics are deployed as Kubernetes *ReplicationControllers* on the *openshift-infra Namespace* or *Project.* This service consists of the following components:

1. **Heapster**[14]: A service for the monitoring and analysis of compute, memory, and network resource utilization and performance for Kubernetes. Collects the information from the Kubelet APIs.

Note   Kubernetes *kubelet* embeds *cAdvisor*[15] which autodiscovers all containers in the machine and collects CPU, memory, filesystem, and network usage statistics. *cAdvisor* also provides the overall machine usage by analyzing the "root" Container on the machine.

2. **Hawkular Metrics**: This is the metric storage engine for Hawkular. It uses the Cassandra database as the metric datastore.

3. **Cassandra**: The Cassandra database is used to store the metrics data.

---

[13]See Release Notes for OpenShift 3.11 at `https://docs.openshift.com/container-platform/3.11/release_notes/ocp_3_11_release_notes.html#ocp-311-major-changes-in-40`

[14]Heapster was deprecated in Kubernetes 1.11 in favor of Metrics Server and has been retired in Kubernetes 1.13. Additional details are available here: `https://github.com/kubernetes-retired/heapster/blob/master/docs/deprecation.md`

[15]Additional information on how *cAdvisors* are embedded in *kubelet* is available at `https://kubernetes.io/docs/tasks/debug-application-cluster/resource-usage-monitoring/#cadvisor`

The interaction between all these components is illustrated in Figure 2-13.

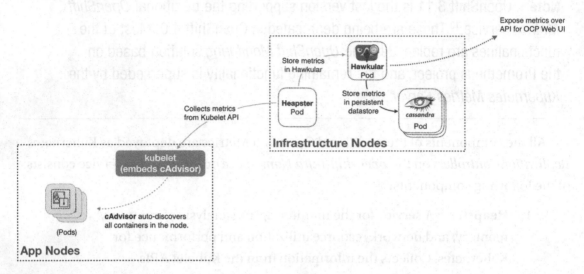

Figure 2-13. *The OpenShift Metrics architecture (deprecated in OCP 4.0)*

Metrics Server

Metrics Server[16] is a cluster-wide aggregator of resource usage data like Container CPU and memory utilization. The Metrics Server collects metrics from the Kubelet API of each node. The resource usage metrics are made available in Kubernetes through the Metrics API. It supersedes the Heapster service in OpenShift 4.0 and beyond.

The *Metrics Server* is considered the prerequisite for some advanced Kubernetes features or capabilities like the *Horizontal Pod Autoscaler (HPA)*, the Kubernetes scheduler, and other functionalities that require access to metrics[17] from nodes and Pods. In OpenShift, this service runs as a *Deployment* which creates a *ReplicaSet* to maintain a *metrics-server Pod* in one of the *Master Nodes*.

---

[16]For more details about the Kubernetes Metrics Server, visit https://kubernetes.io/docs/
tasks/debug-application-cluster/core-metrics-pipeline/#metrics-server

[17]Additional information on use cases and scalability of the Metrics Server is available at https://
github.com/kubernetes/community/blob/master/contributors/design-proposals/
instrumentation/metrics-server.md

Logging

The *OpenShift Logging* service aggregates logs for the OpenShift platform services, *Nodes*, *Containers*, and applications. The OpenShift Logging service shown in Figure 2-14 is comprised of the following components:

- **Elasticsearch (ES)**: A NoSQL database with multitenant full-text search and analytics engine. This component is deployed in the *openshift-logging Namespace* or *Project* as *DeploymentConfig* which creates a *ReplicationController* to run the requested number of *Pods*. The cluster administrator should rightsize[18] the Elasticsearch deployment to the requirements of the specific environment.

- **FluentD**: Data collection software that gathers logs from the *Nodes* and feeds them to the *Elasticsearch* database. This element is deployed in the *openshift-logging Namespace* as a *DaemonSet*. There is a *logging-fluentd Pod* in *every* Node of the cluster.

- **Kibana**: An analytics and visualization Web UI for Elasticsearch. It enables the creation of visualizations and dashboards for monitoring *Container* and *Pods* logs by *Deployment, Namespace, Pod, and Container*. Kibana is deployed in the *openshift-logging Namespace* as a *DeploymentConfig* which creates a *ReplicationController* to run and maintain the *logging-kibana Pod* running on an *Infrastructure Node*.

- **Curator**[19]: Allows administrators to configure scheduled maintenance operations for the Elasticsearch database. These are performed automatically on per-project basis. This component is deployed into the *openshift-logging Namespace* as a *Kubernetes CronJob* object and runs the *logging-curator Pod* on one of the Infrastructure Nodes.

---

[18]For guidelines on rightsizing the Elasticsearch database, visit `https://docs.openshift.com/container-platform/3.11/install_config/aggregate_logging_sizing.html`

[19]For details on how to configure and use Curator, visit `https://docs.openshift.com/container-platform/3.11/install_config/aggregate_logging.html#configuring-curator`

- **Eventrouter**: Watches Kubernetes events, formats them to JSON, and outputs them to STDOUT to be ingested by FluentD. The *logging-eventrouter Pod* is deployed to *default Namespace* or *Project* as a *DeploymentConfig* where it creates a *ReplicationController* and runs the *Pod* on an *Infrastructure Node*.

The first three components together (Elasticsearch, FluentD, and Kibana) are known as the ***EFK*** *stack*.

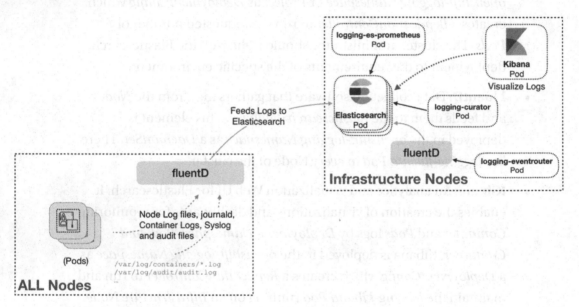

Figure 2-14. *The OpenShift Logging Service*

HA for Data Plane

As mentioned before, there is no official definition of the *OpenShift Data Plane* even though the term is normally used to refer to the traffic forwarding plane of the SDN layer.

As with any other networking architecture, from the SDN layer perspective, we can talk about north-south traffic and east-west traffic. From the OpenShift perspective, the north-south traffic refers to the external traffic arriving into the cluster or the inbound traffic toward the applications hosted on the platform. The east-west traffic refers to the traffic within the cluster.

In a future chapter, we will go into details on how the different SDN options and capabilities move traffic within the cluster (east-west traffic) and the specific features they may provide. For now, this section focuses on the inbound traffic (north-south traffic) arriving to the applications deployed on the cluster. By default, the traffic toward the applications running on the cluster goes through the OpenShift Routers.

HA for OpenShift Router

The *OpenShift Router* is an OpenShift component used to expose *Services* running on the cluster to external clients. It does this by generating a unique *FQDN* and handling requests to it by steering the traffic to the appropriate *Service*. The *OpenShift Routers* are deployed in the *default Namespace* or *Project* as a *DeploymentConfig* which creates a *ReplicationController*. The ReplicationController maintains the number of *router Pod* specified by *openshift_hosted_router_replicas* in the inventory file. These *Routers* are deployed to the *Infrastructure Nodes.* This behavior can be modified by specifying a different *Node* label selector for the Pods using the *openshift_router_selector* variable in the inventory file. If not specified, the default number of replicas is set to one.

In case of failure of a *Router*, the *DeploymentConfig* takes care of correcting the environment by creating a new one.

In a later chapter, we will cover the *OpenShift Router Sharding* capabilities, and we are going to see some of the advanced techniques that can be used to distribute *Routes* among different *Routers* or even dedicate *Routers* to specific *Namespaces* or *Projects*.

HA for Container Registry

The *OpenShift Container Registry (OCR)* is the default internal *Container* image registry used by the cluster to store *Container* images built with one of the supported build strategies, or among other things, to maintain a copy of *Container* images running in the environment.

The OpenShift Container Registry is deployed into the *default Namespace* or *Project* using a *DeploymentConfig* which creates a *ReplicationController* used to run and maintain the desired number of *docker-registry Pod* running. Alternatively, the cluster admin can choose to deploy the OCR as a DaemonSet.[20]

---

[20]Deploying the Registry as a DaemonSet:https://docs.openshift.com/container-platform/3.11/install_config/registry/deploy_registry_existing_clusters.html#registry-daemonset

When not specified, by default, the installer will deploy one *docker-registry Pod* running on the *Infrastructure Nodes*. The number of *docker-registry Pods* to deploy and the *Nodes* selectors to use to deploy the Pod can be specified by using the *openshift_ hosted_registry_replicas* and *openshift_registry_selector* variables, respectively, in the advanced installer *inventory* file.

If no persistent storage options are specified for the registry, the default is to use ephemeral storage and all data will be lost when the *Pod* is restarted.

When using multiple replicas, the persistent storage must support the *ReadWriteMany*[21] storage access mode. The supported storage[22] backends for the Registry range from GlusterFS to S3 compatible services.

Caution   In production environments, the OpenShift Container Registry should NOT use NFS as the storage backend.

Summary

The OpenShift architecture is designed for high availability of every one of its components. Since these elements are built on top of Kubernetes using the Kubernetes constructs, they benefit from the resiliency provided by these. As it can be seen from this chapter, when the OpenShift cluster is deployed with multiple Master, Infrastructure, and Application Nodes, the availability of all the other internal elements of the platform is achieved with Kubernetes itself.

With the abstraction layers created by Kubernetes and the OpenShift platform, Chapter 3 describes the traffic flow with different overlay SDNs when components communicate inside the platform vs. when applications communicate outside the platform.

---

[21]Persistent volume access modes supported by OpenShift are described here: `https://docs. openshift.com/container-platform/3.11/architecture/additional_concepts/storage. html#pv-access-modes`

[22]The full list of supported storage for registry is available at `https://docs.openshift.com/ container-platform/3.11/install_config/registry/deploy_registry_existing_ clusters.html#storage-for-the-registry`

CHAPTER 3

Networking

Chapter 2 covers how high availability is achieved for the core components of the platform. The communication for specific control plane components like the synchronization of the *etcd* database, external connections to the OpenShift Console (in OCP 3.11.x), the communication from the Kubelet to the Kubernetes APIs, and external connections to the cluster's Kubernetes API goes directly to Master's Nodes IPs. Any other intercommunication among components in the cluster uses the OpenShift Networking service.

When considering the *OpenShift Networking* as a whole, there are the *OpenShift SDN plugins* to handle the east-west traffic or the traffic within the cluster and the *OpenShift Router plugins* to handle the north-south traffic, or the inbound traffic destined to *Services* in the cluster.

The default OpenShift software-defined networking (SDN) solution is built on top of Open vSwitch (OVS). With OpenShift, the *cluster admin* is free to choose to deploy with one of the OpenShift native SDN plugins or they can opt to deploy the cluster using a third-party SDN from the supported ecosystem. Should a different SDN is desired, OpenShift supports *Kubernetes CNI-compliant* SDN solutions.

There are multiple Kubernetes CNI-compliant SDN solutions in the market. If considering a third-party SDN, something to keep in mind is the alignment of the release cycle between OpenShift and the third-party SDN solution. The alignment or lack thereof, between the two, will have a direct impact in the supported upgrade cycle for the whole platform.

This chapter provides an overview of the main OpenShift SDN solutions and documents the traffic flow among Pods inside the cluster as well as how these communicate to destination outside the cluster.

© William Caban 2019
W. Caban, *Architecting and Operating OpenShift Clusters*, https://doi.org/10.1007/978-1-4842-4985-7_3

East-West Traffic

For the east-west traffic, out of the box, OpenShift provides the following SDN plugins:

- OpenShift ovs-subnet

- OpenShift ovs-multitenant

- OpenShift ovs-networkpolicy

- OpenShift OVN[1] (future)

- Flannel[2] (limited)

In addition to the native SDN options, at the time of this writing, the following SDN solutions are validated and supported on OpenShift directly by the third-party vendors[3]:

- Big Switch[4]

- Cisco Contiv

- Cisco ACI CNI[5]

- Juniper Contrail

- Nokia Nuage

- Tigera Calico

- VMware NSX-T

- Kuryr SDN[6] (or Kuryr-Kubernetes)

---

[1]The OpenShift Open Virtual Networking (OVN) plugin is considered a development preview. The current capabilities for OCP OVN are similar to the *ovs-networkpolicy*. More information about OVN can be found at the Kubernetes OVN upstream project under the Open vSwitch project: https://github.com/openvswitch/ovn-kubernetes

[2]Flannel is only supported when OCP is deployed over OpenStack environments which are using a VXLAN-based SDN to work around issues with the possible VXLAN over VXLAN encapsulation.

[3]For an updated list of the supported third-party vendor, visit https://docs. openshift.com/container-platform/3.11/install_config/configuring_sdn. html#admin-guide-configuring-sdn-available-sdn-providers

[4]Additional information about Big Switch Big Cloud Fabric Enterprise Cloud (BCF-EC) integration with OpenShift is available here: www.bigswitch.com/tech-partner/red-hat

[5]For more information about the Cisco ACI CNI Plugin for OCP, refer to www.cisco.com/c/en/ us/td/docs/switches/datacenter/aci/apic/white_papers/Cisco-ACI-CNI-Plugin-for-OpenShift-Architecture-and-Design-Guide.pdf

OpenShift SDN

The native *OpenShift Software-Defined Networking (SDN)* configures an *Open vSwitch (OVS)*–based overlay network to provide communication between *Pods* in the cluster. This overlay network uses the *VXLAN* protocol as the SDN encapsulation protocol.

Tip   Standard VLANs provide up to 4094 VLAN IDs to segregate Ethernet traffic, but it requires for every device between two endpoints to be Layer2 devices supporting the IEEE 802.1Q protocol and maintaining the same configuration; hence its support in Cloud and hyperscaled datacenter environments is limited. By default, VLANs cannot work over the Internet, and stretched Layer2 networks are limited. On the other hand, the VXLAN protocol provides 2^{24} or 16,777,216 VXLAN Network IDs (VNIs or VNIDs) and works over any Layer2 or Layer3 transport (including the Internet). It only requires IP reachability between the two endpoints. Because of this and other properties, VXLAN has become the preferred transport protocol for SDN solutions.

Independent from the OpenShift SDN plugin in use, there are some default behaviors. For every node registered into the cluster, OpenShift SDN allocates a /23 subnet (see #2 of Figure 3-1) from the cluster network specified by the *osm_cluster_network_cidr* variable in the *inventory* file of the *openshift-ansible* advanced installer. If not specified, the default cluster network is 10.128.0.0/14. The cluster network subnet assigned to each node is used to assign IPs to the *Pods* at the node.

---

[6]At the time of this writing, the Kuryr SDN is considered Technology Preview; for more information, refer to https://docs.openshift.com/container-platform/3.11/install_config/configuring_kuryrsdn.html

Caution   When considering the value for *osm_cluster_network_cidr*, keep in mind that once a cluster is deployed, the cluster network cannot be arbitrarily reconfigured.

Tip   The *osm_host_subnet_length* variable in the inventory file can be used to specify a different subnet length size, in bits, for the subnets to allocate to each registered node. The default subnet length is 9 which is a subnet of size /23. This is why, by default, OpenShift SDN allocates /23 per node, equivalent to two /24, to each node.

Caution   The host subnet length is one of the attributes that has a direct impact in the maximum number of Pods that can run per node, and its value cannot be reconfigured after deployment.

To identify the cluster network subnet allocated to each Node, execute the *"oc get hostsubnet"* command with a user with *cluster-admin* privilege. The resulting output will be similar to Figure 3-1. The *Host IP* column (#1 in Figure 3-1) is the *Nodes* physical IP address (i.e., the IP Address of *eth0* in the *Node*) and the *Subnet* column (#2 in Figure 3-1) is the cluster network subnet allocated to the corresponding *Node*.

```
$ oc get hostsubnet
NAME                      HOST                      ①  HOST IP          SUBNET        ②  ...
infranode1.demo.internal  infranode1.demo.internal     192.168.0.217    10.1.10.0/23     ...
infranode2.demo.internal  infranode2.demo.internal     192.168.0.30     10.1.8.0/23      ...
master1.demo.internal     master1.demo.internal        192.168.0.176    10.1.4.0/23      ...
master2.demo.internal     master2.demo.internal        192.168.0.201    10.1.2.0/23      ...
master3.demo.internal     master3.demo.internal        192.168.0.10     10.1.0.0/23      ...
node1.demo.internal       node1.demo.internal          192.168.0.5      10.1.6.0/23      ...
node2.demo.internal       node2.demo.internal          192.168.0.40     10.1.12.0/23     ...
node3.demo.internal       node3.demo.internal          192.168.0.48     10.1.14.0/23     ...
```

Figure 3-1. *Sample output showing the cluster network subnet allocation*

When removing or deleting a node from the cluster, the OpenShift SDN frees the corresponding cluster network subnet. This subnet becomes available for future allocations to new nodes.

Note   Unless *Master Nodes* are also configured as *Nodes*, the OpenShift SDN will not configure or allocate a cluster network subnet for the *Master Nodes*. If the *Master Nodes* are not configured as *Nodes*, they do not have access to *Pods* via the SDN.

In every *Node* that is registered as part of a cluster, the *OpenShift SDN* registers the *Node* with the *SDN Master*. The *SDN Master* allocates a cluster network subnet for the new *Node* (see #2 in Figure 3-1). This subnet is stored in the *etcd* database of the cluster (see #2 in Figure 3-2). The *OpenShift SDN* at the *Node* creates the local host *Open vSwitch (OVS)* named *br0* with two interfaces: the *vxlan_sys_4789* in port 1 and *tun0* in port 2 of the OVS *br0* (refer to #4, #5, #8, #9, and #10 in Figure 3-2).

For each Pod in the Node, the local OpenShift SDN creates a *vethXX* interface and assigns it to the OVS br0 (refer to #6 and #8 in Figure 3-2).

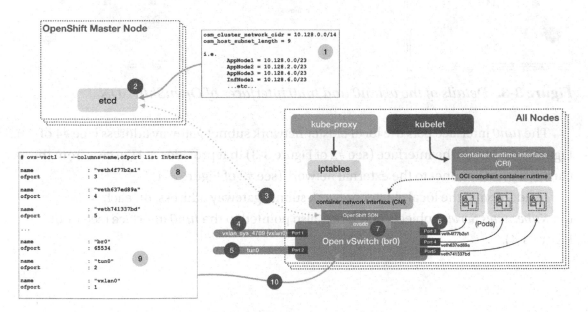

Figure 3-2. *Diagram of the OpenShift SDN*

During the initialization, the local *OpenShift SDN* instance injects an *OpenFlow* entry for every cluster network subnet that has been allocated by the *SDN Master*. After this, the local *OpenShift SDN* of each *Node* monitors the *SDN Master* for subnet updates. Upon detecting an update (i.e., new subnet allocation or deletion of a subnet), the local *OpenShift SDN* injects or removes a corresponding *OpenFlow* entry in the *ovsdb* in *br0*.

The *vxlan_sys_4789* of *br0* is the interface that defines the *VXLAN tunnels*, or the overlay network, that enables the communication between local *Pods* with *Pods* in remote *Nodes* (refer to #1 of Figure 3-3). This interface is known as *vxlan0* interface inside the OVS and that is the name used in the *OpenFlow* entries.

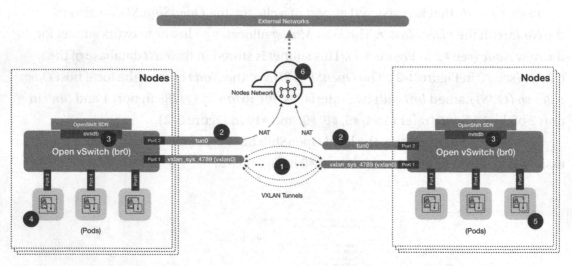

Figure 3-3. *Details of the vxlan0 and tun0 interfaces of OpenShift SDN*

The *tun0* interface gets the local cluster network subnet gateway address (see #4 of Figure 3-4). This is the interface (see #2 of Figure 3-3) that provides *NAT* access from the cluster network subnet to the external network (see #2 of Figure 3-4).

In addition to the local cluster network subnet gateway address, on each *Node* the *Kubernetes Service* objects network is also pointed to the *tun0* interface (see #1 of Figure 3-4).

```
[root@node1 ~]# ip route
default via 192.168.0.1 dev eth0 proto dhcp metric 100
10.1.0.0/16 dev tun0 scope link
...
172.30.0.0/16 dev tun0   1
192.168.0.0/24 dev eth0 proto kernel scope link src 192.168.0.5 metric 100

[root@node1 ~]# $ iptables -t nat -L OPENSHIFT-MASQUERADE
Chain OPENSHIFT-MASQUERADE (1 references)
target     prot opt source              destination
MASQUERADE  all  --  ip-10-1-0-0.demo.internal/16  anywhere   2   /* masquerade pod-to-service and pod-to-external traffic */

$ ip addr
...
2: eth0: <BROADCAST,MULTICAST,UP,LOWER_UP> mtu 9001 qdisc mq state UP group default qlen 1000   3
    link/ether 16:30:3c:26:30:94 brd ff:ff:ff:ff:ff:ff
    inet 192.168.0.5/24 brd 192.168.0.255 scope global noprefixroute dynamic eth0
       valid_lft 3428sec preferred_lft 3428sec
    inet6 fe80::1430:3cff:fe26:3094/64 scope link
       valid_lft forever preferred_lft forever
...
11: tun0: <BROADCAST,MULTICAST,UP,LOWER_UP> mtu 8951 qdisc noqueue state UNKNOWN group default qlen 1000
    link/ether 8e:b9:4d:1c:85:8a brd ff:ff:ff:ff:ff:ff
    inet 10.1.6.1/23 brd 10.1.7.255 scope global tun0
       valid_lft forever preferred_lft forever                                                   4
    inet6 fe80::8cb9:4dff:fe1c:858a/64 scope link
       valid_lft forever preferred_lft forever
...
```

Figure 3-4. *Details of routes and NAT for tun0*

In OpenShift, the *Service* network configuration is set by the *openshift_portal_net* variable in the *inventory* file. If this variable is not defined, the default *Service* network is 172.30.0.0/16.

Tip   After the initial installation of the cluster, the service network can be expanded as long as the existing network is at the beginning of the new network range.[7]

As new *Pods* are created on a host, the local *OpenShift SDN* allocates and assigns an *IP Address* from the cluster network subnet assigned to the *Node* and connects the *vethXX* interface to a port in the *br0* switch. At the same time, the OpenShift SDN injects new OpenFlow entries into the *ovsdb* of *br0* to route traffic addressed to the newly allocated *IP Address* to the correct OVS port connecting the *Pod*.

---

[7]For details on expanding the Service network, refer to https://docs.openshift.com/container-platform/3.11/install_config/configuring_sdn.html#expanding-the-service-network

OpenShift ovs-subnet

The *OpenShift ovs-subnet* is the original *OpenShift SDN* plugin. This plugin provides basic connectivity for the *Pods*. In the OpenShift official documentation, this network connectivity is sometimes referred to as a "flat" Pod network. That may cause some confusion with season network engineers. For any network engineer, the term "flat" network will be interpreted as a network where there are no subnetting and sharing of the same broadcast domain. That would be a very bad network design and would be prone to constant broadcast storms. Fortunately, that is not the case with ovs-subnet.

With the *OpenShift SDN ovs-subnet* plugin, each *Node* still receives a dedicated /23 cluster network subnet (see #1, #2, and #3 of Figure 3-5). Then, the local OpenShift SDN instance sets up OpenFlow entries for each cluster network subnet defined by the SDN Master (#4, #5, and #6 of Figure 3-5 provide a conceptual representation of these).

The reason it is described as a "flat" Pod network is because there are no filters or restrictions and every Pod can communicate with every other Pod and Service in the cluster. So, from the networking perspective, this will be a fully meshed and unfiltered network. In this case, any Pod in Node 1 (#8 of Figure 3-5) will have reachability to the Pods in Node 2 and Node 3 (see #9 and #10 in Figure 3-5) and vice versa.

Note   Even when *Pods* may have reachability to any other *Pod* in the cluster, they will only see open the *Ports* explicitly enabled by the destination *Pod* definition. For example, a *Pod* definition opening TCP Port 8080 will only allow traffic to TCP 8080 to arrive to the container inside the Pod and will block everything else.

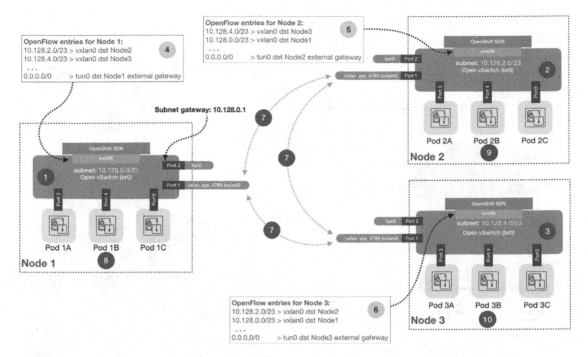

Figure 3-5. *Representation of OpenShift SDN ovs-subnet plugin*

OpenShift ovs-multitenant

With *OpenShift ovs-multitenant* plugin, each *Project* receives a unique *VXLAN ID*, also known as a *Virtual Network ID (VNID)*. All the *Pods* and *Services* of a *Project* are assigned to the corresponding *VNID*. By doing this, it maintains project-level traffic isolation. Meaning, *Pods* and *Services* of one *Project* can only communicate with *Pods* and *Services* in the same *Project*. By definition, there is no way for *Pods* or *Services* from one *Project* to send traffic into another *Project*.

The underlying cluster network subnet allocation remains the same. Each Node receives a dedicated /23 cluster network subnet (see #1, #2, and #3 of Figure 3-6). After this, the local OpenShift SDN instance sets up the OpenFlow entries for each cluster network subnet defined by the SDN Master (see #4, #5, and #6 of Figure 3-6).

After this point, it starts differencing from the other plugins. When using *ovs-multitenant,* the *OpenShift SDN Master* monitors the creation and deletion of *Projects*. Upon the creation of a new *Project*, it allocates and assigns a *VXLAN ID* to the *Project*. This *VXLAN ID* is the one used to isolate the traffic of the *Project* (see #11 of Figure 3-6).

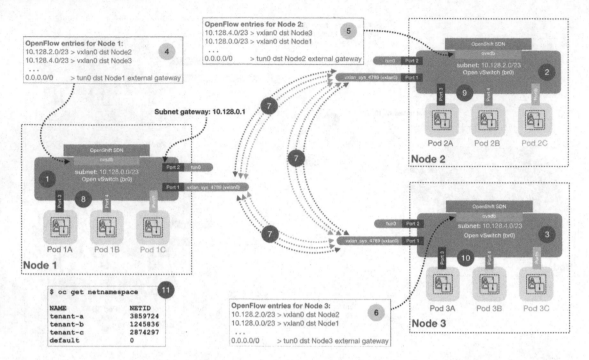

Figure 3-6. *Representation of OpenShift SDN ovs-multitenant plugin*

When a new *Pod* is instantiated in a cluster using the *ovs-multitenant plugin*, during the process of injecting the OpenFlow entries into *br0*, the *OpenShift SDN* includes OpenFlow rules to tag traffic coming from the br0 port connecting the Pod with the VNID corresponding to its Project. In addition, it adds explicit rules to only allow traffic into the Pod if traffic's VNID matches the Pod's VNID or is coming from a privileged VNID 0.

Note   When using *ovs-multitenant*, the VNID=0 is considered privileged traffic that can communicate with any *Project,* and any *Project* can send traffic to a *Project with VNID=0*. OpenShift assigns *Project "default"* to VNID=0 (see #11 of Figure 3-6). Among other *Pods* and *Services*, *Project* "default" contains the *Pods* and *Services* for the internal *Container Registry (OCR)* and the *OpenShift Router.*

When sending traffic across the *vxlan0* interface to a remote *Node,* the traffic is tagged with the correct VNID matching the source Pod Project VNID. The VNID is used as the *VXLAN Tunnel ID* (see #7 of Figure 3-6 where the colors represent the different *VNIDs*). The receiving *Node* uses the *VXLAN Tunnel ID* as the *VNID* tag for the traffic. This guarantees end-to-end isolation of traffic from different projects.

OpenShift ovs-networkpolicy

The *OpenShift ovs-networkpolicy* plugin, fully supported since OpenShift 3.7, is a modern SND that implements the *Kubernetes Network Policies*[8] capabilities. In the default configuration, all *Pods* have reachability to any other *Pod* or *Service* in the cluster.

To restrict traffic to or from a *Pod* or to isolate *Pods,* a *NetworkPolicy* resource must be defined (see #8 in Figure 3-7). Once a *NetworkPolicy* is configured in a *Project* or *Namespace* selecting a particular *Pod*, there will be an implicit *deny-all* rule rejecting all the traffic to that *Pod* and only allowing traffic from connections explicitly allowed by the *NetworkPolicy*. These policies will not impact or affect any other *Pods* in the same *Project,* and those will continue to receive all traffic directed to them.

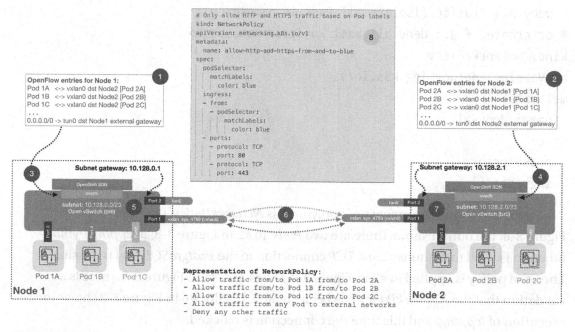

Figure 3-7. Representation of the OpenShift SDN ovs-networkpolicy plugin

For each Node, these network policies are enforced by *OpenFlow* entries in the *bro0* switch (see #1 in Figure 3-7 for representation).

---

[8]Additional detail of *Kubernetes Network Policies* is available at `https://kubernetes.io/docs/concepts/services-networking/network-policies/`

The *NetworkPolicy* resource provides robust network policy mechanisms. As such, it is up to the *cluster-admin* or *Project admin* to define the desired policies for a *Project*. The additive property of these objects enables for multiple *NetworkPolicy* objects to be combined together to create advanced and complex network policies.

As with any other *Kubernetes* resource, the *NetworkPolicy* resource is expressed in YAML format.

Consider Listing 3-1 for an example *NetworkPolicy* definition to deny all traffic from and to any *Pod* in a *Project* or *Namespace*. After applying this policy, all *Pods* in the particular *Project* become isolated.

Listing 3-1. NetworkPolicy to deny all traffic and isolate Pods

```
# Deny All Traffic (isolate all Pods in namespace)
# oc create -f 3.1_deny-all.yaml -n <your-namespace>
kind: NetworkPolicy
apiVersion: networking.k8s.io/v1
metadata:
  name: deny-all
spec:
  podSelector:
  ingress: []
```

Figure 3-8 shows the process of applying this *NetworkPolicy*. On #1 in Figure 3-8, the output shows there are two *Pods*. In #2 in Figure 3-8, a *tcpping Python* function is used to demonstrate a *TCP* connection to the *PostgreSQL Pod* is possible. Then the policy is applied in #3 in Figure 3-8. On #4 and #5 in Figure 3-8, there is a validation that the *NetworkPolicy* has been created. Finally, #6 in Figure 3-8 shows the execution of *tcpping,* and this time the connection is blocked.

```
$ oc get pods -o wide --show-labels
NAME                ... IP          NODE ①       ... LABELS
podcool-1-gl86q     ... 10.128.2.9  ocp-n3.shift.zone  ... app=podcool,deployment=podcool-1,deploymentconfig=podcool
postgresql-1-5s54b  ... 10.129.0.8  ocp-n2.shift.zone  ... deployment=postgresql-1,deploymentconfig=postgresql,name=postgresql


$ oc exec podcool-1-gl86q -- python -c "from tcpping import tcpping ; tcpping(d_host='postgresql',d_port=5432, maxCount=3, DEBUG=True)"
Connected to postgresql[5432]: tcp_seq=0 time=2.92 ms
Connected to postgresql[5432]: tcp_seq=1 time=1.41 ms  ②
Connected to postgresql[5432]: tcp_seq=2 time=1.22 ms

TCP Ping Results: Connections (Total/Pass/Fail/Avg): [3/3/0/1.85] (Failed: 0%)

$ oc create -f deny-all.yaml -n demo-policy
networkpolicy.networking.k8s.io/deny-all created  ③

$ oc get networkpolicy
NAME         POD-SELECTOR   AGE  ④
deny-all     <none>         1m

$ oc describe networkpolicy deny-all  ⑤
Name:         deny-all
Namespace:    demo-policy
Created on:   2019-01-17 18:40:52 -0500 EST
Labels:       <none>
Annotations:  <none>
Spec:
  PodSelector:     <none> (Allowing the specific traffic to all pods in this namespace)
  Allowing ingress traffic:
    <none> (Selected pods are isolated for ingress connectivity)
  Allowing egress traffic:
    <none> (Selected pods are isolated for egress connectivity)
  Policy Types: Ingress

$ oc exec podcool-1-gl86q -- python -c "from tcpping import tcpping ; tcpping(d_host='postgresql',d_port=5432, maxCount=3, DEBUG=True)"
Connection timed out!
Connection timed out!  ⑥
Connection timed out!

TCP Ping Results: Connections (Total/Pass/Fail/Avg): [3/0/3/1001.993] (Failed: 100.00%)
```

Figure 3-8. *Applying NetworkPolicy to isolate Pods by blocking all traffic to them*

Following the same exercise, consider Listing 3-2. This *NetworkPolicy* allows every *Pod* to communicate to any other *Pod* in the same *Project* and enables access to the *default* Project.

Note   When using *NetworkPolicy* resources, the communication with *Project "default"* is required to get to the *OpenShift Routers.* This rule must be explicitly allowed by the defined policy.

Listing 3-2. NetworkPolicy to allow traffic within Pods in the Project and with the default Namespace

```
# Allow traffic between Pods in the same Project and with the default
project (i.e. to access the routers)
# oc label namespace default name=default
# oc create -f 3.2_allow-same-project-and-default.yaml -n <your-namespace>
kind: NetworkPolicy
apiVersion: extensions/v1beta1
```

```
metadata:
  name: allow-same-and-default-namespace
spec:
  ingress:
  - from:
    - podSelector: {}
  - from:
    - namespaceSelector:
        matchLabels:
          name: default
```

Figure 3-9 documents the application of Listing 3-2 *NetworkPolicy* (#1) to restore the communication with the PostgreSQL Pod (#3).

```
$ oc create -f allow-same-and-default-ns.yml -n demo-policy
networkpolicy.extensions/allow-same-and-default-namespace created        1

$ oc describe networkpolicy allow-same-and-default-namespace
Name:          allow-same-and-default-namespace
Namespace:     demo-policy
Created on:    2019-01-17 18:47:50 -0500 EST                  2
Labels:        <none>
Annotations:   <none>
Spec:
  PodSelector:     <none> (Allowing the specific traffic to all pods in this namespace)
  Allowing ingress traffic:
    To Port: <any> (traffic allowed to all ports)
    From:
      PodSelector: <none>
    ----------
    To Port: <any> (traffic allowed to all ports)
    From:
      NamespaceSelector: name=default
  Allowing egress traffic:
    <none> (Selected pods are isolated for egress connectivity)
  Policy Types: Ingress

$ oc exec podcool-1-gl86q -- python -c "from tcpping import tcpping ; tcpping(d_host='postgresql',d_port=5432, maxCount=3, DEBUG=True)"
Connected to postgresql[5432]: tcp_seq=0 time=3.34 ms
Connected to postgresql[5432]: tcp_seq=1 time=4.88 ms
Connected to postgresql[5432]: tcp_seq=2 time=1.09 ms        3

TCP Ping Results: Connections (Total/Pass/Fail/Avg): [3/3/0/3.103] (Failed: 0%)
$
```

Figure 3-9. *Applying NetworkPolicy to allow traffic among Pods and with Project default*

Flannel

Flannel is one of the simplest SDN implementations of the *Kubernetes network model*. It supports various overlay protocols (or backends) ranging from *VXLAN* to *host-gw*, and many others.[9] The OpenShift-supported *Flannel* configuration uses the *host-gw* backend.[10]

Note   In OpenShift, the support of the *Flannel* plugin is limited to deployments of *OpenShift Container Platform* over the Red Hat OpenStack Platform.[11]

The *host-gw* backend requires Layer2 connectivity between the Nodes so *flanneld* can forward the packets to the corresponding *Node* as *next-hop*. The *Flannel* SDN initialization in OpenShift is as follows:

- Each *Node* runs a *flanneld* agent which reads the configuration from the *etcd* database (see #11 of Figure 3-10).

- The *flanneld* agent allocates a unique /24 subnet from the configured *Network* and registers the allocated *Node* host subnet into the *etcd* database (see #12 of Figure 3-10).

- The first IP of the subnet is assigned as the interface *docker0* (#1 of Figure 3-10) which becomes the *default gateway* for the local *Pods*.

- For each allocated host subnet in *etcd*, Flannel host-gw backend injects a subnet route with the remote *Node* eth0 *IP Address* as the *next-hop* gateway address to reach that subnet (see #2 of Figure 3-10).

---

[9]For a complete list of the backend protocols supported by the Flannel SDN, refer to `https://github.com/coreos/flannel/blob/master/Documentation/backends.md`

[10]Additional details about OpenShift and Flannel are available at the following URL (note: a valid Red Hat support subscription is required to access this link): `https://access.redhat.com/documentation/en-us/reference_architectures/2018/html/deploying_and_managing_openshift_3.9_on_red_hat_openstack_platform_10/components_and_considerations#key_considerations`

[11]For more information of OpenShift Flannel, see `https://docs.openshift.com/container-platform/3.11/install_config/configuring_sdn.html#using-flannel`

With *Flannel host-gw* backend, the traffic flow from a Pod in one *Node* to a Pod in another Pod is as follows:

1. The Pod sends traffic to its default gateway. For example, Pod 1A in Node 1 sends traffic to Pod 2C in Node 2 (Figure 3-10). Pod 1A sends traffic to its default gateway, which happens to be the *docker0* interface (#1 of Node 1 in Figure 3-10).

2. From the *docker0* interface, the traffic is routed by the *host routing table* (#5 in Figure 3-10). Since there is a specific route for the destination subnet (#2 in Figure 3-10), the traffic is sent to the registered *next-hop* address (#7 in Figure 3-10) which, in this example, happens to be Node 2 *eth0 IP Address*.

3. Once the traffic is received by the remote Node (Node 2), the destination *IP Address* is evaluated by the host routing table (#9 in Figure 3-10) so the traffic is sent to *docker0* interface which finally forwards the traffic to Pod 2C (#10 in Figure 3-10).

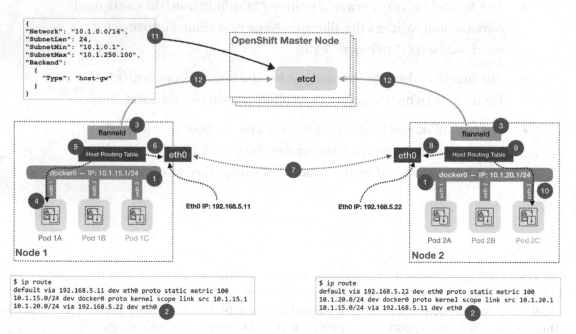

Figure 3-10. *Flannel SDN with host-gw backend in OpenShift*

Because *Flannel* with the *host-gw* backend does not use additional encapsulations, it maintains certain level of performance, and the *host-gw* backend is considered a good option when deploying Kubernetes over virtualized platforms that have their own SDN solutions. This is to avoid the performance penalties which might be experienced when using SDNs over SDNs, resulting in what is known as double encapsulation.

OpenShift with Third-Party SDN

OpenShift configurations with third-party SDN are maintained by their respective third-party vendors. To illustrate the use of third-party SDNs with OpenShift in this section, we focus on the *Open Source Calico*[12] *SDN* solution.

OpenShift with Calico SDN

The *Calico SDN CNI* provides another *SDN* alternative supporting *NetworkPolicy* resources for *ingress* and *egress* policy rules. Calico can be used with or without an encapsulated overlay network. In OpenShift, by default it uses IP over IP encapsulation.

Calico relies on routing principles from the native Linux network stack to move traffic from one *Node* to another. It can be used with Nodes using *Layer2* or *Layer3* connectivity.

As with other *Kubernetes SDN* solutions, *Calico* maintains its configuration and state in the cluster *etcd* database and relies on the *BGP* protocol at each *Node* to communicate the routing information.

Tip   A best practice for large-scale cluster deployments with Calico is to have a dedicated *etcd* instance for it, different from the cluster *etcd*.

Note   If BGP is supported by the *top-of-rack (TOR)* switches interconnecting the cluster, *Calico* can peer with the *TOR* over BGP. The default BGP ASN is 64512. This ASN value is configurable by CLI.[13]

---

[12]Additional information about project Calico can be found at www.projectcalico.org
[13]For information on customizing the BGP ASN number, visit https://docs.projectcalico.org/v3.4/usage/configuration/bgp#configuring-the-default-node-as-number

71

By default, *Calico* allocates a /26 subnet to each *Node,* and as IPs are consumed by the *Node*, it dynamically allocates additional blocks to the *Node*. This is possible thanks to the use of a dynamic routing protocol, in this case BGP, on each *Node*.

Various components come together to create the Calico architecture (see Figure 3-11):

1. ***CNI Plugin***:

   a. **Calico-CNI**: The Calico CNI plugin implements the Kubernetes CNI specification.

   b. **Calico-IPAM**: The Calico IPAM assigns IP address to the Pods.

2. ***calico-node***: The *calico-node* is a privileged container running as *DaemonSet* in every *Node* (see #1 of Figure 3-11). This container has three elements:

   a. ***confd***: Monitors the *etcd* database for state updates and generates the corresponding new *BGP* configuration for *BIRD*.

   b. ***BIRD and BIRD6***: *BGP* agents running at each *Node* and distribute the routes across. *BIRD* is for IPv4 addresses and *BIRD6* for IPv6 IP addresses.

   c. ***Felix***: Agent doing the routing and policy calculation. It writes the corresponding routes and ACLs to the *Node* host routing table and *iptables,* respectively.

3. ***calico-kube-controller***: This container runs as a *Pod* on top of Kubernetes and maintains Calico in sync with *Kubernetes* when using *NetworkPolicy*.

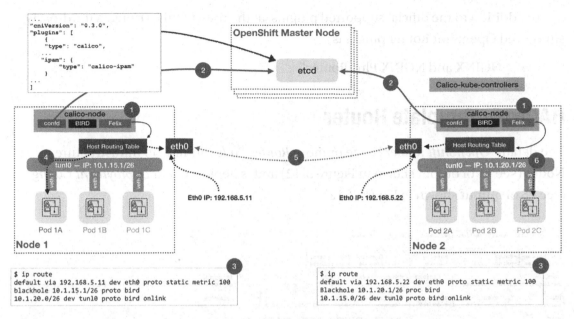

Figure 3-11. *Representation of Calico SDN in OpenShift*

From #3 in Figure 3-11, we can see an extract of the resulting host routing table when using *Calico*. Local Pod-to-Pod traffic has direct communication inside the host. To reach a *Pod* in a remote Node, the traffic from a *Pod* gets to the local *tunl0* interface (#4 in Figure 3-11) and gets routed by the *host routing table* to the *next-hop* IP Address which is the remote *Node*. At the remote *Node,* the packet is routed by the host routing table and delivered to the *tunl0* interface (#6 in Figure 3-11) where it finally reaches the remote *Pod*.

North-South Traffic

When considering the north-south traffic, out of the box, the available *OpenShift Router plugins*[14] are

- HAProxy Template Router (default plugin)
- F5 BIG-IP Router plugin

---

[14]For an updated list of available Router plugins, visit https://docs.openshift.com/container-platform/3.11/architecture/networking/assembly_available_router_plugins.html

In addition to the official supported plugins, at the time of this writing, a third-party supported OpenShift Router plugin is

- NGINX and NGINX Plus Router[15]

HAProxy Template Router

The default *OpenShift Router* is one or more *Router Pods* running on Infrastructure Nodes (see #1 of output shown in Figure 3-12) and is deployed as a *Deployment Config* (see #5 of output shown in Figure 3-12).

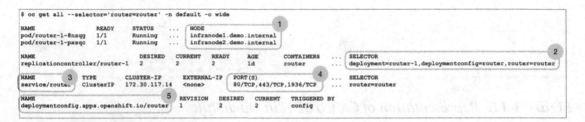

Figure 3-12. *Output showing the elements comprising the OpenShift Router service*

These *Router* container images are based on *HAProxy* (see #6 of *Pod* definition extract shown in Figure 3-13). These *Pods* are defined to share the *Network Namespace* with the host *Infrastructure Node* (see #5 and #8 of extract shown in Figure 3-13).

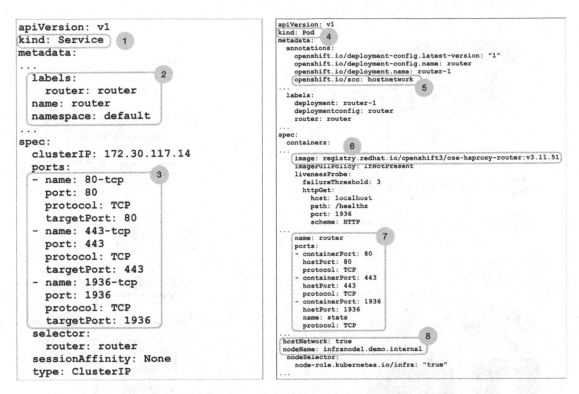

Figure 3-13. *Extract of an OpenShift Router Service and Pod definition*

Sharing the *Network Namespace* enables these *Router Pods* to receive traffic over the *host-network*. By default, the *OpenShift Router* listens on TCP ports 80 (HTTP), 443 (HTTPS), and 1936 (HAProxy Stats) (see #3 and #7 in Figure 3-13). Once the traffic arrives to the Pod, it will match the corresponding Route object (see #1 and #2 of Figure 3-14).

During the creation of the Route resource (#1 in Figure 3-14) and at the addition or removal of a *Pod*, the *OpenShift Router* queries the Service resource (#3 in Figure 3-14) for the Endpoints associated to the *Service* based on label selectors (#5 in Figure 3-14). From here it obtains Endpoint information like name and IP of the *Pods*. The OpenShift Router uses this information to create the corresponding HAProxy configuration to load balance the traffic (#6 in Figure 3-14) destined to the particular *Route* (i.e., myapp-demo-app.example.com) across the available *Pods*.

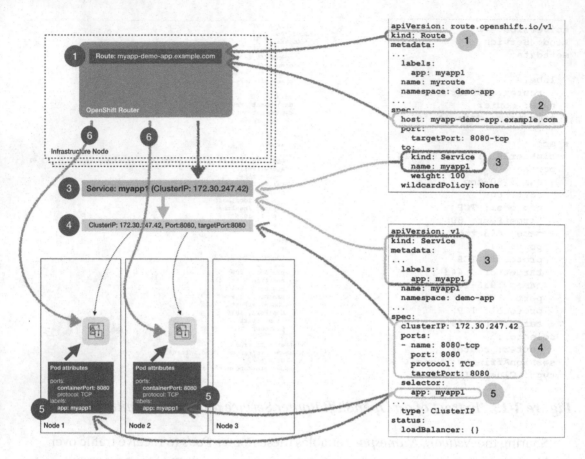

Figure 3-14. *OpenShift Route to Service details*

Summary

OpenShift Networking is comprised of multiple elements that can be grouped into two types of solutions: the solutions that provide the Software-Defined Networking (SDN) to move the east-west traffic, or traffic within the cluster, and the solutions that handle the north-south traffic, or the inbound traffic to applications hosted on the OpenShift cluster.

For both cases, for the east-west traffic and for the north-south traffic, there are the OpenShift native supported plugins and third-party validated plugins supported by those third-party vendors.

The next chapter, Chapter 4, explores the available options for providing storage to components and applications running on the platform.

CHAPTER 4

Storage

Once the networking options are defined for Containers as described in Chapter 3, another essential service is storage. Container storage is ephemeral by design. Initially, Containers were designed for immutable and stateless workloads. Later, the advantages of containerizing stateful applications became apparent. With that came the need to support persistent storage. A similar paradigm happened with Kubernetes; initially, it was designed for stateless applications, but it was rapidly extended to support stateful workloads. Supporting these new types of workloads drove the need to support multiple storage options. The storage options for Kubernetes and OpenShift environments are grouped under two classifications: ephemeral storage and persistent storage.

OpenShift Storage

With *Kubernetes* and *OpenShift*, the on-disk files representing the instance of a *Container* are ephemeral. Meaning, once the *Pod* is destroyed or reinstantiated (i.e., during rolling upgrade), any changes to files or data stored inside those *Container* are destroyed.

The default mount point for the ephemeral storage representing the filesystem and the data inside the Containers is determined by the *Container Runtime* in use. See Tables 4-1 and 4-2 for the default mount points used by *OpenShift* when using *Docker* runtime or *CRI-O* runtime.

© William Caban 2019
W. Caban, *Architecting and Operating OpenShift Clusters*, https://doi.org/10.1007/978-1-4842-4985-7_4

Table 4-1. *OpenShift Mount Points for OpenShift 3.11*

Directory	Notes
/var/lib/docker	When using *Docker* runtime, this mount point is used by active Containers and Pods. This is the local storage where the *Node* maintains a copy of Container images pulled from a *Container Registry*. This mount point is managed by *docker-storage*. It uses the following naming format: /var/lib/docker/overlay2/<layer-id> /var/lib/docker/containers/<container-id> **Note:** When using the CRI-O runtime, this folder is a symbolic link to /var/lib/containers.
/var/lib/ containers	When using the CRI-O runtime, this is the mount point used by active Containers and Pods. This is the local storage where the *Node* maintains a copy of *Container* images pulled from a *Container Registry*. It uses the following naming format: /var/run/containers/storage/overlay-containers/<layer-id> /var/lib/containers/<container-name>/<container-id>
/var/lib/ origin/ openshift. local.volumes	This is the mount point of the ephemeral volume storage for Pods including anything external that is mounted into a Container at runtime. This is also the mount point for environment variables, kube secrets, and any data volumes not backed by a persistent storage volume (PV). It uses the following naming format: /var/lib/origin/openshift.local.volumes/pods/<pod-id>/ containers/<container-name>/<container-id> /var/lib/origin/openshift.local.volumes/pods/<pod-id>/ volumes/<volume-type>/<volume-name>

Table 4-2. *OpenShift Mount Points for OpenShift 4.0[1]*

Directory	Notes
/var/lib/ containers	When using the CRI-O runtime with Red Hat CoreOS (RHCOS), this is the mount point used by active Containers and Pods. This is the local storage where the *Node* maintains a copy of *Container* images pulled from a *Container Registry*. It uses the following naming format: /run/containers/storage/overlay-containers/<pod-id> /var/lib/containers/storage/overlay/<layer-id>
/var/lib/ kubelet/pods	With Red Hat CoreOS (RHCOS), this is the mount point of the ephemeral volume storage for Pods including anything external that is mounted into a Container at runtime. This is also the mount point for environment variables, kube secrets, and any data volumes not backed by a persistent storage volume (PV). It uses the following naming format: /var/lib/kubelet/pods/<pod-uid>/volumes/<volume-type>/<volume-name>

Beyond the default ephemeral storage of the on-disk files representing the instance of a Container, *Kubernetes* has the concept of a *Volume*.[2] A *Kubernetes Volume* is an object that provides a mechanism to provide persistent storage for the *Containers*. A *Volume* and the data on it are preserved across Container restarts and it even outlives any *Containers* within a *Pod*.

Note   A *Volume* is created to provide persistent storage for *Containers* in a *Pod*. There is a special Volume type, *emptyDir*,[3] that is ephemeral in nature as it is created when a *Pod* is assigned to a *Node* but is deleted when the *Pod* is removed from the *Node*.

[1]This information applies to OpenShift 4.0 Beta release. Paths may be subject to change during development and may be different for final release.

[2]Additional information and definitions of Volume from the upstream Kubernetes community are available at https://kubernetes.io/docs/concepts/storage/volumes/

[3]For use cases and details about emptyDir, refer to the Kubernetes upstream documentation at https://kubernetes.io/docs/concepts/storage/volumes/#emptydir

Kubernetes Storage Constructs

Kubernetes maintains strict separations of concerns between the definitions of a *PersistentVolume (PV),* making it available to the *Cluster* (see #1 and #12 in Figure 4-1), to the moment the *PV* is associated to a *Project or Namespace* through a *PersistentVolumeClaim (PVC)* (see #6 and #13 in Figure 4-1). Once the PVC is created associating the PV to the Project or Namespace, it then can be associated as a *Volume* and binds to a mount point in the *Container* (see #10 and #14 in Figure 4-1).

Note   A *PersistentVolume (PV)* is not tied to any *Namespace.* A *PersistentVolumeClaim (PVC)* is associated and created inside a *Project or Namespace.*

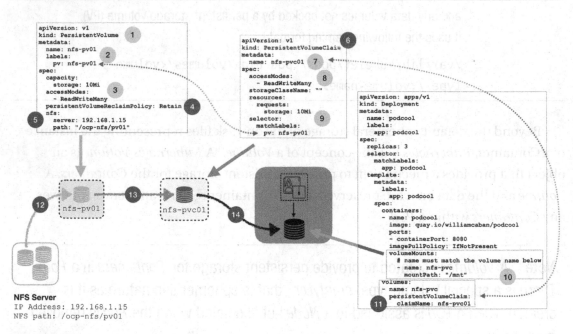

Figure 4-1. *PersistentVolume, PersistentVolumeClaim, and Volumes*

PersistentVolumes (PV) can be provisioned manually by the cluster administrator or the cluster administrator can enable dynamic provisioner plugins which take care of dynamically creating PVs for any PVC's definition configured in a *Namespace.*

Tip   A PVC storage size request (see #9 in Figure 4-1) can bind to a PV with equal or larger storage size (see #3 in Figure 4-1) defined by a PV.

Caution   If there is no PV capable of fulfilling the PVC storage size request, the PVC remain unbound indefinitely.

When the *Volume* is disconnected from the *Container,* the PVC is available for any other *Container* in the same *Namespace* to use. The data remains on the *Volume* and will be available to any future *Container* using the PVC.

When the PVC definition is deleted, the PV is considered to be *released*. The data is handled based on the *reclaimPolicy* of the PV.

PersistentVolume Status

A PersistentVolume (PV) will be in one of the following status (see #5 in Figure 4-2):

- **Available**: The PV has not been claimed by a PVC.

- **Bound**: The PV is associated and claimed by a PVC.

- **Released**: The PVC was deleted but the resource has not been reclaimed by the cluster according to the *reclaimPolicy*.

- **Failed**: The automatic reclamation of the PV has failed.

```
$ oc get pv
NAME                                          CAPACITY  ACCESS MODES  RECLAIM POLICY  STATUS
nfs-pv01                                      10Mi      RWX           Retain          Bound
nfs-pv02                                      10Mi      RWX           Retain          Available
pvc-04ec0d5e-2721-11e9-87a2-001a4a160101      20Gi      RWO           Delete          Bound
pvc-1bb8a09c-2721-11e9-87a2-001a4a160101      2Gi       RWO           Delete          Bound
```

Figure 4-2. Output showing PV's Access Modes, reclaimPolicy, and Status

Reclaim Policy

PersistentVolumes (PV) have an associated *Reclaim Policy* (see #4 in Figure 4-2) which dictates how to handle data after the PV is not *Bound* to a PVC. Kubernetes supports the following Reclaim Policies[4]:

- **Retain**: With this policy the PV is kept after the PV is no longer Bound to a PVC and enables manual reclamation of the resources.

- **Recycle**: *(Depreciated in favor of dynamic provisioning)* This policy performs a basic scrub doing a `"rm -rf /<volume-path>/*"` on the *Volume,* then makes the *Volume* available again for new PVCs.

- **Delete**: This policy removes the PV and the associated storage asset (i.e., AWS EBS, GCE PD, Cinder Volume, Gluster Volume, etc.) when the PV is no longer *Bound* to a PVC.

Note   When no *reclaimPolicy* is specified or when using dynamically provisioned Volumes, the default reclaim policy is *Delete.*

Access Modes

The access mode (see #3 in Figure 4-2) capabilities of a *PersistentVolume (PV)* are dependent on the modes supported by the provider of the storage resource. For example, NFS supports the three available access modes, while AWS EBS only supports one.

The available access modes are detailed in Table 4-3.

Note   A *Volume Access Mode* describes the *Volume's* capability but does not enforce constraints. It is up to the storage provider to enforce this at runtime.

---

[4]Additional details and utilization of the Reclaim Policies are available at the upstream Kubernetes documentation: `https://kubernetes.io/docs/concepts/storage/persistent-volumes/#reclaiming`

Table 4-3. *Volume Access Modes*

Access Mode	Abbreviation	Description
ReadWriteOnce	RWO	The volume can be mounted as read-write only by a single *Node* at a time.
ReadOnlyMany	ROX	The volume can be mounted as read-only by many *Nodes* at a time.
ReadWriteMany	RWX	The volume can be mounted as read-write by many *Nodes* at a time.

OpenShift PersistentVolume Plugins

OpenShift supports multiple storage plugins.[5] Some of these plugins and the access modes are listed in Table 4-4.

Table 4-4. *OpenShift PersistentVolume (PV) Plugins and Supported Access Modes*

PV Plugin Name	Access Mode	Mount Options
NFS	RWO, ROX, RWX	Yes
HostPath	RWO	No
GlusterFS	RWO, ROX, RWX	Yes
Ceph RBD	RWO, ROX	Yes
OpenStack Cinder	RWO	Yes
AWS EBS	RWO	Yes
GCE Persistent Disk	RWO	Yes
iSCSI	RWO, ROX	Yes
FibreChannel	RWO, ROX	No
Azure Disk	RWO	Yes
Azure File	RWO, ROX, RWX	Yes
VMWare vSphere	RWO	Yes

(continued)

---

[5]For an updated list of the supported plugins, visit https://docs.openshift.com/container-platform/3.11/install_config/persistent_storage/index.html#install-config-persistent-storage-index

Table 4-4. (*continued*)

PV Plugin Name	Access Mode	Mount Options
Local	RWO	No
FlexVolume	*FlexVolume* is an out-of-tree plugin interface that enables users to write their own drivers. Because of this, the supported *Access Modes* and *Mount Options* are implementation specific.	
Container Storage Interface (CSI)	*CSI* is an industry standard that enables vendors to develop storage plugins for container orchestration systems (i.e., Kubernetes) in a way that it is portable across CSI-compliant container orchestration systems. Because of this, the supported *Access Modes* and *Mount Options* are implementation specific.	

Since Kubernetes 1.8, the upstream Kubernetes project decided to stop accepting in-tree storage *Volume* plugins. Before this, Volume plugins were linked and distributed as part of the core binaries of Kubernetes. To enable vendors to develop Volume plugins independently from Kubernetes and with their own release cadence, nowadays, instead, it promoted the use of the FlexVolume plugin interface or the use of the Container Storage Interface (CSI) plugin.

The FlexVolume plugin interface has been available since Kubernetes 1.2. The Container Storage Interface (CSI) plugin was introduced in Kubernetes 1.9 and GA in 1.13. These two options are covered in detail in the following sections.

FlexVolume

FlexVolume is known as an out-of-tree plugin interface because it is developed outside the main *Kubernetes* source code. The *FlexVolume* interface enables users to write their own drivers. These drivers can be written in any programming or scripting language.

User-provided driver binaries must be installed in a predefined *Volume* plugin path[6] in every *Node* of the cluster (see #1 in Figure 4-3). The *FlexVolume* driver performing the attach and detach operations must be a self-contained executable with no external dependencies.

---

[6]The standard path for FlexVolume is /usr/libexec/kubernetes/kubelet-plugins/volume/ exec/<vendor>~<driver>/<driver>.

Kubernetes is shipped with a *FlexVolume* in-tree plugin that *kubelet* uses to interact with the user-provided drivers using an exec-based model (see #2 in Figure 4-3). When invoking the binary of the driver, the first command-line argument is an *operation* name followed by parameters for the operation.

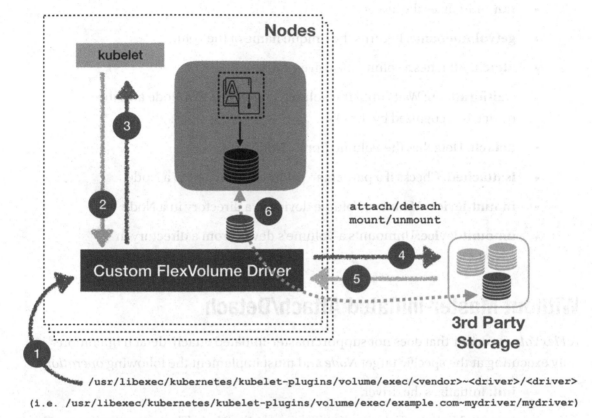

```
/usr/libexec/kubernetes/kubelet-plugins/volume/exec/<vendor>~<driver>/<driver>

(i.e. /usr/libexec/kubernetes/kubelet-plugins/volume/exec/example.com~mydriver/mydriver)
```

Figure 4-3. *FlexVolume plugin architecture*

The FlexVolume driver works in one of two modes:

- *FlexVolume* driver with master-initiated attach/detach operation
- *FlexVolume* driver without the master-initiated attach/detach operation

With Master-Initiated Attach/Detach

A *FlexVolume* driver with master-initiated attach/detach operation[7] must implement the following *operations*:

- **init**: Initializes the driver

- **getvolumename**: Returns the unique name of the volume

- **attach**: Attaches a volume to a given Node

- **waitforattach**: Waits until the Volume is attached to a Node and the device is recognized by the OS

- **detach**: Detaches the Volume from a Node

- **isattached**: Checks if a particular Volume is attached to a Node

- **mountdevice**: Mounts a Volume device to a directory in a Node

- **umountdevice**: Unmounts a Volume's device from a directory in a Node

Without Master-Initiated Attach/Detach

A *FlexVolume* driver that does not support master-initiated attach/detach operations[8] is only executing at the specific target *Node* and must implement the following *operations*:

- **init**: Initializes the driver.

- **mount**: Mounts a Volume to a directory in the *Node*. This operation is responsible for finding the device, attaching the device to the Node, and mounting the device to the correct mount point.

- **umount**: Unmounts a Volume from a directory in the Node. This operation should take care of cleaning up the Volume and detaching the device from the Node.

---

[7]Additional details can be found at https://docs.openshift.com/container-platform/3.11/install_config/persistent_storage/persistent_storage_flex_volume.html#flex-volume-drivers-with-master-initiated-attach-detach

[8]Additional details can be found at https://docs.openshift.com/container-platform/3.11/install_config/persistent_storage/persistent_storage_flex_volume.html#flex-volume-drivers-without-master-initiated-attach-detach

CSI

The *Container Storage Interface (CSI)* was designed to provide a way for vendors to develop storage plugins for any container orchestration platform following the *CSI* specification. This means these plugins are not tied to *Kubernetes* but any *CSI-compliant* platform. *CSI* was introduced into *Kubernetes* as a way to decouple plugin development from Kubernetes releases and prevent bugs from a plugin from affecting other *Kubernetes* critical components.

Contrary to *FlexVolume* plugins that use an exec-based API and assume plugins have access to the root filesystem, the *CSI* plugins use a *gRPC* interface over a unix domain socket.

To support *CSI* plugins, a CSI-compliant plugin interface recommended[9] architecture was defined (Figure 4-4). The CSI plugin interface was included starting in *Kubernetes 1.9* and was made GA in *Kubernetes 1.13*.

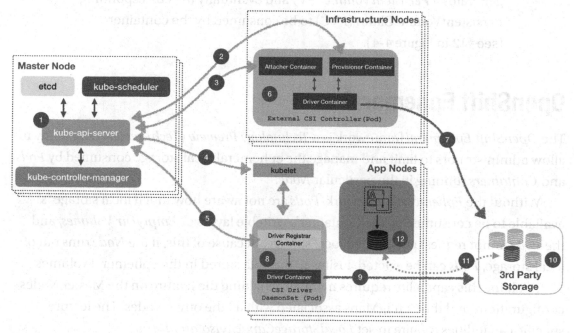

Figure 4-4. CSI plugin recommended architecture

---

[9]Details about recommended deployment mechanisms for CSI plugin on Kubernetes are available at https://github.com/kubernetes/community/blob/master/contributors/design-proposals/storage/container-storage-interface.md#recommended-mechanism-for-deploying-csi-drivers-on-kubernetes

The Kubernetes CSI volume plugin implements the following internal volume interfaces:

- **VolumePlugin**: Mount and unmount of a Volume to a specific path. During the mount operation, Kubernetes generates a unique path and passes it to the CSI Driver DaemonSet (see #4, #5, and #8 in Figure 4-4) for the CSI plugin to mount the volume (see #9 and #11 in Figure 4-4).

- **AttachableVolumePlugin**: Attach and detach of a volume to a given node. This action is handled by the CSI External Controller (see #2, #3, and #6 in Figure 4-4). It is up to the CSI external controller to determine when a CSI Volume must be attached or detached from a particular Node (see #7 and #10 in Figure 4-4). Once the CSI controller determines a Volume should be attached to a Node, it generates a *PersistentVolume (PV)* and eventually the corresponding PersistentVolumeClaim (PVC) to be consumed by the container (see #12 in Figure 4-4).

OpenShift Ephemeral

The *OpenShift Ephemeral* framework is a *Technology Preview (TechPreview)* capability to allow administrators to limit and manage the ephemeral local storage consumed by *Pods* and *Containers* running in the particular *Node*.

Without the *Ephemeral* framework, *Pods* are not aware how much local storage is available to be consumed by the Container's writable layers or *EmptyDir Volumes,* and the *Pod* cannot request guaranteed local storage. Because of this, if the *Node* runs out of local storage, *Pods* can be evicted, losing all the data stored in the ephemeral volumes.

Enabling this capability requires manually enabling the feature on the Master Nodes configurations and the ConfigMaps associated with all the other Nodes. The feature-specific capabilities require to set *LocalStorageCapacityIsolation=true.*[10]

---

[10]For the specific steps toward enabling the LocalStorageCapacityIsolation, refer to `https:// docs.openshift.com/container-platform/3.11/install_config/configuring_ephemeral. html#ephemeral-storage-enabling-ephemeral-storage`

OpenShift Container Storage

The *OpenShift Container Storage (OCS)*[11] brings the software-defined storage capabilities of the *Gluster*[12] *and Heketi*[13] open source projects as a native storage solution into *Containers* environments. It does this by adding a *REST API* interface to front end the *Gluster* services.

The *OpenShift Container Storage (OCS)* supports two deployment modes: converged mode and independent mode (see Figure 4-5).

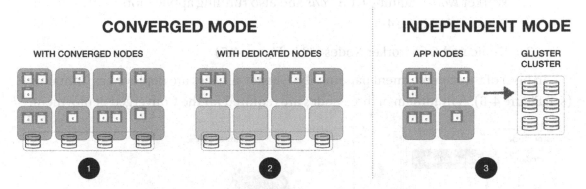

Figure 4-5. *OpenShift Container Storage deployment modes*

Note   During the installation of OCS using the OpenShift advanced installer (openshift-ansible), only one of the OCS modes can be specified. Should both modes be required in a cluster, one of the modes can be installed with the Ansible workflow and the other must be manually configured.[14]

---

[11]Additional information about OCS is available at (an active Red Hat subscription is required to access this link) https://access.redhat.com/documentation/en-us/red_hat_openshift_container_storage/3.11/

[12]The upstream Gluster project is available at www.gluster.org

[13]The Heketi RESTful API for Gluster project is available at https://github.com/heketi/heketi

[14]The Red Hat OpenShift Container Storage (OCS) Deployment Guide provides step-by-step instructions for manual installation of the OCS deployment modes (an active Red Hat subscription is required to access this link): https://access.redhat.com/documentation/en-us/red_hat_openshift_container_storage/3.11/html/deployment_guide/

OCS Converged Mode

The *OCS Converged Mode* deploys a hyperconverged environment with an end result where the *Nodes* are providing *Compute* and storage services to the cluster.

From the technical perspective, *OCS Converged Mode* deploys an environment where the *Gluster* storage *Containers* reside in *Nodes* where it mounts raw disks attached to these *Nodes* that are then used for the *Gluster* service (see #1 and #2 in Figure 4-5).

There are two common deployment patterns with *OCS Converged Mode*:

1. Worker *Nodes* running *OCS Pods* and also running application Pods (#1 in Figure 4-5)

2. Dedicated *OCS* worker Nodes (#2 in Figure 4-5)

In both of these deployment patterns, the Gluster services are deployed as Containers (see Figure 4-6). A minimum of three nodes are required for the Converged deployment.

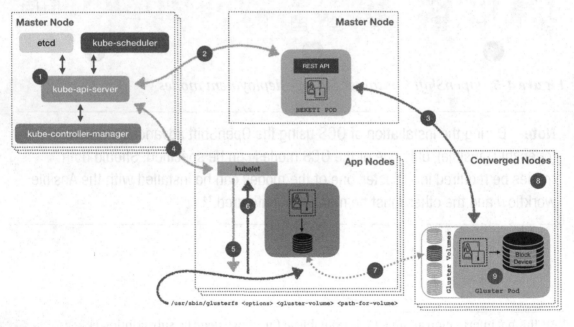

Figure 4-6. *OCS Converged Mode*

Tip   *OCS Converged Mode* is commonly illustrated using *Application Nodes* as the *Converged Nodes,* but it is not limited to those. With the proper planning and design considerations, another option is to deploy *OCS Converged Mode* to *Infrastructure Nodes* instead.

Raw Disks for OCS Converged Mode

The raw block devices for the Gluster service Pods can be provided by Kernel using any supported technology to provide raw block devices to the Node (see Figure 4-7).

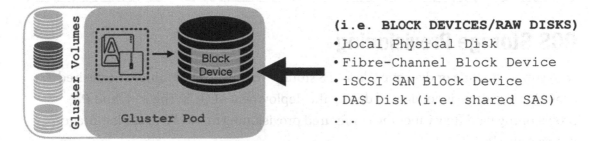

(i.e. BLOCK DEVICES/RAW DISKS)
- Local Physical Disk
- Fibre-Channel Block Device
- iSCSI SAN Block Device
- DAS Disk (i.e. shared SAS)
  ...

Figure 4-7. *OCS Converged Mode block device*

OCS Independent Mode

OCS Independent Mode uses an external or standalone Gluster cluster managed by an instance of Heketi REST API (#3 and #8 Figure 4-8).

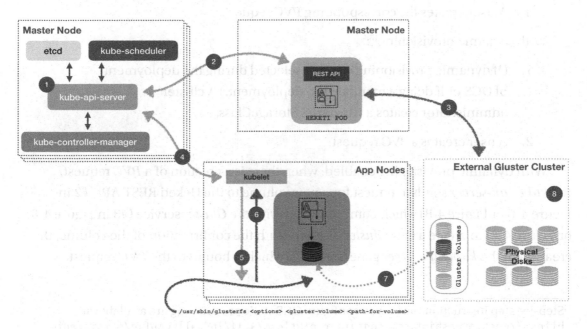

Figure 4-8. *OCS Independent Mode*

> **Note**   Even when the *Heketi* service can run either as a regular system service or as a *Container*, the recommendation is for *Heketi* to be deployed as a *Pod* on *OpenShift* so it can benefit from the HA capabilities of the platform.

OCS Storage Provisioning

OCS supports static or dynamic *GlusterFS* storage volume provisioning. The desired provisioning mode is configured during the deployment of *OCS*. The *PVC* and *PV* provisioning workflow varies the configured provisioning mode. With static storage provisioning[15]:

1. The GlusterFS administrator creates a GlusterFS volume.

2. A user with cluster-admin privileges creates the corresponding GlusterFS Kubernetes Endpoints in the cluster.

3. A user with cluster-admin privileges creates a PV definition.

4. A user creates the corresponding PVC request.

With dynamic provisioning[16]:

1. (If dynamic provisioning was not selected during the deployment of OCS or if doing a manual OCS deployment.) A cluster administrator creates a GlusterFS StorageClass.

2. A user creates a PVC request.

With dynamic provisioning enabled, when there is a creation of a *PVC* request, the *kube-api-server* sends a request for a new volume to the Heketi REST API (#2 in Figure 4-6 or Figure 4-8) which communicates with the *Gluster* service (#3 in Figure 4-6 or Figure 4-8) to create a new *Gluster Volume*. With the confirmation of the volume, the creation of the *kube-api-server* generates a *PV* which is bound to the *PVC* request.

---

[15]Step-by-step instructions on how to configure OCS static provisioning are available at https://docs.openshift.com/container-platform/3.11/install_config/persistent_storage/persistent_storage_glusterfs.html#provisioning-static

[16]Instructions for configuring OCS dynamic provisioning on an existing cluster are available at https://docs.openshift.com/container-platform/3.11/install_config/persistent_storage/persistent_storage_glusterfs.html#provisioning-dynamic

When the *Kubelet* service (#4 in Figure 4-6 or Figure 4-8) receives the mount request, it invokes the *mount.glusterfs* system command (#5 and #6 in Figure 4-6 or Figure 4-8) with the appropriate parameters to mount the volume to the *Container*. When the *Kubelet* receives an unmount volume request, it uses the *umount* system command.

When the *PVC* is deleted, the *PV* is destroyed and a notification is sent to the Heketi service (#2 in Figure 4-6 or Figure 4-8) which in turn notifies *Gluster* service (#3 in Figure 4-6 or Figure 4-8).

Note   After the *PVC* and *PV* objects are destroyed and do not exist in the *Kubernetes* environment, from the *Gluster* cluster perspective, it might not be the case as the action of completely deleting and recycling a *Gluster* volume may take additional time.

Storage Classes

A StorageClass is a Kubernetes construct for cluster administrators to create storage profiles describing the storage options available for the platform. Cluster administrators are free to use the StorageClass to represent storage types, or backup policies, or quality-of-service levels, or replication policies, or encryption policies, or any other arbitrary characteristic or service determined relevant for the organization.

A *StorageClass*[17] configuration consists of a *YAML* file with the following options:

- **Provisioner**: (#3 in Figure 4-9) Determines the volume plugin to use for provisioning PVs under the specified StorageClass.

- **Reclaim Policy**: (#5 in Figure 4-9) Tells the cluster what to do with the *Volume* after it is released. The policy can be either *Delete, Retain, or Recycle*.[18] With dynamically provisioned volumes, the *Reclaim Policy* is *Delete*.

- **Mount Options** (optional): (#6 in Figure 4-9) Mount options for dynamically created *PVs*.

---

[17]The details of StorageClass resources are described in the upstream Kubernetes documentation: `https://kubernetes.io/docs/concepts/storage/storage-classes/#the-storageclass-resource`

[18]The Recycle Reclaim Policy is considered deprecated. `https://kubernetes.io/docs/concepts/storage/persistent-volumes/#recycle`

- **Volume Binding Mode**: (#7 in Figure 4-9) This parameter controls the *Volume* binding and dynamic *Volume* provisioning.

- **Allowed Topologies** (optional): Used to restrict provisioning to specific topologies.

- **Parameters** (optional): (#4 in Figure 4-9) This section is used to set *Provisioner*-specific parameters.

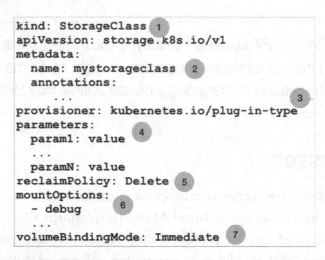

```
kind: StorageClass  1
apiVersion: storage.k8s.io/v1
metadata:
  name: mystorageclass  2
  annotations:
    ...
provisioner: kubernetes.io/plug-in-type    3
parameters:
  param1: value  4
  ...
  paramN: value
reclaimPolicy: Delete  5
mountOptions:
  - debug    6
  ...
volumeBindingMode: Immediate  7
```

Figure 4-9. *Sample StorageClass definition*

Note   A *StorageClass* definition is required for enabling dynamic storage provisioning.

OpenShift with Third-Party Storage

Beyond the list[19] of supported OpenShift software-defined storage (SDS) plugins, because of the availability of the *FlexVolume* and *CSI* plugins, there are many third-party traditional or modern storage solutions supported for OpenShift. This section is a reference (nonexhaustive) list of additional third-party storage vendors. Additional vendors can be found at the OpenShift Primed[20] web site.

---

[19]OpenShift Persistent Volume plugins: https://docs.openshift.com/container-platform/ 3.11/install_config/persistent_storage/index.html

[20]OpenShift Primed technical readiness: www.openshift.com/learn/partners/primed/

DriveScale Composable Platform

The *DriveScale Composable Platform*[21] by *DriveScale* is a composable storage platform that aggregates JBOD chassis behind the *DriveScale Composer*. From there, the raw disks are presented as iSCSI targets.

DriveScale supports dynamic storage provisioning in *OpenShift*. At the moment of this writing, DriveScale has a FlexVolume and a CSI plugin. The *DriveScale FlexVolume* plugin is available at the *Red Hat ISV* registry[22] and the *CSI*[23] plugin is provided directly by them.

From the *OpenShift* perspective, at the creation of a new *PVC*, the *DriveScale FlexVolume* plugin interacts with the *DriveScale Composer* and dynamically allocates disks from the JBOD. It then proceeds to present them directly to the *Node* running the *Container* and mount them as a *Volume* into the *Container*. If the *Pod* is reinstantiated into another *Node*, the plugin takes care of unmounting the disk from the *Node* and mounting it into the new *Node*.

HPE 3PAR

The *HPE 3PAR*[24] storage by *HPE* is an all-flash or hybrid storage array platform with support for data services and quality of services guaranteed for the storage. The LUNs are presented to the *Nodes* over *FibreChannel (FC)* or *iSCSI* protocols.

HPE 3PAR supports dynamic storage provisioning in *OpenShift*. At the time of this writing, HPE provides a *FlexVolume* plugin[25] for *OpenShift*. The HPE *FlexVolume* driver is named *Dory*, and the dynamic provisioner is named *Doryd*. The configuration for the plugin can either be set for FibreChannel (FC) or iSCSI, not both at the time. The *FibreChannel (FC)* protocol is supported for OpenShift bare-metal deployments, and the *iSCSI* protocol is supported for *OpenShift* bare-metal or *OpenShift* over virtualization environments.

---

[21]Additional information about the DriveScale Composable Platform is available at https://drivescale.com/composable-platform/

[22]DriveScale Composable Platform FlexVolume plugin: https://access.redhat.com/containers/?tab=overview#/registry.connect.redhat.com/drivescale/flexvolume

[23]DriveScale CSI plugin: https://github.com/DriveScale/k8s-plugins

[24]Additional information about the HPE 3PAR storage is available at www.hpe.com/us/en/storage/3par.html

[25]Additional information about the HPE 3PAR FlexVolume plugin is available at https://github.com/hpe-storage/python-hpedockerplugin/blob/master/ansible_3par_docker_plugin/README.md

From the *OpenShift* perspective, at the creation of a new *PVC*, the *HPE 3PAR FlexVolume* plugin interacts with the *Doryd* and dynamically allocates LUNs from the HPE 3PAR storage array. *Dory* presents them directly to the *Node* running the *Container* and mounts them as a *Volume* into the *Container*. If the Pod is reinstantiated into another Node, the plugin takes care of unmounting the disk from the *Node* and mounting it into the new *Node*.

HPE Nimble

The *HPE Nimble*[26] storage by *HPE* is an all-flash high-performance storage platform with support for data-at-rest encryption, extreme availability, and sub-millisecond response time. The LUNs are presented to the *Nodes* over the *iSCSI* protocol.

HPE Nimble supports dynamic storage provisioning in *OpenShift*. At the time of this writing, HPE provides a *FlexVolume* plugin[27] for *OpenShift*. The HPE *FlexVolume* is available from the Red Hat ISV registry.[28]

From the *OpenShift* perspective, at the creation of a new *PVC*, the *HPE Nimble FlexVolume* plugin interacts with the *Nimble Dynamic Provisioner* and dynamically allocates LUNs from the HPE Nimble storage. This LUN is presented directly to the *Node* running the *Container* and mounts as a *Volume* into the *Container*. If the Pod is reinstantiated into another Node, the plugin takes care of unmounting the disk from the *Node* and mounting it into the new *Node*.

NetApp Trident

NetApp Trident[29] is an open source project maintained by *NetApp* designed to support the *NetApp* storage portfolio in *Docker* and *Kubernetes* environments. The plugin supports the NFS or iSCSI protocols.

---

[26]Additional information about the HPE 3PAR storage is available at `www.hpe.com/us/en/storage/3par.html`

[27]Additional information about the HPE 3PAR FlexVolume plugin is available at `https://github.com/hpe-storage/python-hpedockerplugin/blob/master/ansible_3par_docker_plugin/README.md`

[28]The HPE Nimble Kube Storage Controller is available at `https://access.redhat.com/containers/?tab=overview#/registry.connect.redhat.com/nimble/kube-storage-controller`

[29]Additional information about NetApp Trident is available in the upstream documentation: `https://netapp-trident.readthedocs.io/en/stable-v19.01/`

NetApp Trident supports dynamic storage provisioning in *OpenShift*. At the time of this writing, by default, *NetApp Trident* provides a plugin which uses the native *Kubernetes iSCSI* and *NFS* plugins and provides an experimental *CSI* plugin[30] implementation.

From the *OpenShift* perspective at the creation of a new PVC, the NetApp Trident plugin provisions the corresponding *LUN* or *Volume* in the storage array and relies in the native *Kubernetes iSCSI* or *NFS* plugins for mounting the Volume into the *Container*.

OpenEBS (OSS, MayaData)

OpenEBS[31] is an open source project supported by MayaData to provide block storage with tiering and replica policies. While it can use any block devices as the backend storage, the OpenEBS Volumes are presented to the Nodes over the iSCSI protocol.

OpenEBS supports dynamic storage provisioning in *OpenShift*. At the time of this writing, *OpenEBS* provides a *FlexVolume* plugin available from the *Red Hat ISV registry*[32] or directly from the upstream[33] project.

From the OpenShift perspective at the creation of a *PVC*, the OpenEBS plugin creates a volume. A volume is represented by a series of Pods. First there is Pod that works as the iSCSI target[34] for the particular volume. This is the target that is presented to the *Node* running the *Container* and mounts as a Volume into the *Container*. Supporting the iSCSI target volume, there is one Pod per replica. For example, if the configuration is set to have three replicas, there will be three Pods, each one representing one of the replicas. This replica Pods provide the actual backend storage for the Volume. The backend storage can be supported by any block device.

---

[30]CSI Trident for Kubernetes: https://netapp-trident.readthedocs.io/en/stable-v19.01/kubernetes/trident-csi.html?highlight=CSI#csi-trident-for-kubernetes

[31]OpenEBS: www.openebs.io

[32]OpenEBS API Server and volume exporter: https://access.redhat.com/containers/#/product/54cd9cf908d9f6b7

[33]OpenEBS project documentation: https://docs.openebs.io/docs/next/installation.html

[34]For additional information around the constructs of OpenEBS, refer to the upstream documentation in GitHub: https://github.com/openebs/openebs/blob/master/contribute/design/README.md#openebs-volume-container-aka-jiva-aka-data-plane

Summary

The use of storage in *Kubernetes* and *OpenShift* environments can be grouped under two classifications: ephemeral storage and persistent storage. The different use cases of ephemeral storage rely on the underlying *Node* filesystem. When working with persistent storage, there are new constructs in play. OpenShift and Kubernetes provide an extensible plugin framework that enables third-party storage providers to onboard their solutions developing plugins at their own phase and independently, without having to coordinate releases with the *Kubernetes* core project.

There are many more persistent storage providers and plugins for OpenShift. The *OpenShift Primed* web site is good place to find additional ones understanding the ecosystem supporting OpenShift and Kubernetes is much larger than the list there.

Once the Containers have networking and storage services, containerized applications can start serving requests. To benefit from the HA capabilities of the platform, the traffic to these applications should consider the use of load balancers. Chapter 5 explores various configuration options to steer traffic to the cluster using load balancers.

CHAPTER 5

Load Balancers

As seen in Chapters 1 through 4, the OpenShift platform integrates and builds on top of Kubernetes to provide an environment to run and scale containerized applications reliably. To maintain the most resiliency and benefit the most from the HA capabilities of the platform, the infrastructure hosting the cluster should use load balancers to steer the traffic to the Nodes in the cluster serving the application at a given time. This chapter explores various configuration options when using load balancers with OpenShift.

Load Balancer Overview

When considering the use of external Load Balancers with the OpenShift platform, there are general target areas or traffic types. Each type of traffic will have different requirements based on the desired outcome and the capabilities of the external device or virtual appliance used at load balancing. The use cases for load balancer can be grouped in, at least, the following three types:

- **Load balancing traffic to the *Master Nodes*** (#1 in Figure 5-1): This load balancer should be present for any highly available deployment. For small deployments and lab environments, OpenShift provides the option to deploy a software load balancer based on HAProxy. (Refer to "HA for Masters Services" section in Chapter 2).

- **Load balancing traffic to the *Infrastructure Nodes*** (#2 in Figure 5-1): This is the load balancer handling the traffic to applications running on the cluster and using the *OpenShift Router* as their ingress endpoint. This load balancer is recommended for any highly available deployment even though it can be as simple as a round-robin DNS resolution for the apps wildcard subdomain.

99

© William Caban 2019
W. Caban, *Architecting and Operating OpenShift Clusters*, https://doi.org/10.1007/978-1-4842-4985-7_5

- **Load balancing traffic directly to *Application Nodes* or Pods** (#3, #4, and #5 in Figure 5-1): This load balancer only exists in nonstandard deployments requiring specialized networking interaction between the client and the application *Nodes* or directly with the *Pods*.

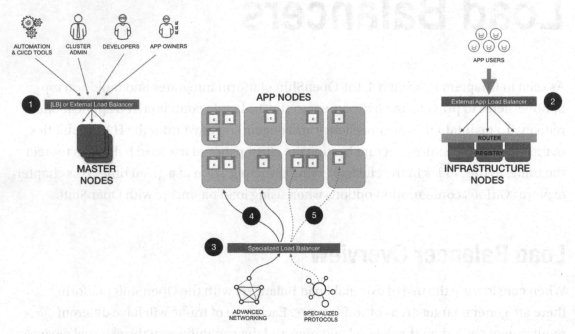

Figure 5-1. *OpenShift and Load Balancers*

Load Balancer Considerations

There are many load balancer options in the market. Instead of focusing on a particular software or hardware solution, let's focus on the basic requirements for each type of traffic and destination in an OpenShift cluster.

Considerations for Master Nodes

As presented during the discussion of *High Availability for Master Nodes* in *Chapter* 2, these *Nodes* are the ones exposing the *Kubernetes APIs*, the web interface for the *Developer* or *Application Console*, the *Service Portal,* and the *Operations Console* (see #1 in Figure 5-1). From the perspective of web sessions, the *Master Nodes* are stateless, meaning it does not matter which *Master* receives the request during interactions with the *API*. There are no special requirements for persistent sessions or sticky sessions. Because of this, the load balancing service functioning as the front end for the *Master Nodes* can use simple load balancing algorithms (i.e., source IP, round-robin, etc.) to distribute the load among the *Master Nodes*.

Refer to *Chapter* 2 for details on the requirements for load balancers for *Master Nodes*.

Considerations for Infrastructure Nodes

Traffic load balancing for the *Infrastructure Nodes* refers to a load balancer handling the traffic destined to the *OpenShift Routers* (see #2 in Figure 5-1) which serve as the main ingress point for any external traffic destined to applications and services running on the cluster. A simple *DNS round-robin* resolution can be used to spread traffic across *Infrastructure Nodes* and, from that perspective, an external load balancer for traffic destined to these *Nodes* is optional. Normally, production environments prefer to have more advanced load balancing capabilities to distribute the traffic among the *OpenShift Routers*. In those cases, an external load balancer is used.

This external load balancer for the *OpenShift Routers* should be configured in passthrough mode (see Listings 5-1 and 5-2). This means the load balancer will do *connection tracking* and *Network Address Translation (NAT)*, but the *TCP* connections are not terminated by the load balancer; instead, they are forwarded to one of the *Router* instances at the *Infrastructure Node*s (see #1 in Figure 5-2).

Listing 5-1. Passthrough configuration example with NGINX

```
# NOTE: extract from nginx.conf
<snip>
stream {
    # Passthrough required for the routers
    upstream ocp-http {
        # Worker Nodes running OCP Router
        server worker-0.ocp.example.com:80;
        server worker-1.ocp.example.com:80;
    }
    upstream ocp-https {
        # Worker Nodes running OCP Router
        server worker-0.ocp.example.com:443;
        server worker-1.ocp.example.com:443;
    }
```

```
    server {
        listen 443;
        proxy_pass ocp-https;
    }

    server {
        listen 80;
        proxy_pass ocp-http;
    }
}
<snip>
```

Listing 5-2. Passthrough configuration example with HAProxy

```
# NOTE: extract from haproxy.cfg
<snip>
frontend ocp-http
    bind *:8080
    default_backend ocp-http
    mode tcp
    option tcplog

backend ocp-http
    balance source
    mode tcp
    server worker-0 192.168.1.15:80 check
  server worker-1 192.168.1.16:80 check

frontend ocp-https
    bind *:443
    default_backend ocp-https
    mode tcp
    option tcplog

backend ocp-https
    balance source
    mode tcp
```

```
      server worker-0 192.168.1.15:443 check
      server worker-1 192.168.1.16:443 check
<snip>
```

At the *OpenShift Router,* this traffic is matched with a *Route* (see #3 in Figure 5-2), and it is load balanced among the *Pods* of the corresponding *Service* object (see #4 in Figure 5-2).

The *OpenShift Router* supports *roundrobin, leastconn,* and *source* as the load balancing algorithms or load balancing strategies.[1] The *source* is considered the default load balancing strategy.

The default load balancing strategy and other *OpenShift Router* parameters can be configured by setting the corresponding *Environment Variable* for the *OpenShift Router DeploymentConfig.*[2]

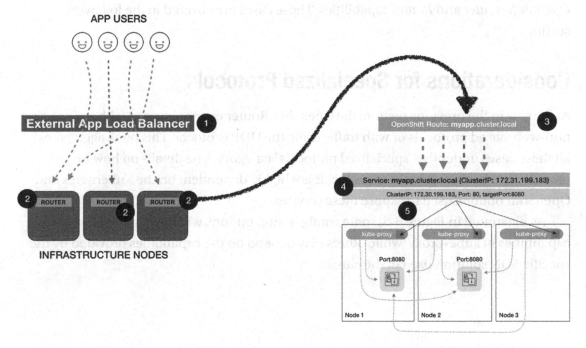

Figure 5-2. *Traffic flow from external load balancers to OpenShift Routers*

---

[1]The supported load balancing strategies are described here: https://docs.openshift.com/container-platform/3.11/architecture/networking/routes.html#load-balancing

[2]A list of available Environment Variables to fine-tune the OpenShift Router is available at https://docs.openshift.com/container-platform/3.11/architecture/networking/routes.html#env-variables

103

Note   The specific behavior of the traffic at the *Router* level may be different if using third-party *Router* plugins.

The *OpenShift Router* supports the following protocols:

- HTTP
- HTTPS with SNI[3]
- WebSockets
- TLS with SNI

Any traffic for protocols outside these web protocols cannot make use of the *OpenShift Router* and *Routes* capabilities. Those cases are covered in the following section.

Considerations for Specialized Protocols

As we saw in the previous section, the OpenShift Router cannot be used with traffic using non-web-based protocols or with traffic using the UDP protocol. This book aggregates all these cases under the "specialized protocols" category. The details on how to provide load balancing to these protocols are highly dependent on the Kubernetes and OpenShift options used to expose these services.

As illustrated in Figure 5-3, some configuration options will rely on the native capabilities of kube-proxy, while others may depend on the capabilities provided by the specific SDN solution used in the cluster.

---

[3]Standard Name Indication (SNI) is an extension of the TLS protocol. With this extension, the client indicates the *hostname* it is trying to contact at the start of the *handshaking* process.

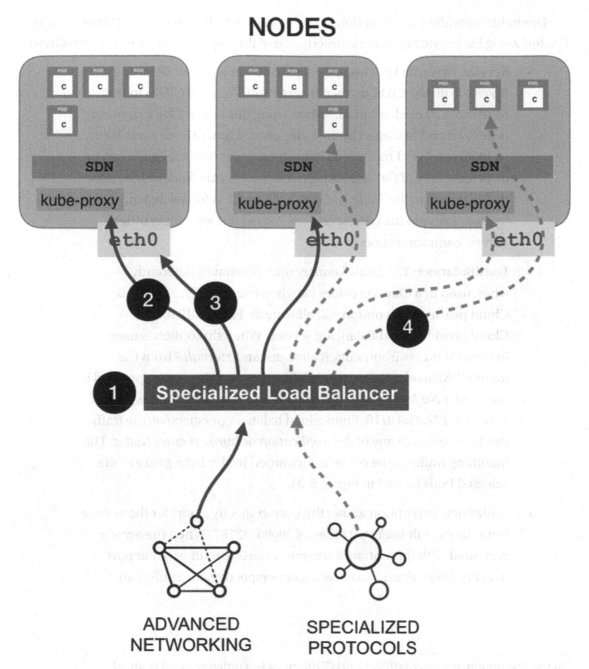

Figure 5-3. *Representation of load balancer for non-HTTP/HTTPS/TLS protocols*

OpenShift provides several options to support non-web-based or UDP-based traffic. The following list provides a general description of the options and their functionalities:

- **Service External IP**: This option allocates an *External IP* for the *Service* from the CIDR defined by *externalIPNetworkCIDRs* in the *Master Nodes* configuration.[4] When using this option, the *ExternalIP* is defined and managed by the kube-proxy agent in each node (see #2 in Figure 5-3). From a load balancer perspective, the traffic can be directed to any of the *Application* or *Infrastructure Nodes*. Once the traffic arrives to the *Node*, the incoming traffic is forwarded internally by *kube-proxy* to the corresponding *Pods* as it does for any other *Service* communication.

- **LoadBalancer**: The *LoadBalancer* option behaves differently when used in a Cloud provider vs. when used locally. At a Public Cloud provider, this option will allocate an ExternalIP for the Cloud provider Load Balancing service. When this option is used in non-Cloud environments, it allocates an *ExternalIP* from the *ingressIPNetworkCIDR* network. When this variable is not specified in the *Master Nodes* configuration,[5] the default network for this type of *Service* is 172.29.0.0/16. From a load balancer perspective, the traffic can be directed to any of the *Application* or *Infrastructure Nodes*. The incoming traffic to the *Nodes* is forwarded by the *kube-proxy* to the selected Pods (see #2 in Figure 5-3).

- **nodePort**: This option allows the user to specify a port for the *Service* from the default *nodePort* range of 30000–32767. When the *Service* is created with this option, *kube-proxy* starts listening to that port in every *Node*. From a load balancer perspective, the traffic can

---

[4]To use this option, the *externalIPNetworkCDIRs* must be configured and enabled: `https://docs.openshift.com/container-platform/3.11/dev_guide/expose_service/expose_internal_ip_service.html`

[5]To customize the ExternalIPs for this option, use the *ingressIPNetworkCIDR* variable in the *Master Node* configuration: `https://docs.openshift.com/container-platform/3.11/admin_guide/tcp_ingress_external_ports.html#unique-external-ips-ingress-traffic-configure-cluster`

be directed to any of the *Application* or *Infrastructure Nodes*. The incoming traffic to the *Nodes* is forwarded by the *kube-proxy* to the selected Pods (see #2 in Figure 5-3).

- **hostPort**: This option allows the user to bind a *Pod* to any *Port* of the *Node,* and the *Container* will be exposed to the external network as <hostIP>:<hostPort>, where *hostIP* is the physical IP of the *Node* running the particular *Pod*, and *hostPort* is the port number specified in the *Pod* definition. The load balancer for this option needs to be configured to send traffic to the physical IP of the *Node* running the *Pod* (see #3 in Figure 5-3). A consideration when using this option is that the *hostIP* of the <hostIP>:<hostPort> pair will change if the *Pod* recreated in another *Node*.

- **hostNetwork**: This option enables the Pod to have full visibility of the Node network interfaces. This is the equivalent of the *Pod* sharing the network namespace with the *Node*. This option is not recommended for running application. It is normally used by SDN plugins and other network functions deployed as DaemonSets or privileged containers.

- **IP Failover**: The *IP Failover*[6] option is an OpenShift-specific capability which enables the creation of a *Virtual IP address (VIP)* for the applications. When this configuration is enabled, OpenShift deploys *Keepalived* privileged containers to handle the particular *VIP*. These *Keepalived Pods* for the IP Failover capability can be deployed cluster-wide or in a subset of Nodes matching a particular label. These *Pods* use the *VRRP* protocol to maintain the *VIP* address active. Only one of the *Keepalived Pods* will be active or in *MASTER* state serving the *VIP* address at a time; the others will be on standby or in *BACKUP* state. The *VRRP* protocol is used to determine which *Pod* gets to be active for a particular *VIP*. From a load balancer perspective, the *Node* with the active Pod serving the VIP address is the only one capable of handling the traffic destined to that VIP address.

---

[6]For configuration requirements for the OpenShift IP Failover capability, refer to
`https://docs.openshift.com/container-platform/3.11/admin_guide/high_availability.`
`html#configuring-ip-failover`

In addition to the options described here, there are other techniques which are more relevant to *Cloud* environments. One of these options is the *LoadBalancer* which requires external support by a Cloud provider. In this case, Kubernetes interacts with the *Cloud* platform to provision a *Cloud Load Balancer* with an *External IP* for the *Service*. Another option are SDNs like Calico or MacVLAN which can be configured to expose the *Pods IPs* to the upstream networking equipment enabling direct access to the *Pods* from the external networks (see #4 in Figure 5-3). In this case, it is up to the networking team to manage the network traffic directed to the *Pods*.

Summary

Configuring a load balancer service in *OpenShift* for *Master Nodes* and *OpenShift Routers* at the *Infrastructure Nodes* can be a simple pass-through load balancing configuration. These can be considered web-friendly protocols: HTTP, HTTPS, TLS, and WebSockets. Supporting UDP or non-web-friendly protocols with Kubernetes and OpenShift requires the use of a different set of objects and capabilities. The particular load balancer configuration for these use cases requires an understanding of the workload, the option being used, and the level of exposure of the *Services* and *Pods* to the external networks.

Having a base understanding of how the networking, storage, and traffic routing options work for OpenShift, Chapter 6 will focus on putting all this knowledge together for a successful deployment of a cluster.

CHAPTER 6

Deployment Architectures

Having an understanding of the OpenShift components and platform as seen in the previous chapters provides the basis for understanding some of the configuration options that are set during the installation.

OpenShift (OCP) provides the ability to customize the deployment architecture. The exact customization is highly dependent on the version and release, so it is necessary to group the deployment process in two main categories:

- **OCP 3.11 release**: This is considered a long-term release. At the time of this writing, the latest subrelease is 3.11.99.[1] The 3.11.x advanced deployment methodology uses the OpenShift Ansible installer, and it is supported in any x86 platform where RHEL is supported.

Note At the time of this writing, version 3.11.x is considered to be Technology Preview or Development Preview for Microsoft Windows Server 2019, Power 8 and Power 9. This book does not cover any of these operating systems and architectures.

- **OCP 4.0 release**: This is considered the new major release of OpenShift that brings a new deployment and management paradigm. At the time of this writing, the latest version is 4.0 Beta 3. This means OCP 4.0 is still in active development and has not reached the general availability (GA).

---

[1]For details about the latest 3.11.x release, visit https://docs.openshift.com/container-platform/3.11/release_notes/ocp_3_11_release_notes.html#ocp-3-11-98

© William Caban 2019
W. Caban, *Architecting and Operating OpenShift Clusters*, https://doi.org/10.1007/978-1-4842-4985-7_6

Note   At the time of this writing, 4.0 is considered beta and it is available for AWS with minimal customization. This book covers the AWS deployment architecture.

This chapter presents the most common scenarios that can be used to start deploying OpenShift clusters, and as you'll see, both versions have their advantages and disadvantages, and independent from the deployment methodology, each one provides ways to highly customize the environment to fit the organization's need.

Before going into the two deployment approaches, let's quickly review Minishift, a development tool for Windows, MacOS, and Linux that enables developers to run an OpenShift environment in their workstations.

Minishift

Currently the *Minishift* development tool is a distribution based on OCP 3.11.x or OKD 3.11.x that runs as a Virtual Machine (VM).

Minishift can be downloaded as part of the *Red Hat Container Development Kit (CDK)*,[2] which includes additional Red Hat development tools and middleware. Alternatively, the upstream Minishift from the *OKD* community can be obtained from the *Minishift Git*[3] repository.

Visit the *Minishift* documentation[4] for installation details for a specific platform. The following are common steps to fine-tune Minishift:

- Allocate a minimum of two vCPUs to Minishift (see #2 in Figure 6-1).

- Allocate at least 8 GB to Minishift (see #2 in Figure 6-1).

- To access additional software from the Red Hat Subscription, define and export the corresponding environment variables (see #4 in Figure 6-1).

---

[2]For information of and to download the Red Hat CDK, refer to `https://developers.redhat.com/products/cdk/overview/`

[3]The upstream Minishift project documentation is available at `https://github.com/minishift/minishift/releases`

The Red Hat CDK documentation is available at (requires access to the Red Hat portal) `https://access.redhat.com/documentation/en-us/red_hat_container_development_kit/3.7/`

[4]Upstream Minishift documentation: `https://docs.okd.io/latest/minishift/getting-started/index.html`

- Activate additional add-ons as needed (see #5 in Figure 6-1).

```
$ minishift setup-cdk  ①

$ minishift config set cpus 2  ②
$ minishift config set memory 8GB

$ minishift config view  ③
- cpus                   : 2
- image-caching          : true
- iso-url                : file:///your/home/.minishift/cache/iso/minishift-rhel7.iso
- memory                 : 8GB
- ocp-tag                : vlatest
- openshift-version      : vlatest
- vm-driver              : xhyve


$ export MINISHIFT_USERNAME=<RED_HAT_USERNAME>  ④
$ export MINISHIFT_PASSWORD=<RED_HAT_PASSWORD>

$ minishift addons list  ⑤
- admin-user                 : enabled    P(0)
- anyuid                     : enabled    P(0)
- eap-cd                     : enabled    P(0)
- registry-route             : enabled    P(0)
- xpaas                      : enabled    P(0)
- che                        : disabled   P(0)
- htpasswd-identity-provider : disabled   P(0)


$ minishift start  ⑥
```

Figure 6-1. *Minishift configuration*

Minishift provides the developer experience similar to OCP (see Figure 6-2). From the platform perspective, there are certain *Minishift* defaults and characteristics that are different from an actual OCP cluster. For example, by default, *Minishift* enables any user to run Containers in privilege mode. In OCP, this behavior is discouraged and the cluster administrator must disable security for a user or group to allow them to run Containers in privilege mode. Another distinct characteristic is that the default identity provider with *Minishift* allows users to log in with any *username* and using any *password.* If the *username* does not exist, *Minishift* will automatically provision that user in the environment. In an OCP cluster, the user authentication is handled by the *identity provider,* and when the access is granted, if the functionality is enabled, it proceeds to create the user.

111

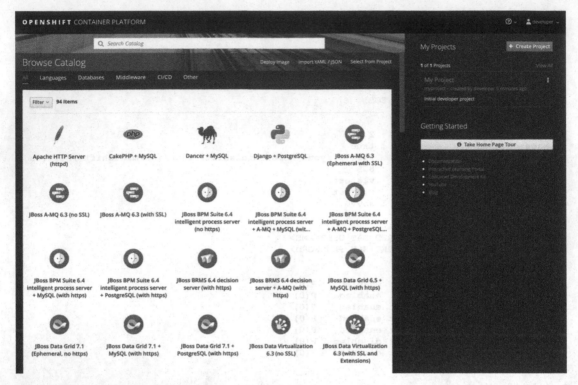

Figure 6-2. *Minishift developer experience*

OCP 3.11 Deployment Architectures

The examples in this section have been tested and validated with *OpenShift (OCP)* *3.11.69, 3.11.82, and 3.11.98*. To identify the latest subrelease of 3.11, refer to the last section of the *Release Notes*[5] as these are updated regularly with any new subrelease.

Prerequisites

OpenShift requires certain preparation of the infrastructure and configuration of ancillary datacenter services before deployment. Refer to Table 6-1 for a summary of a prescribed VM configuration used by this section. This table is a recommendation and it does not represent the minimum requirements. The list of minimum requirements is available at the official OpenShift prerequisites[6] documentation.

---

[5]For details about the latest 3.11.x releases, visit `https://docs.openshift.com/container-platform/3.11/release_notes/ocp_3_11_release_notes.html`

[6]OpenShift prerequisites: `https://docs.openshift.com/container-platform/3.11/install/prerequisites.html`

Table 6-1. *OpenShift 3.11 Nodes Configurations (Recommendation)*

Node	Node Requirements
Masters	• 8 vCPUs • Minimum 16GB RAM (recommended 32GB RAM) • Disk 100GB • /var should have 80GB free
App Nodes	• 8 vCPUs • 32GB RAM (recommended 64GB RAM) • Disk 100GB • /var should have 80GB free A Converged or Hyperconverged App Nodes must include at least a dedicated disk for OCS: • OCS Disk 500GB Raw/Unformatted (any block device) *Note: A minimum of three hyperconverged or converged nodes are required for OpenShift Container Storage (OCS)*
Infrastructure	• 8 vCPUs • 32GB RAM • Disk 100GB • /var should have 80GB free
Bastion	• 2 vCPUs • 8GB RAM • Disk 40GB
LB	• 2 vCPUs • 8GB RAM • Disk 40GB

Operating System—Minimal Installation

All *Nodes* must be configured with the following setup:

- RHEL 7.6 Minimum installation (using Red Hat standard image).

    - Recommended "Minimum" profile installation

- *RHEL* image should not have customizations from post-installation scripts.

- *SELinux* must be set to *enforcing*.

- Firewall should be enabled and running.

- Time synchronization enabled.

General Requirements for the Cluster

- All Nodes should[7] be on the same network.

- All Nodes must have identical MTU.

- All Nodes must have unfiltered communication to each other.

- All Nodes require Internet access during the installation.[8]

    - Nodes access and download RPMs and Containers from the Red Hat repository and Red Hat Container registries.

- Nodes must use static IP address.

- Nodes must have an FQDN resolvable to their IP by the DNS servers in /etc/resolv.conf.

---

[7]OpenShift supports deployment across multiple networks. There must be unrestricted reachability among the nodes for a deployment across networks. To avoid issues with external routing or firewalls, this section assumes the nodes are in the same network.

[8]Disconnected install is possible following the official documentation: https://docs.openshift. com/container-platform/3.11/install/disconnected_install.html

- Allocate a wildcard subdomain for application (i.e., *.apps.ocp. example.com). DNS servers in /etc/resolv.conf must be able to resolve any name under the application subdomain (i.e., test.apps. ocp.example.com) to the *Infrastructure Nodes* or the *Nodes* hosting the *OpenShift Router*.

Note   Installation requires *root* or *sudo* SSH access to *Nodes* from *Bastion* (or *Master Node* when not using *Bastion Node*).

SDN Subnets

OpenShift SDN uses an internal default network address. Validate there are no conflicts with the default IP address range of the internal SDN networks:

- **Containers Network** (osm_cluster_network_cidr): 10.1.0.0/16
- **Services Network** (openshift_portal_net): 172.30.0.0/16

These subnets are internal to the OCP cluster. These are NOT visible outside the cluster. Should there be an existing IP subnet within the range of any of these two subnets, a new set of private /16 networks should be designated for these purposes.

(Optional) Subnets for Hosting Apps with Non-Web-Based or Specialized Protocols

If the cluster will be hosting applications that need to present non-HTTP/HTTPS/TLS protocols to services outside the cluster, there are two additional CIDR network ranges to consider:

- 172.29.0.0/16 (ingressIPNetworkCIDR)
- <undefined CIDR> (externalIPNetworkCIDR)

These subnets are NOT internal to the OCP cluster. When deploying on-premise, the external network devices must be configured to route them to the OCP Nodes.

Registry Service Account and Token

When deploying the *Red Hat OpenShift Container Platform (OCP)*, the installation requires a *Service Account* and a *Token* to access and download *OCP* containers from *registry.redhat.io*. Before the installation, create a new Registry Service Account and generate a *Token* at https://access.redhat.com/terms-based-registry/

The username will have the format "<number>|<custom_string>" and a corresponding *Token* string will be generated. These credentials are required for the installation.

Note   This step is not necessary when deploying the OKD upstream project.

Activate and Assign OpenShift Subscriptions

Each Node must have an active RHEL and OpenShift subscription. Register each Node with a subscription following the steps in Listing 6-1.

Listing 6-1. Register RHEL and OpenShift subscriptions

```
Register each Node with RHSM
$ subscription-manager register --username=<user_name>
--password=<password>
Pull subscriptions
$ subscription-manager refresh
Identify the available OpenShift subscriptions
$ subscription-manager list --available --matches '*OpenShift*'
Assign a subscription to the node
$ subscription-manager attach --pool=<pool_id>
Disable all RHSM repositories
$ subscription-manager repos --disable="*"
Enable only repositories required by OpenShift
$ subscription-manager repos \
    --enable="rhel-7-server-rpms" \
    --enable="rhel-7-server-extras-rpms" \
    --enable="rhel-7-server-ose-3.11-rpms" \
```

```
--enable="rhel-7-server-ansible-2.6-rpms"
```
Upgrade each Node to the latest version of the OS
```
$ yum -y update
```

Prepare OCP 3.11.x Installer on Bastion

Install the OpenShift Ansible installer on the Bastion Node as per Listing 6-2.

Listing 6-2. Install OpenShift Ansible installer on Bastion

```
$ yum -y install atomic-openshift-clients openshift-ansible
```

Enable Password-less SSH

Enable password-less SSH for the OpenShift Ansible installer from the *Bastion Node* to all the other *Nodes* as per Listing 6-3.

Listing 6-3. (Example) Enable password-less SSH from Bastion

Generate key pair at Bastion Node
```
$ ssh-keygen
```
Install public key to all Nodes
```
$ for host in master.ocp.example.com \
inf1.ocp.example.com \
inf2.ocp.example.com \
app1.ocp.example.com \
app2.ocp.example.com \
app3.ocp.example.com \
do ssh-copy-id -i ~/.ssh/id_rsa.pub $host; \
Done
```

OpenShift Ansible Inventory File

The *OpenShift Ansible* installer uses a series of *Ansible Playbooks* to deploy an *OpenShift Cluster*. *Ansible* uses a hosts inventory file to group managed target and set variables for *Ansible Roles* and *Playbooks*.

This provides the ability to highly customize the deployment of an OpenShift cluster. The official *OpenShift* inventory[9] file documentation provides a list of variables available for the customization of the inventory file. There are far more variables than the ones documented in the referenced document. These are additional variables that can be used to fine-tune an inventory file. These additional customizations are documented in the corresponding section of each one of the feature or capabilities.

The fact that there cannot be a single page with all the possible variables available for customization speaks to the degree of fine-tuning that can be achieved for an *OpenShift* cluster. At the same time, having too many options may be cumbersome for someone new to *OpenShift*.

This book describes the configurations for the most common features and the most relevant variables that may be used in the organizations starting with *OpenShift*. There are multiple approaches for deploying these—from starting with a bare minimum deployment of OCP and enabling features over time to the option of doing a deployment enabling all the desired features at the install time.

The following subsections use a single inventory file enabling the most common features in an OCP cluster at install time. During production configurations, the infrastructure and operations teams can choose a more layered approach for the deployment.

Defining the OpenShift Release

The *inventory_file* is an *Ansible inventory* configuration. The first part of it is used to configure some basic information for *Ansible* itself and for the openshift-ansible playbooks. Lines 13–15 on Figure 6-3 are *Ansible* parameters to identify the username Ansible will use to connect to the *Nodes*. This user should be *root* or have *sudo* privileges. When using a regular user with *sudo* privileges, line 15 on Figure 6-3 configures *Ansible* to use sudo when connecting to the target *Node*.

---

[9]For additional details on how to configure the inventory file, visit the official documentation at
 `https://docs.openshift.com/container-platform/3.11/install/configuring_inventory_`
 `file.html`

118

```
 8   [OSEv3:vars]
 9
10   #############################################################################
11   ### Ansible Vars
12   #############################################################################
13   timeout=60
14   ansible_user={{CHANGEME_ANSIBLE_SSH_USER}}
15   ansible_become=yes
16
17   #############################################################################
18   ### OpenShift Basic Vars
19   #############################################################################
20   # Deployment type
21   openshift_deployment_type=openshift-enterprise
22
23   # WARNING: only disable these checks in LAB/TEST environments
24   #openshift_disable_check="disk_availability,memory_availability"
25
26   # OpenShift Version:
27   openshift_release=3.11.98
28
29   # Deploy Operator Lifecycle Manager (OLM)
30   openshift_enable_olm=true
31
32   # firewalld recommended for new installations (default is iptables)
33   #os_firewall_use_firewalld=true
34
```

Figure 6-3. *Inventory file—defining OpenShift Type and Release*

Line 21 on Figure 6-3 is identifying the deployment as OpenShift Container Platform (OCP) by setting the value to openshift-enterprise. When using OKD, this value is set to origin.

Line 27 on Figure 6-3 is identifying the exact subrelease to use. In this example, it is using OCP 3.11.98. This value should be as specific as possible to ease cluster upgrades among minor releases.

Tip   When specifying the OpenShift release, avoid the use of generic version numbers (i.e., 3.11) or generic tags like latest.

Even when considered Technology Preview in OCP 3.11.x, it is recommended to enable the OpenShift Operator Lifecycle Manager (Line 30 on Figure 6-3) to take full advantage of the benefits from the *Kubernetes Operators* capabilities.

By default *OpenShift* uses *iptables* for internal functionalities and Kubernetes resources like *firewall, kube-proxy, and Services,* among others. By enabling the configuration in line 33 on Figure 6-3, *OpenShift* can use *firewallD* instead.

Registry Definitions and Access

During the installation, the *openshift-ansible* installer pulls a series of Container Images from Red Hat repositories. To access these repositories requires a valid subscription, a service account and subscription (see *"Registry Service Account and Token"* section at the beginning of this chapter).

```
35   #############################################################################
36   ### OpenShift Registries Locations
37   #############################################################################
38
39   # NOTE: Need credentials from: https://access.redhat.com/terms-based-registry/
40   oreg_url=registry.redhat.io/openshift3/ose-${component}:${version}
41   oreg_auth_user={{CHANGEME_REGISTRY_SERVICE_ACCOUNT}}
42   oreg_auth_password={{CHANGEME_SERVICE_KEY}}
43
44   # For Operator Framework Images
45   openshift_additional_registry_credentials=[{'host':'registry.connect.redhat.com','user':'{{CHANGEME_REGISTRY_SERVICE_ACCOUNT}}',
     'password':'{{CHANGEME_SERVICE_KEY}}','test_image':'mongodb/enterprise-operator:0.3.2'}]
46
47   # NOTE: accept insecure registries and registries with self-signed certs
48   # setup for lab environment
49   openshift_docker_hosted_registry_insecure=true
50   #openshift_docker_insecure_registries=<registry_hostname>
51   #openshift_docker_blocked_registries=<registry_hostname>
52
53   # Update examples to point to oreg_url -- enable if using disconnected install
54   #openshift_examples_modify_imagestreams=false
55
56   #############################################################################
57   ### Enable dynamic storage provisioning
58   #############################################################################
59   # https://docs.openshift.com/container-platform/3.11/install_config/persistent_storage/dynamically_provisioning_pvs.html
60   # Note: required for OCS dynamic provisioning
61
62   openshift_master_dynamic_provisioning_enabled=true
63
```

Figure 6-4. *Inventory file—Container Registries and Registry Service Account*

The *Registry Service Account* and the corresponding token should be set in the variables shown in lines 41, 42, and 45 on Figure 6-4.

To support dynamic storage provisioning with OCS or any other supported storage plugin, the configuration in line 62 on Figure 6-4 must be enabled. When dynamic provisioning is not enabled, a user with cluster-admin privileges must manually create and define the *Persistent Volumes (PV)* resources.

Red Hat OpenShift Container Storage

The *Red Hat OpenShift Container Storage (RHOCS or OCS)* provides *Container-native Gluster-based* storage. OCS can be deployed during the OCP installation as the default storage class (see line 74 on Figure 6-5).

```
64  ##############################################################################
65  ### OpenShift Container Storage (OCS)
66  ##############################################################################
67  # https://github.com/openshift/openshift-ansible/tree/release-3.11/roles/openshift_storage_glusterfs
68
69  # Deploy OCS glusterfs and create StorageClass
70  # Note: default namespace = glusterfs
71  #openshift_storage_glusterfs_namespace=openshift-storage
72
73  openshift_storage_glusterfs_storageclass=true
74  openshift_storage_glusterfs_storageclass_default=true
75
76  # Enable Glusterfs Block Storageclass
77  openshift_storage_glusterfs_block_deploy=false
78  #openshift_storage_glusterfs_block_host_vol_create=true
79  # NOTE: host_vol_size is effectively an upper limit on the size of glusterblock volumes
80  # unless you manually create larger GlusterFS block-hosting volumes
81  #openshift_storage_glusterfs_block_host_vol_size=100
82  #openshift_storage_glusterfs_block_storageclass=true
83  #openshift_storage_glusterfs_block_storageclass_default=false
84
85  #
86  # Enable Glusterfs S3 (Tech Preview)
87  #
88
89  #openshift_storage_glusterfs_s3_deploy=true
90  #openshift_storage_glusterfs_s3_account=s3testvolume
91  #openshift_storage_glusterfs_s3_user=s3adminuser
92  #openshift_storage_glusterfs_s3_password=s3adminpass
93  #openshift_storage_glusterfs_s3_pvc=dynamic
94  # Size (Gi) of glusterfs backed PVC used for S3 object data storage
95  #openshift_storage_glusterfs_s3_pvc_size=2
96  # Size (Gi) of glusterfs backed PVC used for S3 object metadata storage
97  #openshift_storage_glusterfs_s3_meta_pvc_size=1
98
99  # GlusterFS version
100 openshift_storage_glusterfs_version=v3.11
101 openshift_storage_glusterfs_block_version=v3.11
102 openshift_storage_glusterfs_s3_version=v3.11
103 openshift_storage_glusterfs_heketi_version=v3.11
104
```

Figure 6-5. *Inventory file—Red Hat OpenShift Container Storage (RHOCS or OCS)*

OCS can be deployed supporting *GlusterFS* (line 73 on Figure 6-5), *Gluster-Block* (line 77 on Figure 6-5), and *Glusterfs S3* (line 89 on Figure 6-5).

Note   The Gluster-Block and Glusterfs S3 modes require GlusterFS.

The release cadence of OCS is not tied to OCP. When deploying OCS as part of the deployment, it is highly recommended to specify the exact subrelease tag to use for the corresponding service containers (lines 111, 114, 117, and 120 on Figure 6-6).

```
105     # NOTE: https://docs.openshift.com/container-platform/3.11/install_config/persistent_storage/
        persistent_storage_glusterfs.html#install-advanced-installer
106
107     # NOTE: Using specific sub-releases tags for fixed bugs
108     # https://access.redhat.com/containers/?tab=tags#/registry.access.redhat.com/rhgs3/rhgs-server-rhel7
109
110     # Container image to use for glusterfs pods
111     openshift_storage_glusterfs_image="registry.access.redhat.com/rhgs3/rhgs-server-rhel7:v3.11.2"
112
113     # Container image to use for glusterblock-provisioner pod
114     openshift_storage_glusterfs_block_image="registry.access.redhat.com/rhgs3/rhgs-gluster-block-prov-rhel7:v3.11.2"
115
116     # Container image to use for Gluster S3
117     openshift_storage_glusterfs_s3_image="registry.redhat.io/rhgs3/rhgs-s3-server-rhel7:v3.11.2"
118
119     # Container image to use for heketi pods
120     openshift_storage_glusterfs_heketi_image="registry.access.redhat.com/rhgs3/rhgs-volmanager-rhel7:v3.11.2"
121
122     ## If using a dedicated glusterfs_registry storage cluster
123     # openshift_storage_glusterfs_registry_version=v3.11
124     # openshift_storage_glusterfs_registry_block_version=v3.11
125     # openshift_storage_glusterfs_registry_s3_version=v3.11
126     # openshift_storage_glusterfs_registry_heketi_version=v3.11
127
```

Figure 6-6. *Inventory file—setting up specific subrelease tag for OCS containers*

Web Console Access and Wildcard Apps Domain

The default setup in OCP is for the web console and the Kubernetes API to listen on port 8443 on each Master node. This can be modified to match the standard HTTPS port (see lines 132 and 133 on Figure 6-7).

In addition to the listening port, the *Master* configuration requires an FQDN the *Master Node* or cluster of *Master Nodes (if using multimaster configuration)* will answer to handle requests to the API or web consoles. This variable is the `openshift_master_cluster_hostname` (see line 136 on Figure 6-7). When using a single Master, this value can be the FQDN of the Master Node. When using multimaster configuration, this value must be set to an FQDN that represents all the Masters (usually this can be a Virtual IP or VIP address load balancing the traffic toward the Master Nodes).

When using an external *Load Balancer* service or device, the FQDN of the northbound VIP address must be specified in the inventory file using the variable `openshift_master_cluster_public_hostname` (see line 140 on Figure 6-7).

```
128    #######################################################################
129    ### OpenShift Master Vars
130    #######################################################################
131
132    openshift_master_api_port=443
133    openshift_master_console_port=443
134
135    # Internal cluster name
136    openshift_master_cluster_hostname=ocp-int.example.com
137
138    # Note: use if using different internal & external FQDN (ie. using LB)
139    # set the external cluster name here
140    openshift_master_cluster_public_hostname=ocp-ext.example.com
141
142    # NOTE: Specify default wildcard domain for applications
143    openshift_master_default_subdomain=apps.example.com
144
145    # Configure custom certificates
146    # https://docs.openshift.com/container-platform/3.11/install_config/certificate_customization.html
147
148    # Audit log
149    # https://docs.openshift.com/container-platform/3.11/install_config/
       master_node_configuration.html#master-node-config-audit-config
150    openshift_master_audit_config={"enabled": true, "auditFilePath": "/var/lib/origin/audit-ocp.log",
       "maximumFileRetentionDays": 7, "maximumFileSizeMegabytes": 10, "maximumRetainedFiles": 3}
151
```

Figure 6-7. *Inventory file—web console and wildcard domains*

The *OpenShift Routers* at *Infrastructure Nodes* require a wildcard subdomain it will use to dynamically build a *URL* or *Route* for applications running on the platform and exposing a service outside the cluster (see line 143 on Figure 6-7).

Audit Logs

When audit logs are required as part of the deployment, the inventory file provides a way to enable this functionality with the desired specific configuration (see line 150 on Figure 6-7).

Configuring the SDN

The OpenShift SDN default configuration uses the 10.1.0.0/16 network as the overlay network and 172.30.0.0/16 as the network for the Service Kubernetes resources. These networks can be set to something different before the installation by defining the variables `osm_cluster_network_cidr` and `openshift_portal_net` (see lines 156 and 157 on Figure 6-8).

```
152    #######################################################################
153    ### OpenShift Network Vars
154    #######################################################################
155    # Defaults
156    #osm_cluster_network_cidr=10.1.0.0/16
157    #openshift_portal_net=172.30.0.0/16
158
159    # OpenShift SDN with NetworkPolicy
160    os_sdn_network_plugin_name='redhat/openshift-ovs-networkpolicy'
161
162    # If using Calico SDN
163    #os_sdn_network_plugin_name=cni
164    #openshift_use_calico=true
165    #openshift_use_openshift_sdn=false
166
```

Figure 6-8. *Inventory file—OpenShift SDN parameters*

OpenShift SDN supports multiple modes. The recommended OpenShift SDN mode is the OVS with NetworkPolicy support (see line 160 on Figure 6-8).

Alternatively, there are other CNI plugins, like Calico SDN, which can be enabled as the SDN provider (see lines 163–165 on Figure 6-8).

Identity Providers

OpenShift supports multiple identity providers. To prevent installation failures due to missing parameters or configurations with external identity providers, the deployment can use the *htpasswd* identity provider (line 177 on Figure 6-9) with inline user definitions (line 181 on Figure 6-9) or using an external *htpassword* file (see line 184 on Figure 6-9).

```
167    ##############################################################################
168    ### OpenShift Authentication Vars
169    ##############################################################################
170    # Available Identity Providers
171    # https://docs.openshift.com/container-platform/3.11/install_config/configuring_authentication.html
172
173    ########################
174    # htpasswd Authentication
175    ########################
176    # NOTE: read initial identities in htpasswd format from /root/htpasswd.openshift
177    openshift_master_identity_providers=[{'name': 'htpasswd_auth', 'login': 'true', 'challenge': 'true', 'kind':
       'HTPasswdPasswordIdentityProvider'}]
178
179    # To define initial users directly in the inventory file:
180    # Note: user==password for this example
181    openshift_master_htpasswd_users={'ocpadmin':'$apr1$ZuJlQr.Y$6abuePAhKG0iY8QDNWoq80',
       'developer':'$apr1$QE2hKzLx$4ZeptR1hHNP538zRh/Pew.'}
182
183    # To use external htpassword file:
184    #openshift_master_htpasswd_file=/root/htpasswd.openshift
185
```

Figure 6-9. *Inventory file—configuration for identity providers*

Cluster Monitoring (Prometheus)

To enable *Cluster Monitoring* using the *Prometheus Operator,* set the openshift_
cluster_monitoring_operator_install variable (see line 196 on Figure 6-10).

```
190    ########################
191    # Cluster Monitoring
192    ########################
193    # https://docs.openshift.com/container-platform/3.11/install_config/prometheus_cluster_monitoring.html
194
195    # Enable Prometheus, Grafana & Alertmanager
196    openshift_cluster_monitoring_operator_install=true
197    openshift_cluster_monitoring_operator_node_selector={"node-role.kubernetes.io/infra":"true"}
198
199    # Setup storage allocation for Prometheus services
200    openshift_cluster_monitoring_operator_prometheus_storage_capacity=20Gi
201    openshift_cluster_monitoring_operator_alertmanager_storage_capacity=2Gi
202
203    # Enable persistent dynamic storage for Prometheus services
204    openshift_cluster_monitoring_operator_prometheus_storage_enabled=true
205    openshift_cluster_monitoring_operator_alertmanager_storage_enabled=true
206
207    # Storage class to use if persistent storage enabled
208    # NOTE: it will use storageclass default if storage class not specified
209    #openshift_cluster_monitoring_operator_prometheus_storage_class_name='glusterfs-storage-block'
210    #openshift_cluster_monitoring_operator_alertmanager_storage_class_name='glusterfs-storage-block'
211
212    # For custom config Alertmanager
213    # https://docs.openshift.com/container-platform/3.11/install_config/
       prometheus_cluster_monitoring.html#configuring-alertmanager
214
```

Figure 6-10. *Inventory file—Cluster Monitoring with Prometheus Operator*

Cluster Metrics (EFK Stack) and Logging

The traditional *OpenShift Cluster Metrics* are collected by the EFK Stack (ElasticSearch, FluentD, and Kibana). After OCP 3.11, the Hawkular API functionality (see line 225 on Figure 6-11) is being superseded by the Prometheus API.

The Horizontal Pod Autoscaler (HPA) functionality depends on the openshift-metrics-server which is deployed by enabling the metrics install in the inventory file (see line 220 on Figure 6-11).

Note   In OCP 4.x releases, the *metrics-server* uses metrics from Prometheus instead.

```
215    ########################
216    # Cluster Metrics
217    ########################
218
219    # Deploy Metrics Server (used by HPA)
220    openshift_metrics_install_metrics=true
221
222    # Start metrics cluster after deploying the components
223    openshift_metrics_start_cluster=true
224
225    openshift_metrics_hawkular_nodeselector={"node-role.kubernetes.io/infra": "true"}
226    openshift_metrics_cassandra_nodeselector={"node-role.kubernetes.io/infra": "true"}
227    openshift_metrics_heapster_nodeselector={"node-role.kubernetes.io/infra": "true"}
228
229    # Store Metrics for 2 days
230    openshift_metrics_duration=2
231
232    # Settings for Lab environment
233    openshift_metrics_cassandra_pvc_size=10Gi
234    openshift_metrics_cassandra_replicas=1
235    openshift_metrics_cassandra_limits_memory=2Gi
236    openshift_metrics_cassandra_limits_cpu=1000m
237
238    # User gluster-block or glusterfs (dynamic)
239    #openshift_metrics_cassandra_pvc_storage_class_name='glusterfs-storage-block'
240    openshift_metrics_cassandra_storage_type=dynamic
241
```

Figure 6-11. Inventory file—Cluster Metrics (with EFK Stack)

Installing the *Cluster* logging capabilities (line 246 on Figure 6-12) also provides the ability to enable the event-router (line 247 on Figure 6-12) which watches for Kubernetes events and streams them into the ElasticSearch in the EFK Stack.

```
242   ########################
243   # Cluster Logging
244   ########################
245
246   openshift_logging_install_logging=true
247   openshift_logging_install_eventrouter=true
248
249   openshift_logging_es_pvc_dynamic=true
250   openshift_logging_es_pvc_size=20Gi
251   #openshift_logging_es_pvc_storage_class_name='glusterfs-storage-block'
252
253   openshift_logging_es_memory_limit=4Gi
254   openshift_logging_es_cluster_size=1
255
256   # minimum age (in days) Curator uses for deleting log records
257   openshift_logging_curator_default_days=1
258
259   openshift_logging_kibana_nodeselector={"node-role.kubernetes.io/infra": "true"}
260   openshift_logging_curator_nodeselector={"node-role.kubernetes.io/infra": "true"}
261   openshift_logging_es_nodeselector={"node-role.kubernetes.io/infra": "true"}
262   openshift_logging_eventrouter_nodeselector={"node-role.kubernetes.io/infra": "true"}
263
264   # NOTE: If want to config a dedicated Elasticsearch for operation logs
265   # https://docs.openshift.com/container-platform/3.11/install_config/aggregate_logging.html#aggregated-ops
266
```

Figure 6-12. *Inventory file—Cluster Logging*

By default, the backend components of the metrics and logging services are deployed to the *Infrastructure Nodes*. Configuring the variables in lines 225 to 227 and the variables in lines 259 to 262 on Figure 6-12, these components can be deployed to other *Nodes*.

OpenShift Router and OpenShift Container Registry

The OpenShift Router and the OpenShift Container Registries are deployed to the Infrastructure Nodes. To select different Nodes, specify different Node selectors (see lines 272, 273, and 285 on Figure 6-13).

For the default *OpenShift Router* configurations, the number of *Routers* should be equal to the number of Infrastructure Nodes (see line 276 on Figure 6-13).

To determine the number of Container Registry replicas, consult the documentation as it should take the Container backend storage into consideration. If unsure, set it to one (see line 278 on Figure 6-13).

Note   In this case (see line 283 on Figure 6-13), when using Glusterfs as the storage backend for the *Container Registry*, the storage stores three copies of every container stored in the *Registry*.

```
267    ##########################################################################
268    ### OpenShift Router and Registry Vars
269    ##########################################################################
270
271    # default selectors for router and registry services
272    openshift_router_selector='node-role.kubernetes.io/infra=true'
273    openshift_registry_selector='node-role.kubernetes.io/infra=true'
274
275    # NOTE: Qty should match number of infra nodes
276    openshift_hosted_router_replicas=3
277
278    openshift_hosted_registry_replicas=1
279    openshift_hosted_registry_pullthrough=true
280    openshift_hosted_registry_acceptschema2=true
281    openshift_hosted_registry_enforcequota=true
282
283    openshift_hosted_registry_storage_kind=glusterfs
284    openshift_hosted_registry_storage_volume_size=10Gi
285    openshift_hosted_registry_selector="node-role.kubernetes.io/infra=true"
286
```

Figure 6-13. *Inventory file—OpenShift Router and Registry*

OpenShift Service Catalog and Service Brokers

The *Service Catalog* (line 292 on Figure 6-14) is required for the *Template Service Broker (TSB)* (line 296 on Figure 6-14) and the *Ansible Service Broker (ASB)* (line 301 on Figure 6-14).

```
287    ##########################################################################
288    ### OpenShift Service Catalog
289    ##########################################################################
290
291    # Servie Catalog
292    openshift_enable_service_catalog=true
293
294    # Template Service Broker (TSB)
295    # Note: requires Service Catalog
296    template_service_broker_install=true
297    openshift_template_service_broker_namespaces=['openshift']
298
299    # Ansible Service Broker (ASB)
300    # Note: requires TSB
301    ansible_service_broker_install=true
302    ansible_service_broker_local_registry_whitelist=['.*-apb$']
303
```

Figure 6-14. *Inventory file—OpenShift Service Catalog and Template Service Broker*

OpenShift Nodes

The core definition of the inventory file is the definition of the Nodes and their respective roles. Each Node type configuration is invoked by the definition of the groups in lines 309 to 313 on Figure 6-15. The required section or group definitions are *masters, etcd,* and *nodes.*

```
304    #############################################################################
305    ### OpenShift Hosts
306    #############################################################################
307
308    [OSEv3:children]
309    lb
310    masters
311    etcd
312    nodes
313    glusterfs
314
315    [lb]
316    lb1.example.com
317
318    [masters]
319    master1.example.com
320    master2.example.com
321    master3.example.com
322
323    [etcd]
324    master1.example.com
325    master2.example.com
326    master3.example.com
327
328    [nodes]
329    ## Master Nodes
330    master1.example.com openshift_node_group_name='node-config-master' openshift_node_problem_detector_install=true
331    master2.example.com openshift_node_group_name='node-config-master' openshift_node_problem_detector_install=true
332    master3.example.com openshift_node_group_name='node-config-master' openshift_node_problem_detector_install=true
333
334    ## Infrastructure Nodes
335    infranode1.example.com openshift_node_group_name='node-config-infra' openshift_node_problem_detector_install=true
336    infranode2.example.com openshift_node_group_name='node-config-infra' openshift_node_problem_detector_install=true
337    infranode3.example.com openshift_node_group_name='node-config-infra' openshift_node_problem_detector_install=true
338
339    ## App/Worker nodes
340    node1.example.com openshift_node_group_name='node-config-compute' openshift_node_problem_detector_install=true
341    node2.example.com openshift_node_group_name='node-config-compute' openshift_node_problem_detector_install=true
342    node3.example.com openshift_node_group_name='node-config-compute' openshift_node_problem_detector_install=true
343
344    ## Node Groups and custom Node Groups
345    # https://docs.openshift.com/container-platform/3.11/install/
       configuring_inventory_file.html#configuring-inventory--node-group-configmaps
346
347    [glusterfs]
348    ## App/Worker nodes with OCS hyperconverged
349    node1.example.com glusterfs_devices='[ "/dev/xvdd", "dev/xvde", ... ]'
350    node2.example.com glusterfs_devices='[ "/dev/xvdd", "dev/xvde", ... ]'
351    node3.example.com glusterfs_devices='[ "/dev/xvdd", "dev/xvde", ... ]'
```

Figure 6-15. Inventory file—OpenShift Node definition

The *[lb]* section and group (lines 309, 315, and 316 on Figure 6-15) are required when deploying a multimaster configuration and using *openshift-ansible* to deploy and configure the optional software load balancer for the cluster of *Master Nodes*. Comment this section when using a third-party load balancer or deploying a single Master configuration.

The *[masters]* and *[etcd]* sections (lines 318 to 326 on Figure 6-15) must list all the Master Nodes.

Note   The most common configurations use the *Master Nodes* as the *etcd Nodes*. Should dedicated *etcd* Nodes required, they should be listed in the *[etcd]* section.

The *[nodes]* section should list all the *Master, Infrastructure, and Application Nodes* in the cluster. The *Master Nodes* should be tagged with the node-config-master group name (see details in lines 330 to 332 on Figure 6-15). The Infrastructure Nodes should be tagged with the node-config-infra group name (see details in lines 335 to 337 on Figure 6-15). The *Application Nodes* should be tagged with the node-config-compute group name (see details in lines 340 to 342 on Figure 6-15).

When deploying *OCS* in converged or hyperconverged mode, the *[glusterfs] section* should be defined (see lines 313 and 347 to 351 on Figure 6-15) listing the Nodes providing the raw devices or disks, to be used by OCS (see details in lines 349 to 351 on Figure 6-15).

Sample Deployment Scenarios

Note   This section will focus on three common infrastructure setups (see Table 6-2) and document a prescribed deployment configuration for each one of them. There are many other possible configurations not covered in this book.

Table 6-2. *Sample OpenShift 3.11 Deployment Architectures in This Section*

	Masters	App Nodes	Infr Nodes	LB
All-in-One	1	N/A	N/A	N/A
Non-HA	1	3 or more	1	N/A
Full HA	3	3 or more	2 or 3	1 or more

Single Node Deployment (All-in-One)

Note   This All-in-One (AIO) (see Figure 6-16) is not an officially supported OCP deployment. The AIO configuration is considered a testing or development environment. The Master, Infrastructure and Application Roles are deployed to a single node (see Table 6-3).

Table 6-3. *Sample OpenShift 3.11 All-in-One*

Node Role	FQDN	Node IP Address
Master, Infra., and App Nodes	ocp.example.com	192.168.1.10
Bastion	bastion.ocp.example.com	192.168.1.5
Apps wildcard domain	*.apps.ocp.example.com	CNAME MASTER

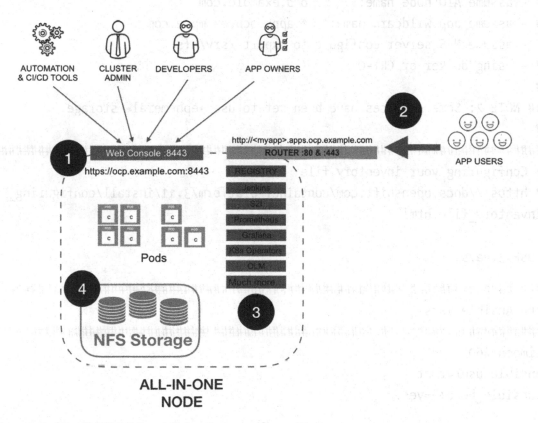

Figure 6-16. *OCP 3.11.x All-in-One configuration*

The All-in-One configuration executes all the OCP roles in a single Node. This particular example is using an internal NFS server as the persistent storage. The openshift-ansible installer will configure additional exports for the NFS based on the inventory file.

The corresponding Ansible inventory file for the All-in-One deployment will be similar to Listing 6-4.

Note   Using NFS as the persistent storage for infrastructure components like *Registry, Metrics, Logging,* and so on is an unsupported configuration.

Listing 6-4. Ansible inventory file for All-in-One deployment

```
#########################################################################
#
## All-in-One (AIO) SERVER WITH EMBEDDED NFS:
# - assume AIO node name:       ocp.example.com
# - assume app wildcard name:   *.apps.ocp.example.com
# - assume NFS server configure to export /srv/nfs
# - using docker or CRI-O
#
## NOTE 2: Some services have been set to use *ephemeral* storage
#
#########################################################################
# Configuring your inventory file
# https://docs.openshift.com/container-platform/3.11/install/configuring_
inventory_file.html


[OSEv3:vars]

#########################################################################
### Ansible Vars
#########################################################################
timeout=60
ansible_user=root
#ansible_become=yes
```

```
##############################################################################
### OpenShift Basic Vars
##############################################################################
# Deployment type
openshift_deployment_type=openshift-enterprise
#openshift_deployment_type=origin

# WARNING: only disable these checks in LAB/TEST environments(Do not use in
production)
openshift_disable_check="disk_availability,memory_availability"

# OpenShift Version(Always use sub-release for smoother upgrades):
openshift_release=3.11.98

# Deploy Operator Lifecycle Manager (Tech Preview)
openshift_enable_olm=true

# Enable NFS support for infrastructure components (unsupported)
openshift_enable_unsupported_configurations=true

##############################################################################
### Enable CRI-O
##############################################################################

#openshift_use_crio=True
#openshift_use_crio_only=False
#openshift_crio_enable_docker_gc=True

##############################################################################
### OpenShift Registries Locations
##############################################################################

# NOTE: Need credentials from: https://access.redhat.com/terms-based-
registry/
oreg_url=registry.redhat.io/openshift3/ose-${component}:${version}
oreg_auth_user={{REGISTY_USER}}
oreg_auth_password={{REGISTRY_TOKEN}}
```

```
# For Operator Framework Images
openshift_additional_registry_credentials=[{'host':'registry.connect.
redhat.com','user':'{{REGISTY_USER}}','password':'{{REGISTRY_
TOKEN}}','test_image':'mongodb/enterprise-operator:0.3.2'}]

# Update examples to point to oreg_url
# NOTE: change this if using disconnected install
openshift_examples_modify_imagestreams=false

# NOTE: accept insecure registries and registries with self-signed certs
# setup for lab environment
openshift_docker_hosted_registry_insecure=true

##############################################################################
### OpenShift Master Vars
##############################################################################

openshift_master_api_port=8443
openshift_master_console_port=8443

# Internal cluster name
openshift_master_cluster_hostname=ocp.example.com

# Default wildcard domain for applications
openshift_master_default_subdomain=apps.ocp.example.com

##############################################################################
### OpenShift Network Vars
##############################################################################
# Defaults
#osm_cluster_network_cidr=10.1.0.0/16
#openshift_portal_net=172.30.0.0/16

os_sdn_network_plugin_name='redhat/openshift-ovs-networkpolicy'

##############################################################################
### OpenShift Authentication Vars
##############################################################################
```

```
# htpasswd Authentication(Non-Priviledge UI User until formal identity
provider is used. For now htpasswd identity provider)
# NOTE: read initial identities in htpasswd format from /root/htpasswd.
openshift
openshift_master_identity_providers=[{'name': 'htpasswd_auth', 'login':
'true', 'challenge': 'true', 'kind': 'HTPasswdPasswordIdentityProvider'}]

# Using an external htpasswd file use this:
#openshift_master_htpasswd_file=/home/cloud-user/htpasswd.openshift
# Embedding users in the configuration file use this syntax
# Note: user==password for this example
openshift_master_htpasswd_users={'ocpadmin':'$apr1$ZuJlQr.Y$6abuePAhKGOiY8Q
DNWoq80','developer':'$apr1$QE2hKzLx$4ZeptR1hHNP538zRh/Pew.'}

#####################################################################
### OpenShift Metrics and Logging Vars
#####################################################################

##########################
# Prometheus Cluster Monitoring
##########################
# https://github.com/openshift/openshift-docs/blob/master/install_config/
monitoring/configuring-openshift-cluster-monitoring.adoc
# https://github.com/openshift/openshift-docs/tree/enterprise-3.11/install_
config/monitoring

openshift_cluster_monitoring_operator_install=true
#openshift_prometheus_node_selector={"node-role.kubernetes.io/
infra":"true"}

# NOTE: Setup for lab environment
# Enable persistent storage of Prometheus time-series data (default false)
openshift_cluster_monitoring_operator_prometheus_storage_enabled=false
# Enable persistent storage of Alertmanager notifications (default false)
openshift_cluster_monitoring_operator_alertmanager_storage_enabled=false
```

```
########################
# Cluster Metrics
########################
# https://github.com/openshift/openshift-docs/blob/enterprise-3.11/install_
config/cluster_metrics.adoc

openshift_metrics_install_metrics=true

# Store Metrics for 1 days
openshift_metrics_duration=1

openshift_metrics_storage_kind=nfs
openshift_metrics_storage_access_modes=['ReadWriteOnce']
openshift_metrics_storage_nfs_directory=/srv/nfs
openshift_metrics_storage_nfs_options='*(rw,root_squash)'
openshift_metrics_storage_volume_name=metrics
openshift_metrics_storage_volume_size=10Gi
openshift_metrics_storage_labels={'storage': 'metrics'}

# cassandra -- ephemeral storage (for testing)
openshift_metrics_cassandra_storage_type=emptydir
openshift_metrics_cassandra_replicas=1
openshift_metrics_cassandra_limits_memory=2Gi
openshift_metrics_cassandra_limits_cpu=800m
openshift_metrics_cassandra_nodeselector={"node-role.kubernetes.io/infra":
"true"}

# hawkular
openshift_metrics_hawkular_limits_memory=2Gi
openshift_metrics_hawkular_limits_cpu=800m
openshift_metrics_hawkular_replicas=1
openshift_metrics_hawkular_nodeselector={"node-role.kubernetes.io/infra":
"true"}

# heapster
openshift_metrics_heapster_limits_memory=2Gi
openshift_metrics_heapster_limits_cpu=800m
openshift_metrics_heapster_nodeselector={"node-role.kubernetes.io/infra":
"true"}
```

```
#########################
# Cluster Logging
#########################
# https://github.com/openshift/openshift-docs/blob/enterprise-3.11/install_
config/aggregate_logging.adoc

# install logging
openshift_logging_install_logging=true

# logging curator
openshift_logging_curator_default_days=1
openshift_logging_curator_cpu_limit=500m
openshift_logging_curator_memory_limit=1Gi
openshift_logging_curator_nodeselector={"node-role.kubernetes.io/infra":
"true"}

# Configure a second ES+Kibana cluster for operations logs
# Fluend splits the logs accordingly
openshift_logging_use_ops=false

# Fluentd
openshift_logging_fluentd_cpu_limit=500m
openshift_logging_fluentd_memory_limit=1Gi
# collect audit.log to ES
openshift_logging_fluentd_audit_container_engine=false

# persistent storage for logs
openshift_logging_storage_kind=nfs
openshift_logging_storage_access_modes=['ReadWriteOnce']
openshift_logging_storage_nfs_directory=/srv/nfs
openshift_logging_storage_nfs_options='*(rw,root_squash)'
openshift_logging_storage_volume_name=logging
openshift_logging_storage_volume_size=10Gi
openshift_logging_storage_labels={'storage': 'logging'}

# eventrouter
openshift_logging_install_eventrouter=true
```

```
openshift_logging_eventrouter_nodeselector={"node-role.kubernetes.io/
infra": "true"}

# Elasticsearch (ES)
# ES cluster size (HA ES >= 3)
openshift_logging_es_cluster_size=1
# replicas per shard
#openshift_logging_es_number_of_replicas=1
# shards per index
#openshift_logging_es_number_of_shards=1
openshift_logging_es_cpu_limit=500m
openshift_logging_es_memory_limit=1Gi
# PVC size omitted == ephemeral vols are used
#openshift_logging_es_pvc_siz=10G
openshift_logging_es_nodeselector={"node-role.kubernetes.io/infra": "true"}

# Kibana
openshift_logging_kibana_cpu_limit=500m
openshift_logging_kibana_memory_limit=1Gi
openshift_logging_kibana_replica_count=1
# expose ES? (default false)
openshift_logging_es_allow_external=false
openshift_logging_kibana_nodeselector={"node-role.kubernetes.io/infra":
"true"}

##########################################################################
### OpenShift Router and Registry Vars
##########################################################################

# NOTE: Qty should NOT exceed the number of infra nodes
openshift_hosted_router_replicas=1

openshift_hosted_registry_replicas=1
openshift_hosted_registry_pullthrough=true
openshift_hosted_registry_acceptschema2=true
openshift_hosted_registry_enforcequota=true
```

```
openshift_hosted_registry_storage_kind=nfs
openshift_hosted_registry_storage_access_modes=['ReadWriteMany']
openshift_hosted_registry_storage_nfs_directory=/srv/nfs
openshift_hosted_registry_storage_nfs_options='*(rw,root_squash)'
openshift_hosted_registry_storage_volume_name=registry
openshift_hosted_registry_storage_volume_size=10Gi
openshift_hosted_registry_selector="node-role.kubernetes.io/infra=true"

####################################################################
### OpenShift Service Catalog Vars
####################################################################

# default=true
openshift_enable_service_catalog=true

# default=true
template_service_broker_install=true
openshift_template_service_broker_namespaces=['openshift']

# default=true
ansible_service_broker_install=true
ansible_service_broker_local_registry_whitelist=['.*-apb$']

####################################################################
### OpenShift Cockpit Vars and plugins
####################################################################

# Disable cockpit
osm_use_cockpit=false

####################################################################
### OpenShift Hosts
####################################################################
[OSEv3:children]
nfs
masters
etcd
nodes
```

```
[nfs]
ocp.example.com

[masters]
ocp.example.com

[etcd]
ocp.example.com

[nodes]
## All-In-One with CRI-O
#ocp.example.com openshift_node_group_name='node-config-all-in-one-crio'
openshift_node_problem_detector_install=true
ocp.example.com openshift_node_group_name='node-config-all-in-one'
openshift_node_problem_detector_install=true

#
# END OF FILE
#
```

Non-HA Control Plane Deployment

Table 6-4. *Sample OpenShift 3.11 Non-HA Control Plane*

Node Role	FQDN	Node IP Address
Master	ocp.example.com	192.168.1.10
Infr Node	inf1.ocp.example.com	192.168.1.15
App Node	node1.ocp.example.com	192.168.1.21
App Node	node2.ocp.example.com	192.168.1.22
App Node	node3.ocp.example.com	192.168.1.23
Bastion	bastion.ocp.example.com	192.168.1.5
Apps wildcard domain	*.apps.ocp.example.com	CNAME INFR NODE

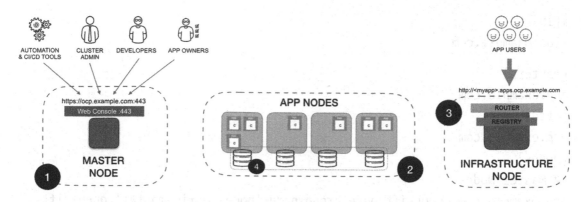

Figure 6-17. *OCP 3.11.x Non-HA Control Plane configuration*

Listing 6-5. Ansible Inventory file for Non-HA Control Plane deployment (fragment)

```
# Use the inventory file from Listing 6-6 with the following modifications
#<snip>
################################################################################
### OpenShift Master Vars
################################################################################
#<snip>
# Internal cluster name
openshift_master_cluster_hostname=ocp.example.com

#<snip>
#openshift_master_cluster_public_hostname=ocp-ext.example.com

#<snip>
# NOTE: Qty should match number of infra nodes
openshift_hosted_router_replicas=1

#<snip>
[OSEv3:children]
#lb
masters
etcd
nodes
glusterfs
```

```
#[lb]
#lb1.example.com

[masters]
ocp.example.com
[etcd]
ocp.example.com
[nodes]
## Master Nodes
ocp.example.com openshift_node_group_name='node-config-master' openshift_
node_problem_detector_install=true
## Infrastructure Nodes
inf1.example.com openshift_node_group_name='node-config-infra' openshift_
node_problem_detector_install=true

#<snip>
#
# END OF FILE
#
```

Full-HA Control Plane Deployment

Table 6-5. Sample OpenShift 3.11 Full-HA Control Plane

Node Role	FQDN	Node IP Address
LB	lb.ocp.example.com	192.168.1.10
(public_hostname)	console.ocp.example.com	CNAME LB (outside)
(cluster_hostname)	ocp-int.ocp.example.com	CNAME LB (inside)
Master Node	master1.ocp.example.com	192.168.1.11
Master Node	master2.ocp.example.com	192.168.1.12
Master Node	master3.ocp.example.com	192.168.1.13
Infr Node	inf1.ocp.example.com	192.168.1.15
Infr Node	inf2.ocp.example.com	192.168.1.16

(*continued*)

Table 6-5. *(continued)*

Node Role	FQDN	Node IP Address
Infr Node	inf3.ocp.example.com	192.168.1.17
App Node	node1.ocp.example.com	192.168.1.21
App Node	node2.ocp.example.com	192.168.1.22
App Node	node3.ocp.example.com	192.168.1.23
App Node	nodeX.ocp.example.com	192.168.1.XX
Bastion	bastion.ocp.example.com	192.168.1.5
Apps wildcard domain	*.apps.ocp.example.com	CNAME ENT LB

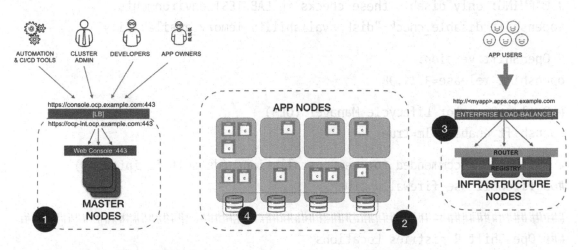

Figure 6-18. *OCP 3.11.x Full-HA Control Plane configuration*

Listing 6-6. Ansible inventory file for Full-HA Control Plane deployment

```
#
# openshift-ansible inventory file for OpenShift Container
Platform  3.11.98
#

# Details on configuring your inventory file
# https://docs.openshift.com/container-platform/3.11/install/configuring_
inventory_file.html

[OSEv3:vars]
```

143

```
##############################################################################
### Ansible Vars
##############################################################################
timeout=60
ansible_user={{CHANGEME_ANSIBLE_SSH_USER}}
ansible_become=yes

##############################################################################
### OpenShift Basic Vars
##############################################################################
# Deployment type
openshift_deployment_type=openshift-enterprise

# WARNING: only disable these checks in LAB/TEST environments
#openshift_disable_check="disk_availability,memory_availability"

# OpenShift Version:
openshift_release=3.11.98

# Deploy Operator Lifecycle Manager (OLM)
openshift_enable_olm=true

# firewalld recommended for new installations (default is iptables)
#os_firewall_use_firewalld=true

##############################################################################
### OpenShift Registries Locations
##############################################################################

# NOTE: Need credentials from: https://access.redhat.com/terms-based-
registry/
oreg_url=registry.redhat.io/openshift3/ose-${component}:${version}
oreg_auth_user={{CHANGEME_REGISTRY_SERVICE_ACCOUNT}}
oreg_auth_password={{CHANGEME_SERVICE_KEY}}

# For Operator Framework Images
openshift_additional_registry_credentials=[{'host':'registry.connect.
redhat.com','user':'{{CHANGEME_REGISTRY_SERVICE_ACCOUNT}}','password':'{{CH
ANGEME_SERVICE_KEY}}','test_image':'mongodb/enterprise-operator:0.3.2'}]
```

```
# NOTE: accept insecure registries and registries with self-signed certs
# setup for lab environment
openshift_docker_hosted_registry_insecure=true
#openshift_docker_insecure_registries=<registry_hostname>
#openshift_docker_blocked_registries=<registry_hostname>

# Update examples to point to oreg_url -- enable if using disconnected
install
#openshift_examples_modify_imagestreams=false

############################################################################
### Enable dynamic storage provisioning
############################################################################
# https://docs.openshift.com/container-platform/3.11/install_config/
persistent_storage/dynamically_provisioning_pvs.html
# Note: required for OCS dynamic provisioning

openshift_master_dynamic_provisioning_enabled=true

############################################################################
### OpenShift Container Storage (OCS)
############################################################################
# https://github.com/openshift/openshift-ansible/tree/release-3.11/roles/
openshift_storage_glusterfs

# Deploy OCS glusterfs and create StorageClass
# Note: default namespace = glusterfs
#openshift_storage_glusterfs_namespace=openshift-storage

openshift_storage_glusterfs_storageclass=true
openshift_storage_glusterfs_storageclass_default=true

# Enable Glusterfs Block Storageclass
openshift_storage_glusterfs_block_deploy=false
#openshift_storage_glusterfs_block_host_vol_create=true
# NOTE: host_vol_size is effectively an upper limit on the size of
glusterblock volumes
# unless you manually create larger GlusterFS block-hosting volumes
#openshift_storage_glusterfs_block_host_vol_size=100
```

```
#openshift_storage_glusterfs_block_storageclass=true
#openshift_storage_glusterfs_block_storageclass_default=false

#
# Enable Glusterfs S3 (Tech Preview)
#

#openshift_storage_glusterfs_s3_deploy=true
#openshift_storage_glusterfs_s3_account=s3testvolume
#openshift_storage_glusterfs_s3_user=s3adminuser
#openshift_storage_glusterfs_s3_password=s3adminpass
#openshift_storage_glusterfs_s3_pvc=dynamic
# Size (Gi) of glusterfs backed PVC used for S3 object data storage
#openshift_storage_glusterfs_s3_pvc_size=2
# Size (Gi) of glusterfs backed PVC used for S3 object metadata storage
#openshift_storage_glusterfs_s3_meta_pvc_size=1

# GlusterFS version
openshift_storage_glusterfs_version=v3.11
openshift_storage_glusterfs_block_version=v3.11
openshift_storage_glusterfs_s3_version=v3.11
openshift_storage_glusterfs_heketi_version=v3.11

# NOTE: https://docs.openshift.com/container-platform/3.11/install_config/
persistent_storage/persistent_storage_glusterfs.html#install-advanced-
installer

# NOTE: Using specific sub-releases tags for fixed bugs
# https://access.redhat.com/containers/?tab=tags#/registry.access.redhat.
com/rhgs3/rhgs-server-rhel7

# Container image to use for glusterfs pods
openshift_storage_glusterfs_image="registry.access.redhat.com/rhgs3/rhgs-
server-rhel7:v3.11.2"

# Container image to use for glusterblock-provisioner pod
openshift_storage_glusterfs_block_image="registry.access.redhat.com/rhgs3/
rhgs-gluster-block-prov-rhel7:v3.11.2"
```

```
# Container image to use for Gluster S3
openshift_storage_glusterfs_s3_image="registry.redhat.io/rhgs3/rhgs-s3-
server-rhel7:v3.11.2"

# Container image to use for heketi pods
openshift_storage_glusterfs_heketi_image="registry.access.redhat.com/rhgs3/
rhgs-volmanager-rhel7:v3.11.2"

## If using a dedicated glusterfs_registry storage cluster
# openshift_storage_glusterfs_registry_version=v3.11
# openshift_storage_glusterfs_registry_block_version=v3.11
# openshift_storage_glusterfs_registry_s3_version=v3.11
# openshift_storage_glusterfs_registry_heketi_version=v3.11

#####################################################################
### OpenShift Master Vars
#####################################################################

openshift_master_api_port=443
openshift_master_console_port=443

# Internal cluster name
openshift_master_cluster_hostname=ocp-int.example.com

# Note: use if using different internal & external FQDN (i.e. using LB)
# set the external cluster name here
openshift_master_cluster_public_hostname=ocp-ext.example.com

# NOTE: Specify default wildcard domain for applications
openshift_master_default_subdomain=apps.example.com

# Configure custom certificates
# https://docs.openshift.com/container-platform/3.11/install_config/
certificate_customization.html

# Audit log
# https://docs.openshift.com/container-platform/3.11/install_config/master_
node_configuration.html#master-node-config-audit-config
```

147

```
openshift_master_audit_config={"enabled": true, "auditFilePath": "/
var/lib/origin/audit-ocp.log", "maximumFileRetentionDays": 7,
"maximumFileSizeMegabytes": 10, "maximumRetainedFiles": 3}

############################################################################
### OpenShift Network Vars
############################################################################
# Defaults
#osm_cluster_network_cidr=10.1.0.0/16
#openshift_portal_net=172.30.0.0/16

# OpenShift SDN with NetworkPolicy
os_sdn_network_plugin_name='redhat/openshift-ovs-networkpolicy'

# If using Calico SDN
#os_sdn_network_plugin_name=cni
#openshift_use_calico=true
#openshift_use_openshift_sdn=false

############################################################################
### OpenShift Authentication Vars
############################################################################
# Available Identity Providers
# https://docs.openshift.com/container-platform/3.11/install_config/
configuring_authentication.html

#########################
# htpasswd Authentication
#########################
# NOTE: read initial identities in htpasswd format from /root/htpasswd.
openshift
openshift_master_identity_providers=[{'name': 'htpasswd_auth', 'login':
'true', 'challenge': 'true', 'kind': 'HTPasswdPasswordIdentityProvider'}]

# To define initial users directly in the inventory file:
# Note: user==password for this example
openshift_master_htpasswd_users={'ocpadmin':'$apr1$ZuJlQr.Y$6abuePAhKGOiY8Q
DNWoq80','developer':'$apr1$QE2hKzLx$4ZeptR1hHNP538zRh/Pew.'}
```

```
# To use external htpasswd file:
#openshift_master_htpasswd_file=/root/htpasswd.openshift

############################################################################
### OpenShift Cluster Monitoring, Metrics and Logging Vars
############################################################################

##########################
# Cluster Monitoring
##########################
# https://docs.openshift.com/container-platform/3.11/install_config/
prometheus_cluster_monitoring.html

# Enable Prometheus, Grafana & Alertmanager
openshift_cluster_monitoring_operator_install=true
openshift_cluster_monitoring_operator_node_selector={"node-role.kubernetes.
io/infra":"true"}

# Setup storage allocation for Prometheus services
openshift_cluster_monitoring_operator_prometheus_storage_capacity=20Gi
openshift_cluster_monitoring_operator_alertmanager_storage_capacity=2Gi

# Enable persistent dynamic storage for Prometheus services
openshift_cluster_monitoring_operator_prometheus_storage_enabled=true
openshift_cluster_monitoring_operator_alertmanager_storage_enabled=true

# Storage class to use if persistent storage enabled
# NOTE: it will use storageclass default if storage class not specified
#openshift_cluster_monitoring_operator_prometheus_storage_class_
name='glusterfs-storage-block'
#openshift_cluster_monitoring_operator_alertmanager_storage_class_
name='glusterfs-storage-block'

# For custom config Alertmanager
# https://docs.openshift.com/container-platform/3.11/install_config/
prometheus_cluster_monitoring.html#configuring-alertmanager
```

```
#########################
# Cluster Metrics
#########################

# Deploy Metrics Server (used by HPA)
openshift_metrics_install_metrics=true

# Start metrics cluster after deploying the components
openshift_metrics_start_cluster=true

openshift_metrics_hawkular_nodeselector={"node-role.kubernetes.io/infra":
"true"}
openshift_metrics_cassandra_nodeselector={"node-role.kubernetes.io/infra":
"true"}
openshift_metrics_heapster_nodeselector={"node-role.kubernetes.io/infra":
"true"}

# Store Metrics for 2 days
openshift_metrics_duration=2

# Settings for Lab environment
openshift_metrics_cassandra_pvc_size=10Gi
openshift_metrics_cassandra_replicas=1
openshift_metrics_cassandra_limits_memory=2Gi
openshift_metrics_cassandra_limits_cpu=1000m

# User gluster-block or glusterfs (dynamic)
#openshift_metrics_cassandra_pvc_storage_class_name='glusterfs-storage-block'
openshift_metrics_cassandra_storage_type=dynamic

#########################
# Cluster Logging
#########################

openshift_logging_install_logging=true
openshift_logging_install_eventrouter=true

openshift_logging_es_pvc_dynamic=true
openshift_logging_es_pvc_size=20Gi
#openshift_logging_es_pvc_storage_class_name='glusterfs-storage-block'
```

```
openshift_logging_es_memory_limit=4Gi
openshift_logging_es_cluster_size=1

# minimum age (in days) Curator uses for deleting log records
openshift_logging_curator_default_days=1

openshift_logging_kibana_nodeselector={"node-role.kubernetes.io/infra":
"true"}
openshift_logging_curator_nodeselector={"node-role.kubernetes.io/infra":
"true"}
openshift_logging_es_nodeselector={"node-role.kubernetes.io/infra": "true"}
openshift_logging_eventrouter_nodeselector={"node-role.kubernetes.io/
infra": "true"}

# NOTE: If want to config a dedicated Elasticsearch for operation logs
# https://docs.openshift.com/container-platform/3.11/install_config/
aggregate_logging.html#aggregated-ops

#############################################################################
### OpenShift Router and Registry Vars
#############################################################################

# default selectors for router and registry services
openshift_router_selector='node-role.kubernetes.io/infra=true'
openshift_registry_selector='node-role.kubernetes.io/infra=true'

# NOTE: Qty should match number of infra nodes
openshift_hosted_router_replicas=3

openshift_hosted_registry_replicas=1
openshift_hosted_registry_pullthrough=true
openshift_hosted_registry_acceptschema2=true
openshift_hosted_registry_enforcequota=true

openshift_hosted_registry_storage_kind=glusterfs
openshift_hosted_registry_storage_volume_size=10Gi
openshift_hosted_registry_selector="node-role.kubernetes.io/infra=true"
```

```
############################################################################
### OpenShift Service Catalog
############################################################################

# Servie Catalog
openshift_enable_service_catalog=true

# Template Service Broker (TSB)
# Note: requires Service Catalog
template_service_broker_install=true
openshift_template_service_broker_namespaces=['openshift']

# Ansible Service Broker (ASB)
# Note: requires TSB
ansible_service_broker_install=true
ansible_service_broker_local_registry_whitelist=['.*-apb$']


############################################################################
### OpenShift Hosts
############################################################################

[OSEv3:children]
lb
masters
etcd
nodes
glusterfs

[lb]
lb1.example.com

[masters]
master1.example.com
master2.example.com
master3.example.com

[etcd]
master1.example.com
master2.example.com
master3.example.com
```

```
[nodes]
## Master Nodes
master1.example.com openshift_node_group_name='node-config-master'
openshift_node_problem_detector_install=true
master2.example.com openshift_node_group_name='node-config-master'
openshift_node_problem_detector_install=true
master3.example.com openshift_node_group_name='node-config-master'
openshift_node_problem_detector_install=true

## Infrastructure Nodes
inf1.example.com openshift_node_group_name='node-config-infra' openshift_
node_problem_detector_install=true
inf2.example.com openshift_node_group_name='node-config-infra' openshift_
node_problem_detector_install=true
inf3.example.com openshift_node_group_name='node-config-infra' openshift_
node_problem_detector_install=true

## App/Worker nodes
node1.example.com openshift_node_group_name='node-config-compute'
openshift_node_problem_detector_install=true
node2.example.com openshift_node_group_name='node-config-compute'
openshift_node_problem_detector_install=true
node3.example.com openshift_node_group_name='node-config-compute'
openshift_node_problem_detector_install=true

## Node Groups and custom Node Groups
# https://docs.openshift.com/container-platform/3.11/install/configuring_
inventory_file.html#configuring-inventory--node-group-configmaps

[glusterfs]
## App/Worker nodes with OCS hyperconverged
node1.example.com glusterfs_devices='[ "/dev/xvdd", "dev/xvde", ... ]'
node2.example.com glusterfs_devices='[ "/dev/xvdd", "dev/xvde", ... ]'
node3.example.com glusterfs_devices='[ "/dev/xvdd", "dev/xvde", ... ]'

#
# END OF FILE
#
```

Deploying OpenShift

Once the *openshift-ansible* inventory file is defined, the process to install OpenShift from the *Bastion Node* is as shown in Listing 6-7.

Listing 6-7. Deploying OpenShift

```
# The following steps assume the openshift-inventory file configuration is
saved as ./inventory_file in the local directory

# Step 1: Validate Bastion Node can reach all the Nodes
$ ansible all -i inventory_file -m ping

# Step 2: Once Step 1 completes without errors, install pre-requisites
$ ansible-playbook -i inventory_file /usr/share/ansible/openshift-ansible/
playbooks/prerequisites.yml

# Step: 3: Once Step 2 completes without errors, deploy the OpenShift
cluster
$ansible-playbook -i inventory_file /usr/share/ansible/openshift-ansible/
playbooks/deploy_cluster.yml
```

> **Tip**   If the installation process fails during the initial deployment, it is recommended to follow the uninstall procedure, correct the inventory file, and redeploy again.

Uninstalling OpenShift

The openshift-ansible provides playbooks to uninstall an OpenShift deployment. To remove any traces of OpenShift, follow the steps described in Listing 6-8.

> **Tip**   If the installation process fails during the initial deployment, it is recommended to uninstall and redeploy again.

Listing 6-8. Uninstalling OpenShift

```
# The following steps assume the openshift-inventory file configuration is
saved as ./inventory_file in the local directory

# Step 1: Uninstall the OpenShift deployment and delete data on OCS disks.
ansible-playbook -i inventory_file -e "openshift_storage_glusterfs_wipe=true"
/usr/share/ansible/openshift-ansible/playbooks/adhoc/uninstall.yml

# Step 2: Remove any leftovers configuration files
ansible nodes -i inventory_file -m file -a "dest=/etc/origin state=absent"

#(optional): If the installation was using 3rd party CNI plugins remove any
leftovers from the CNI configuration
ansible nodes -i inventory_file -m file -a "dest=/etc/cni state=absent"
```

Bastion Node as Admin Jumphost

Once the deployment is completed, OpenShift has a special account "system:admin" with cluster-admin privileges that can be used to configure the platform. By default, this privileged account is only available when logged in as root to a Master Node.

To use the Bastion Node for cluster-admin configurations, it is possible to copy the certificate credentials (/root/.kube/config) from a Master Node into the Bastion Node to enable the use of the "system:admin" account from the Bastion Node. Listing 6-9 documents a way to copy these credentials to the Bastion Node using the information from the inventory file.

Listing 6-9. Bastion Node

```
# The following step assume the openshift-inventory file configuration is
saved as ./inventory_file in the local directory
$ ansible -i inventory_file masters[0] -b -m fetch -a "src=/root/.kube/
config dest=/root/.kube/config flat=yes"
```

OpenShift 4.x Deployments (AWS)

The examples in this section have been tested and validated with OpenShift (OCP) 4.0 Developer Preview 3 on AWS.

Prerequisites

OpenShift 4.0 on AWS requires minimum preparation of the AWS environment.

1. Create a new DNS zone for OCP in AWS Route53[10] service.

    a. Note: Entries created in the Route53 zone are expected to have full resolution from the Nodes.

2. Prepare Bastion Node.

    a. Configure the AWS credentials in the Bastion Node as per AWS CLI[11] documentation.

    b. Test the AWS configuration executing a query to validate the DNS zone is listed of the following command:

        i. aws route53 list-hosted-zones

    c. Download the OpenShift 4 installer[12] from the OpenShift portal.

        i. At the time of this writing, the official portal to download the installer is https://cloud.openshift.com/clusters/install

        ii. Note: The OpenShift 4 installer is a single Go binary that can be executed from any Linux or MacOS machine.

---

[10]AWS Route53: https://console.aws.amazon.com/route53

[11]AWS CLI Configuration: https://docs.aws.amazon.com/cli/latest/userguide/cli-chap-configure.html#cli-quick-configuration

[12]The latest beta installer is available at https://github.com/openshift/installer/releases

    d. Download the *Pull Secret* for the OpenShift subscriptions.

        i. At the time of this writing, the *Pull Secret* is generated and available at the *Developer Preview* site: `https://cloud.openshift.com/clusters/install`

    e. Download and install the OpenShift 4 client (the *oc* client) from the official mirror[13] site.

OpenShift 4.x Deployment Architecture

The OpenShift 4.x deployment architecture uses the *openshift-install* command to deploy OCP 4.x to the desired environment using one of two modes:

- **User Provisioned Infrastructure (UPI)**: In this mode, the Nodes are manually provisioned with a set of prerequisites. Then, by a configuration process that has not been published, feed this information to the *openshift-install* for it to deploy the OpenShift cluster.

  - At the time of this writing, this mode is not yet available under the Developer Preview release.

- **Installer Provisioned Infrastructure (IPI)**: In this mode, the Nodes are provisioned by the installer, and OpenShift is deployed as a series of Kubernetes Operators on top of the provisioned Nodes.

  - During the IPI installation, the installer provisions a *bootstrap Node* it will use to instantiate the *Master Nodes* and the *Worker Nodes*. Once the cluster is instantiated, the *bootstrap Node* is destroyed.

OCP4 Deployment to AWS (IPI Mode)

When deploying OCP4 into AWS, it uses the IPI mode. By default, this process deploys an architecture of three Master Nodes and three Worker Nodes. The deployment automatically distributes these *Nodes* across different *AWS Availability Zones (AZ)* in the same *AWS Region* (see Figure 6-19).

---

[13]OpenShift 4 client can be downloaded from `https://mirror.openshift.com/pub/openshift-v4/clients/oc/4.1/`

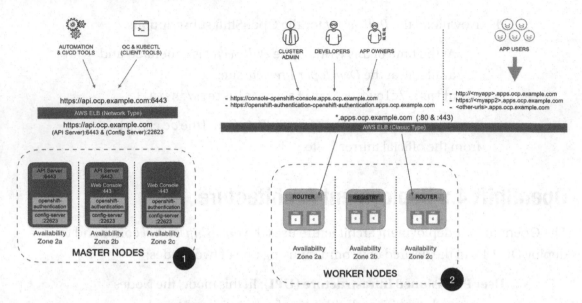

Figure 6-19. OCP4 Deployment to AWS (IPI Mode)

Note   In OCP4 the *Application Nodes* are known as *Worker Nodes*. Both terms are interchangeable.

As seen in Figure 6-19, the basic deployment does not use dedicated Infrastructure Nodes and instead deploys two *OpenShift Router* instances into the *Worker Nodes*. The Service resource definition for the Routers uses the *Kubernetes LoadBalancer* resource to provision a classic AWS ELB load balancer to distribute the traffic among the OpenShift Routers. This ELB receives the HTTP and HTTPS traffic to applications served by the wildcard subdomain.

Note   The wildcard subdomain is automatically configured by the installer following the format *.apps.<ocp-route53-dns-zone>

Another difference from the OCP 3.11.x architecture is that only the Kubernetes API server is exposed to the outside world directly from the *Master Nodes*. All other services, including the *Web Consoles*, are published as *Routes*.

> **Note**   There is an *openshift-config-server* service that is accessible directly on Master Nodes but, when using IPI mode, this is not exposed outside the cluster.

Installing OCP4 on AWS

Standard Deployment

The standard OCP4 deployment is the single liner described in Listing 6-10 which will prompt for basic information and proceed with the deployment.

Listing 6-10. Installing OpenShift 4 (standard)

```
# Assuming prerequisites in place.
$ openshift-install create cluster
? SSH Public Key /Users/wcabanba/.ssh/id_rsa.pub
? Platform aws
? Region us-west-2
? Base Domain example.com
? Cluster Name ocp4demo1
? Pull Secret [? for help] ****<snip>*******
INFO Creating infrastructure resources...
INFO Waiting up to 30m0s for the Kubernetes API at https://api.ocp.example.
com:6443...
INFO API v1.12.4+0ba401e up
INFO Waiting up to 30m0s for the bootstrap-complete event...
INFO Destroying the bootstrap resources...
INFO Waiting up to 30m0s for the cluster at https://api.ocp.example.
com:6443 to initialize...
INFO Waiting up to 10m0s for the openshift-console route to be created...
INFO Install complete!
INFO Run 'export KUBECONFIG=/path/to/ocp4demo1/auth/kubeconfig' to manage
the cluster with 'oc', the OpenShift CLI.
INFO The cluster is ready when 'oc login -u kubeadmin -p <snip>' succeeds
(wait a few minutes).
```

```
INFO Access the OpenShift web-console here: https://console-openshift-
console.apps.ocp.example.com
INFO Login to the console with user: kubeadmin, password: <snip>
```

Customizing Standard Deployment

There is some minor customization possible by generating the installer configuration file and editing parameters on it before running the installation.

The OCP4 installer provides the `--dir` flag to read or write the configuration parameters to it. This provides a way to maintain multiple configurations on different folders. To generate the installation configuration, follow the steps in Listing 6-11.

Listing 6-11. Generating the OCP4 installation file

```
# Assuming prerequisites in place.
$ openshift-install create install-config --dir ocp4demo1
? SSH Public Key /Users/wcabanba/.ssh/id_rsa.pub
? Platform aws
? Region us-west-2
? Base Domain example.com
? Cluster Name ocp
? Pull Secret [? for help] ****<snip>*******
```

This command will prompt for any missing information it requires to generate the configuration. The resulting configuration is similar to Listing 6-12.

Listing 6-12. The OCP4 installation file

```
apiVersion: v1beta4
baseDomain: example.com
compute:
- name: worker
  platform: {}
  replicas: 3
controlPlane:
  name: master
  platform: {}
  replicas: 3
```

```
metadata:
  creationTimestamp: null
  name: ocp
networking:
  clusterNetwork:
  - cidr: 10.128.0.0/14
    hostPrefix: 23
  machineCIDR: 10.0.0.0/16
  networkType: OpenShiftSDN
  serviceNetwork:
  - 172.30.0.0/16
platform:
  aws:
    region: us-west-2
    type: m4.large
pullSecret: <snip>
sshKey: |
  ssh-rsa <snip>
```

From the output shown in Listing 6-12, it is relatively easy to identify core areas that can be modified. From the output, it is clear where to change the number of replicas to have more workers or change the Workers instance type. Additional customization attributes can be found in the official OCP4 documentation.[14].

To deploy using the customization, point the installer to the directory when executing the installation. The exact flags when invoking the command are shown in Listing 6-13.

Listing 6-13. The deploying OCP4 with customizations

```
# Assuming prerequisites are in place
$ openshift-install create cluster --dir ocp4demo1
INFO Consuming "Install Config" from target directory
INFO Creating infrastructure resources.
<snip>
```

The rest of the output and process is similar to the one shown in Listing 6-10.

---

[14]AWS Customizations: https://docs.openshift.com/container-platform/4.0/installing/installing_aws/installing-aws-customizations.html

Deployment Progress

As part of the initial configuration for the environment, the installer extends the DNS zone on AWS Route53 designated for OCP (see #1 on Figure 6-20) and creates a subdomain for the new cluster using the cluster name as the subdomain (see #2 on Figure 6-20).

In addition to the default AWS resources in the VPC (see #3 on Figure 6-20), the installer allocates Elastic IPs, creates an ELB load balancer, and creates security groups for the Nodes (see #4 on Figure 6-20).

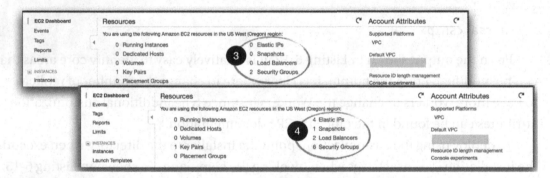

Figure 6-20. *OCP4 installation—allocating subdomain and EC2 resources*

The installer continues by creating the Bootstrap and Master Nodes (see #1 on Figure 6-21). The process takes several minutes.

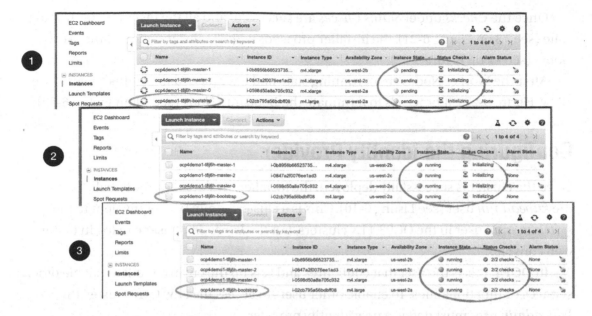

Figure 6-21. *OCP4 installation—BootStrap and Master Nodes*

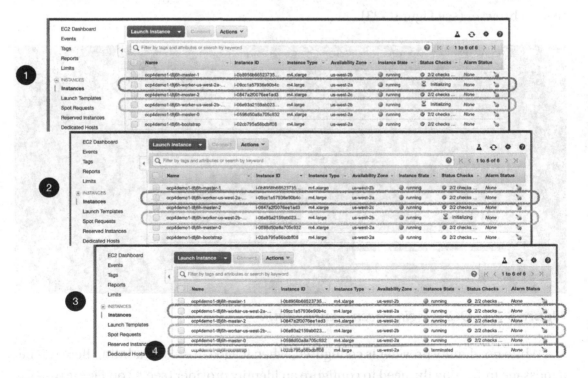

Figure 6-22. *OCP4 installation—Worker Nodes*

Once the *Checks* under *Status Checks* are successful and all the instances in running state (see #3 on Figure 6-21), the installer proceeds with the instantiation of the *Worker Nodes* (see #1 on Figure 6-22).

After the Worker Nodes are in running state and have passed the Status Checks (see #3 on Figure 6-22), it proceeds to terminate the Bootstrap Node (see #4 on Figure 6-22).

Configuring the Identity Provider

Once the cluster is successfully deployed, the installer displays the credentials for the *kubeadmin* user (see Listing 6-10). This is a cluster-admin user equivalent to the *system:admin* user in the OCP3.11.x clusters, but the *kubeadmin* user can log in to the web console.

In OCP4, this is the user that configures and sets up the environment to enable other services or functionalities. To enable other users to access the new OCP cluster, the *kubeadmin* user must define a new identity provider.

Identify the console URL returned by the installer (see Listing 6-10) and access it using a browser (see Figure 6-23).

Figure 6-23. *OCP4 login screen—kubeadmin*

While no identity provider is configured, when logged in as kubeadmin, there will be a message indicating the need to configure an identity provider (see #2 on Figure 6-24).

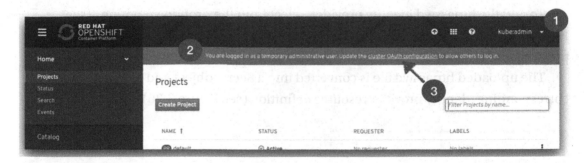

Figure 6-24. *OCP4 OAuth configuration*

From the same message, there is a link to the OAuth configuration (see #3 on Figure 6-24).

At the OAuth configuration, the existing identity provider can be modified or a new identity provider can be added (see Figure 6-25). At the time of this writing, the Developer Preview version provides a wizard to configure the htpasswd and the OpenID identity providers.

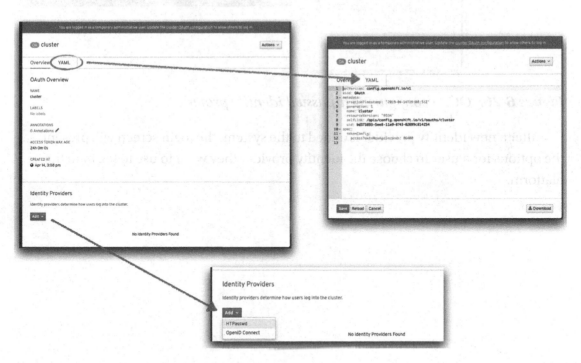

Figure 6-25. *OCP4 adding identity provider*

To add the htpasswd identity provider, select from the dropdown options (see Figure 6-25), and a simple screen will provide a way to set up the name for the identity provider and to upload the htpasswd file with the new user identities (see Figure 6-26).

The uploaded htpasswd file is converted into a Secret object and associated to the corresponding identity provider resource definition (see Figure 6-26).

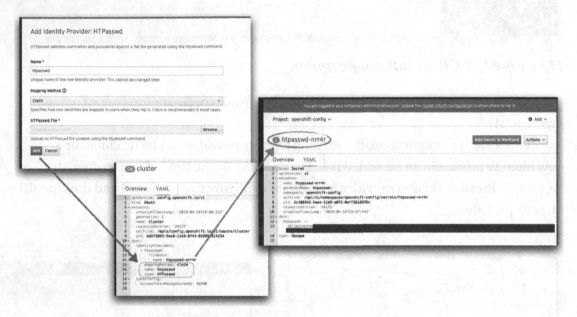

Figure 6-26. *OCP4 configuring htpasswd identity provider*

After a new identity provider is added to the system, the login screen will present the options for a user to choose the identity provider they want to use to log in to the platform.

Figure 6-27. *OCP4 login screen with htpasswd identity provider*

Summary

There are many ways to deploy OpenShift 3.11.x and OpenShift 4 clusters. This chapter presented the most common scenarios that can be used to start deploying OpenShift clusters.

With OCP 3.11.x, there is the option of using a huge single inventory file to set up the parameters and features required for the deployment. The deployment model of OCP 3.11.x requires the pre-provisioning of the Nodes before starting a deployment. This model allows for the cluster administrators to have fine control of the deployment and features to enable since the very beginning.

OCP 4.x brings a paradigm shift which focuses on deploying the core components in an HA configuration without much customization during the installation. Once the cluster is operational, the cluster-admin user *kubeadmin* can be used to configure and set up the parameters for all the features and elements required by the implementation.

Both deployment approaches have their advantages and disadvantages. Independent from the deployment methodology, both provide ways to highly customize the environment to fit the organization's need.

Once the cluster is deployed, new users can be created, and further tuning of the platform is possible. OpenShift supports granular role-based access control (RBAC) capabilities while supporting self-service for regular users. These and other administrative tasks are covered in Chapter 7.

CHAPTER 7

Administration

After deploying OpenShift platform as presented in Chapter 6, the administrative tasks of the platform start. The interaction with an OpenShift cluster is governed by the role-based access control (RBAC) objects. The RBAC determines whether a User is authorized to perform a given action within a Project. A User is an account that is used to interact with the OpenShift API. A User will be associated to one or more Groups that are used to assign privileges to multiple users at the same time.

This chapter focuses on the main tasks of user management (basic user management, groups, virtual users, and service accounts), security, quotas, and templates, which are powerful features for enabling self-service capabilities.

User and Groups

There are several types of users in OpenShift. The default user types are documented in Table 7-1.

© William Caban 2019
W. Caban, *Architecting and Operating OpenShift Clusters*, https://doi.org/10.1007/978-1-4842-4985-7_7

Table 7-1. *OpenShift Virtual Groups*

User Type	Description
Regular users	Regular users are represented by the *User* object. This is the most common way users interact with OpenShift.
System users	This type of user is usually created automatically during the deployment and is used by the platform to interact with the OpenShift API.
Service accounts	The service accounts users are represented by the *ServiceAccount* object. These are special system users associated with projects. The service accounts can be created automatically during Project creation or by a *Project* administrator.

Examples of some of the *system users* created during the deployment of OpenShift are

- Cluster administrators (i.e., system:admin)

- Per-node users (i.e., system:node:node1.ocp.example.com)

- An anonymous user (system:anonymous)

During the creation of a new *Project*, OpenShift creates three service accounts that are used when executing certain actions in the *Project*:

- system:serviceaccount:<project-name>:deployer

- system:serviceaccount:<project-name>:builder

- system:serviceaccount:<project-name>:default

To access *OpenShift*, every user must be authenticated (i.e., using access tokens, certificates, etc.). The policy associated to the *User* object determines what the user is authorized to do in the cluster. When the user is authenticated, the policy associated to the *User* dictates the authorizations. When the API receives a request with no authentication or invalid authentication, these requests are processed as a request by the anonymous user *system:anonymous*.

Virtual Groups and Virtual Users

OpenShift provisions a series of system groups as the base classification for any user interacting with the platform. These special groups are referred to as *Virtual Groups*. Similarly, there is a special *Virtual User* used to identify for anonymous interactions. Table 7-2 lists the *Virtual Groups* and *Virtual Users*.

Table 7-2. *OpenShift Virtual Groups*

Virtual Group or Virtual User	Description
system:authenticated	This *Virtual Group* represents all the authenticated users.
system:authenticated:oauth	This *Virtual Group* represents authenticated users with an OAuth access token.
system:unauthenticated	This *Virtual Group* represents all the unauthenticated users.
system:anonymous	This *Virtual User* is used in conjunction with the system:unauthenticated *Virtual Group* to represent an unauthenticated user interacting with the OpenShift API.

Authentication, Authorization, and OpenShift RBAC

The OpenShift Master has a built-in OAuth server[1] used by the users to obtain an access token to interact with the API. The request for an OAuth token must specify the OAuth client that will receive and use the token (see Table 7-3).

Table 7-3. *OpenShift OAuth Clients*

OAuth Clients	Description
openshift-web-console	Request tokens to use for the web console
openshift-browser-client	Token requests at https://<master>/oauth/token/request with a user-agent that can handle interactive logins
openshift-challenging-client	Token requests with a user-agent that supports OAuth *WWW-Authenticate* challenges.

When a new OAuth Token request arrives to the OAuth server (#2 on Figure 7-1), the OAuth server uses the identity provider to determine the identity of the user making the request (#3 on Figure 7-1). Once the user identity is established, it maps the identity to the corresponding *User* (#4 on Figure 7-1). After successfully mapping the identity to the *User*, the OAuth server creates a token for that *User* and returns it to the original requester.

---

[1]OpenShift OAuth Server: https://docs.openshift.com/container-platform/3.11/
  architecture/additional_concepts/authentication.html#oauth

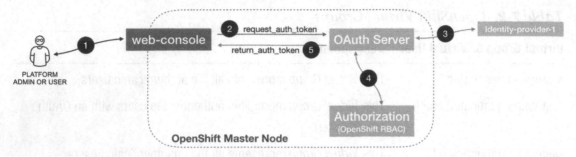

Figure 7-1. *Sample flow for an OAuth Token request*

Note   OpenShift supports the use of Service Account as OAuth clients[2] and the addition of OAuth client[3] definitions.

RBAC

The RBAC objects determine if a user is allowed to perform a specific action within a *Project*. The RBAC authorization is comprised of Rules, Roles, and Bindings (see Table 7-4 for more details).

Table 7-4. *Authorization Constructs*

Construct	Description
Rules	Represent the *Verbs* permitted on a set of Kubernetes and OpenShift objects.
Roles	Represent a collection of policy *Rules*. *Users* and *Groups* can be associated to multiple *Roles* at the same time.
Bindings	Represent the association of *Users* or *Groups* with a *Role*.
Verb	The *Verbs* are get, list, create, update, delete, delete collection, or watch.
Identity	Represents the *User Name* and the list of *Groups* the *User* belongs to.

---

[2]Using Service Account as OAuth client: https://docs.openshift.com/container-platform/
3.11/architecture/additional_concepts/authentication.html#service-accounts-as-
oauth-clients

[3]To define additional OAuth clients, refer to https://docs.openshift.com/container-
platform/3.11/architecture/additional_concepts/authentication.html#oauth-clients

There are two levels of RBAC authorization in an OpenShift Cluster (see Table 7-5 for details).

Table 7-5. *Levels of RBAC Authorizations*

Construct	Description
Cluster RBAC	Refers to *Roles* and *Bindings* that are applicable cluster-wide and not scoped to a particular *Project*. *Cluster Role Bindings* can only reference *Cluster Roles* (*Roles* that exist cluster-wide).
Local RBAC	Refers to *Roles* and *Bindings* scoped to a particular *Project*. *Local Role Bindings* can reference *Cluster Roles* or *Local Roles* (*Roles* that only exist in a *Project*).

Default Cluster Roles

OpenShift predefines a series of default *Cluster Roles* (see Table 7-6) that can be bound to *Users* or *Groups*. In addition, a cluster-admin user can define additional *Roles*.

Table 7-6. *Default Cluster Roles*

Default Cluster Role	Description
cluster-admin	A super-user that can perform any action on any Project. **Note:** When the *cluster-admin Role* is bound to a *User* with a *Local Binding*, that user will have full control over quota and actions on every resource in the *Project*.
admin	A Project manager. **Note:** When used in a *Local Binding*, a *User* with *admin Role* will have rights to view and modify any resource in the *Project* (except for Quota).
basic-user	A user that can get basic information about *Projects* and *Users*.
cluster-status	A user that can get basic cluster status information.
edit	A user that can modify most objects in a *Project* but does not have rights to view or modify *Roles* or *Bindings*.
self-provisioner	A user that can create their own *Projects*.
view	A user who can see, but not modify, most objects in a *Project*. They cannot view or modify *Roles* or *Bindings*.
cluster-reader	A user who can *read*, but not *view*, objects in the cluster.

Security Context Constraints

OpenShift provides granular control of the actions and access of a *Pod* with the capabilities provided by the *Security Context Constraints (SCC)*.

The SCC objects define the conditions that a Pod must met in order to be accepted into the system. The SCC controls the following:

1. Ability to run privileged *Containers*

2. Additional capabilities that can be requested by a *Container*

3. Ability to use *Host* directories as Volumes

4. *SELinux* context of the *Container*

5. The User ID

6. The use of *Host* namespaces and networking

7. Allocating an *FSGroup*[4] that owns the *Pod's* Volumes

8. Configuring allowable supplemental *Groups*

9. Requiring the use of a *read-only* root filesystem

10. Controlling the usage of *Volume types*

11. Configuring allowable *SECCOMP* profiles

OpenShift defines seven default SCC in a cluster. These default SCC are listed on Figure 7-2.

```
 1  $ oc get scc
 2  NAME               PRIV    CAPS  SELINUX     RUNASUSER          FSGROUP    SUPGROUP    PRIORITY   READONLYROOTFS  VOLUMES
 3  anyuid             false   []    MustRunAs   RunAsAny           RunAsAny   RunAsAny    10         false           [configMap downwardAPI emptyDir persistentVolumeClaim projected secret]
 4  hostaccess         false   []    MustRunAs   MustRunAsRange     MustRunAs  RunAsAny    <none>     false           [configMap downwardAPI emptyDir hostPath persistentVolumeClaim projected secret]
 5  hostmount-anyuid   false   []    MustRunAs   RunAsAny           RunAsAny   RunAsAny    <none>     false           [configMap downwardAPI emptyDir hostPath nfs persistentVolumeClaim projected secret]
 6  hostnetwork        false   []    MustRunAs   MustRunAsRange     MustRunAs  MustRunAs   <none>     false           [configMap downwardAPI emptyDir persistentVolumeClaim projected secret]
 7  node-exporter      false   []    RunAsAny    RunAsAny           RunAsAny   RunAsAny    <none>     false           [*]
 8  nonroot            false   []    MustRunAs   MustRunAsNonRoot   RunAsAny   RunAsAny    <none>     false           [configMap downwardAPI emptyDir persistentVolumeClaim projected secret]
 9  privileged         true    [*]   RunAsAny    RunAsAny           RunAsAny   RunAsAny    <none>     false           [*]
10  restricted         false   []    MustRunAs   MustRunAsRange     MustRunAs  RunAsAny    <none>     false           [configMap downwardAPI emptyDir persistentVolumeClaim projected secret]
11
```

Figure 7-2. *List of default SCC*

By default, authenticated users are granted access to the *restricted SCC* (line #10 on Figures 7-2 and 7-3), while cluster administrators, Nodes, and the build controller are granted the *privileged SCC* (line #9 on Figure 7-2).

---

[4]The FSGroup defines Pod's "file system group" ID, for more information refer to the documentation at https://docs.openshift.com/container-platform/3.11/install_config/persistent_storage/pod_security_context.html#fsgroup

```
1    $ oc get --export scc/restricted -o yaml
2    allowHostDirVolumePlugin: false
3    allowHostIPC: false
4    allowHostNetwork: false
5    allowHostPID: false
6    allowHostPorts: false
7    allowPrivilegeEscalation: true
8    allowPrivilegedContainer: false
9    allowedCapabilities: null
10   apiVersion: security.openshift.io/v1
11   defaultAddCapabilities: null
12   fsGroup:
13     type: MustRunAs
14   groups:
15   - system:authenticated
16   kind: SecurityContextConstraints
17   metadata:
18     annotations:
19       kubernetes.io/description: restricted denies access to all host features and requires
20         pods to be run with a UID, and SELinux context that are allocated to the namespace.  This
21         is the most restrictive SCC and it is used by default for authenticated users.
22     creationTimestamp: null
23     name: restricted
24     selfLink: /apis/security.openshift.io/v1/securitycontextconstraints/restricted
25   priority: null
26   readOnlyRootFilesystem: false
27   requiredDropCapabilities:
28   - KILL
29   - MKNOD
30   - SETUID
31   - SETGID
32   runAsUser:
33     type: MustRunAsRange
34   seLinuxContext:
35     type: MustRunAs
36   supplementalGroups:
37     type: RunAsAny
38   users: []
39   volumes:
40   - configMap
41   - downwardAPI
42   - emptyDir
43   - persistentVolumeClaim
44   - projected
45   - secret
```

Figure 7-3. *The "restricted SCC" definition*

As it can be seen from the *restricted SCC* definition (Figure 7-3), this SCC enforces the following restrictions:

- Pods cannot run as privileged (line #8 on Figure 7-3).

- Pods cannot use Host directory Volumes (lines #39 to #45 on Figure 7-3).

- Pods run as a user in a preallocated range of UID (lines #32 and #33 on Figure 7-3).

- Pods run with a preallocated SELinux MCS label (lines #34 and #35 on Figure 7-3).

- Pods can use any supplemental Group (lines #36 and #37 on Figure 7-3).

The SCC strategies[5] are settings and strategies that fall into three categories:

- Controlled by a boolean (default to the most restrictive value)

- Controlled by an allowable set specifying the allowed values

- Controlled by a strategy in which a mechanism generates the value and ensures the value is allowed (see Table 7-7)

Table 7-7. *SCC Strategies*

SCC Strategy	Options
RUNASUSER	MustRunAs, MustRunAsRange, MustRunAsNonRoot, RunAsAny
SELINUXCONTEXT	MustRunAs, RunAsAny
SUPPLEMENTALGROUPS	MustRunAs, RunAsAny
FSGROUP	MustRunAs, RunAsAny
volumes	azureFile, azureDisk, flocker, flexVolume, hostPath, emptyDir, gcePersistentDisk, awsElasticBlockStore, gitRepo, secret, nfs, iscsi, glusterfs, persistentVolumeClaim, rbd, cinder, cephFS, downwardAPI, fc, configMap, vsphereVolume, quo byte, photonPersistenDisk, projected, portworxVolume, scaleIO, storageos, "*", none

---

[5]Details about the SCC Strategies: https://docs.openshift.com/container-platform/3.11/architecture/additional_concepts/authorization.html#authorization-SCC-strategies

SECCOMP Profiles

SECCOMP (secure computing mode) is a security facility in the Linux Kernel that allows a system administrator to limit access by Containers to the system features. The combination of restricted and allowed calls are arranged in profiles. Different profiles can be passed to different *Containers*. This provides a fine-grained control over the *syscalls* available from a *Container*.

Note   SECCOMP is a Kernel feature, and as such, it must be enabled[6] on the system.

To enable SECCOMP for a Pod, the following annotations are required in the Pod configuration:

- `seccomp.security.alpha.kubernetes.io/pod: <unconfined>`

- `container.seccomp.security.alpha.kubernetes.io/<container_name>: <localhost/profile_name>`

In addition, edit the `/etc/origin/node/node-config.yaml` to define the `seccomp-profile-root` directory where the local SECCOMP profiles will be stored. (See Listing 7-1.)

Listing 7-1. Defining SECCOMP profiles directory

```
# Edit /etc/origin/node/node-config.yaml
kubeletArguments:
  ...
  seccomp-profile-root:
    - "/path/to/seccomp/profiles"
# Restart the Node services
$ sudo systemctl restart atomic-openshift-node
```

To control the *SECCOMP* profiles that may be used in the *OpenShift* platform and to set the default *SECCOMP* profile, configure the *SCC* with the `seccompProfiles` field. When using a custom SECCOMP profile, the format for the field is `localhost/<profile name>`. (See Listing 7-2.)

---

[6]To check if SECCOMP is enabled, consult the documentation at https://docs.openshift.com/container-platform/3.11/admin_guide/seccomp.html#seccomp-enabling-seccomp

Listing 7-2. Configuring SECCOMP in SCC profiles

```
seccompProfiles:
- localhost/<profile-name>
```

Enabling Unsafe SYSCTL

When SYSCTL are *namespaced*, their value can be set independently for each *Pod*. This is a requirement for *SYSCTLS* to be accessible in a *Pod* within *Kubernetes*.

A SYSCTL is considered safe for a Pod if

- Does not influence any other *Pod* on the *Node*

- Does not harm the *Node's* health

- Does not gain *CPU* or *memory* resources outside the resource limits of a *Pod*

All safe[7] SYSCTLS are enabled by default. All other SYSCTLS are considered unsafe and are disabled by default. A user with cluster-admin privileges can manually enable unsafe SYSCTLS on a per-node basis.

Enabling unsafe sysctls requires modifying the `kubeletArguments` on the `/etc/origin/node/node-config.yaml` in the Nodes that will be supporting the unsafe SYSCTLS (see Listing 7-3).

Listing 7-3. Enabling unsafe SYSCTLS

```
# Edit /etc/origin/node/node-config.yaml
kubeletArguments:
  ...
  allowed-unsafe-sysctls:
    - "kernel.msg*,net.ipv4.route.min_pmtu"
# Restart the Node services
$ sudo systemctl restart atomic-openshift-node
```

The configuration of SYSCTLS for a Pod is done by setting the values under the securityContext in the Pod configuration (see Listing 7-4).

---

[7]For additional information of safe vs. unsafe sysctls, refer to `https://docs.openshift.com/container-platform/3.11/admin_guide/sysctls.html#safe-vs-unsafe-sysclts`

Note   There is no distinction between safe and unsafe sysctls in the Pod configuration.

Listing 7-4. Example setting SYSCTLS for Pod

```
apiVersion: v1
kind: Pod
metadata:
  name: sysctl-example
spec:
  securityContext:
    sysctls:
    - name: kernel.shm_rmid_forced
      value: "0"
    - name: net.ipv4.route.min_pmtu
      value: "552"
    - name: kernel.msgmax
      value: "65536"
...
```

Note   A Pod using unsafe SYSCTLS will fail to run on any *Node* where the unsafe SYSCTLS have not been explicitly enabled.

Identity Providers

Configuring the identity provider[8] for the built-in OAuth server can be done during the installation or after the installation.

---

[8]Additional details on configuring identity providers: https://docs.openshift.com/container-platform/3.11/install_config/configuring_authentication.html#identity-providers-configuring

The OpenShift 3.11.x supported identity providers are

- **Deny All**: Default identity provider. Denies access for all usernames and passwords.

- **Allow All**: Allows access to any non-empty username with any non-empty password to log in. Used for testing purposes. (Used as default if running without a master configuration file.)

- **HTPasswd**: Validates usernames and passwords against a flat file generated using *htpasswd*.

- **Keystone**: Uses the OpenStack identity project for authentication.

- **LDAP**: Validates usernames and password against an LDAPv3 server using simple bind authentication.

- **Basic Authentication** (remote): Allows users to log in to OpenShift with credentials validated against a remote identity provider. (Must use an HTTPS connection to remote server.)

- **Request Header**: Identifies users from request header values like X-Remote-User.

- **GitHub**: Uses the OAuth authentication from GitHub.

- **GitLab**: Uses the OAuth authentication from GitLab (versions 7.7.0 to 11.0). If using GitLab version 11.1 or later, use the OpenID Connect.

- **Google**: Uses Google's OpenID Connect integration.

- **OpenID Connect**: Integrates with an OpenID Connect identity provider.

The configuration of the identity provider uses a `mappingMethod` to define how new identities are mapped to users when they log in to *OpenShift*. The value will be one of the following:

- **claim**: Provisions a user with the identity's preferred user name. Fails if a user with that user name is already mapped to another identity. (This is the default configuration.)

- **lookup**: Looks up an existing identity, user identity mapping, and user. It does not provision users or identities if they don't exist. Using this method requires cluster administrators to set up identities and users manually or by an external process.

- **generate**: Provisions a user with the identity's preferred user name. If a user with the preferred user name already exists, a unique user name is generated (i.e., username2).

- **add**: Provisions a user with the identity's preferred user name. If a user with that user name already exists, the identity is mapped to the existing user. (Required when multiple identity providers are configured that identify the same set of users.)

Managing Users and Groups

The creation of a user depends on the configuration of the mappingMethod in the *identity provider*. The manual creation of a user is as shown in Listing 7-5.

Listing 7-5. Manual creation of a user

```
$ oc create user <username> --full-name="User Name"
```

Managing the roles, groups, and SCC for a user can be done with the oc client command with the options as shown in Figure 7-4.

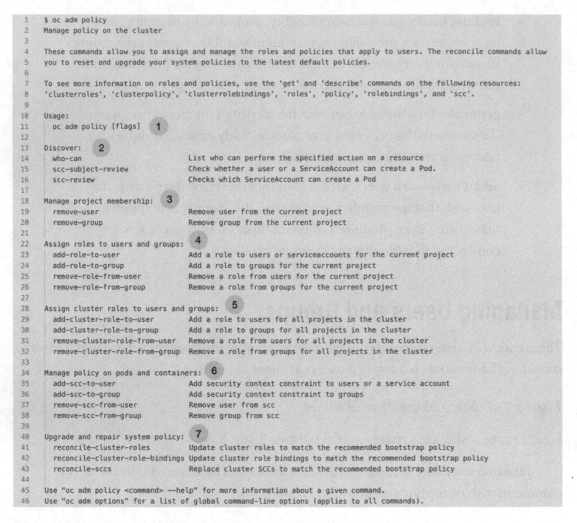

```
1    $ oc adm policy
2    Manage policy on the cluster
3
4    These commands allow you to assign and manage the roles and policies that apply to users. The reconcile commands allow
5    you to reset and upgrade your system policies to the latest default policies.
6
7    To see more information on roles and policies, use the 'get' and 'describe' commands on the following resources:
8    'clusterroles', 'clusterpolicy', 'clusterrolebindings', 'roles', 'policy', 'rolebindings', and 'scc'.
9
10   Usage:
11     oc adm policy [flags]    1
12
13   Discover:    2
14     who-can                          List who can perform the specified action on a resource
15     scc-subject-review               Check whether a user or a ServiceAccount can create a Pod.
16     scc-review                       Checks which ServiceAccount can create a Pod
17
18   Manage project membership:    3
19     remove-user                      Remove user from the current project
20     remove-group                     Remove group from the current project
21
22   Assign roles to users and groups:    4
23     add-role-to-user                 Add a role to users or serviceaccounts for the current project
24     add-role-to-group                Add a role to groups for the current project
25     remove-role-from-user            Remove a role from users for the current project
26     remove-role-from-group           Remove a role from groups for the current project
27
28   Assign cluster roles to users and groups:    5
29     add-cluster-role-to-user         Add a role to users for all projects in the cluster
30     add-cluster-role-to-group        Add a role to groups for all projects in the cluster
31     remove-cluster-role-from-user    Remove a role from users for all projects in the cluster
32     remove-cluster-role-from-group   Remove a role from groups for all projects in the cluster
33
34   Manage policy on pods and containers:    6
35     add-scc-to-user                  Add security context constraint to users or a service account
36     add-scc-to-group                 Add security context constraint to groups
37     remove-scc-from-user             Remove user from scc
38     remove-scc-from-group            Remove group from scc
39
40   Upgrade and repair system policy:    7
41     reconcile-cluster-roles          Update cluster roles to match the recommended bootstrap policy
42     reconcile-cluster-role-bindings  Update cluster role bindings to match the recommended bootstrap policy
43     reconcile-sccs                   Replace cluster SCCs to match the recommended bootstrap policy
44
45   Use "oc adm policy <command> --help" for more information about a given command.
46   Use "oc adm options" for a list of global command-line options (applies to all commands).
```

Figure 7-4. *Manage user roles, groups, and SCC*

Using Service Accounts

Service Accounts (SA) provide a flexible way to control API access without sharing a regular *User* credential.

The user name of a *Service Account (SA)* is derived from its Project and name (see Listing 7-6). The *Service Account* can be granted *Roles* (see Listing 7-6) as any other user in the system.

Listing 7-6. Assigning Roles to Service Account

```
# Format of a Service Account name
system:serviceaccount:<project-name>:<name>
# Assigning Role to a Service Account
$ oc policy add-role-to-user <role-name> system:serviceaccount:<project-
name>:<name>
# Assigning Role to a Service Account from the Project it belongs to
$ oc policy add-role-to-user <role-name> -z <SA-name>
```

Each Service Account belongs to two groups:

- `system:serviceaccount`
- `system:serviceaccount:<project-name>`

During the creation of a new *Service Account,*[9] the system ensures to add two secrets to it (see Listing 7-7):

- An API token
- Credentials for the OpenShift Container Registry

Note   The generated API token and registry credentials do not expire. If the secret is deleted, a new one is automatically generated to replace it.

Listing 7-7. Creating a Service Account

```
# Creating a Service Account name
$ oc create sa sa-demo (or) oc create serviceaccount sa-demo
serviceaccount/sa-demo created
$ oc describe sa sa-demo
Name:              sa-demo
Namespace:         demo
Labels:            <none>
Annotations:       <none>
```

---

[9]Additional information about Service Accounts `https://docs.openshift.com/container-platform/3.11/dev_guide/service_accounts.html`

Image pull secrets: sa-demo-dockercfg-rj875

Mountable secrets: sa-demo-token-xph4v

                      sa-demo-dockercfg-rj875

Tokens: sa-demo-token-txlcq

                      sa-demo-token-xph4v

Events: <none>

To associate a *ServiceAccount* to a *Pod,* use the serviceAccountName under the *Pod's* spec definition (see Listing 7-8).

Listing 7-8. Creating a Service Account

```
apiVersion: v1
kind: Pod
metadata:
  name: demo-pod
spec:
  serviceAccountName: sa-demo
  ...
```

The API tokens from the ServiceAccount associated to the Pod are mounted as a file at /var/run/secrets/kubernetes.io/serviceaccount/token inside the *Container*.

Note   The default *ServiceAccount* is used when no explicit *ServiceAccount* is specified in the Pod definition.

Quotas and Limit Ranges

Quotas and *Limit Ranges* are objects that can be set by a cluster administrator to limit the number of objects or amount of compute resources that are used by a particular *Project*. While *LimitRanges* specify the limits of compute resources in a *Project* on per-object basis, *Quotas* act as the upper limit for the total compute resources or number of objects in the Project.

LimitRange object can set up compute resource constraints in a *Project* at the following level:

- Pod

- Container

- Image

- ImageStream

- PersistentVolumeClaim

To apply a *LimitRange*[10] to a *Project,* create the object definition with the specification (see definition in Figure 7-5).

```
1    $ oc create -f demo-limit-range.yaml -n demo
2    limitrange/demo-limit-range created
3
4    $ oc describe limitrange demo-limit-range
5    Name:                    demo-limit-range
6    Namespace:               demo
7    Type                     Resource                 Min    Max   Default Request   Default Limit   Max Limit/Request Ratio
8    ----                     --------                 ---    ---   ---------------   -------------   -----------------------
9    Pod                      cpu                      200m   2     -                 -               -
10   Pod                      memory                   6Mi    1Gi   -                 -               -
11   Container                memory                   4Mi    1Gi   100Mi             200Mi           -
12   Container                cpu                      100m   2     200m              300m            10
13   openshift.io/Image       storage                  -      1Gi   -                 -               -
14   openshift.io/ImageStream openshift.io/image-tags  -      20    -                 -               -
15   openshift.io/ImageStream openshift.io/images      -      30    -                 -               -
```

Figure 7-5. *Creating and verifying LimitRange*

All resource creation or modification requests are checked against the *LimitRange* in the *Project.* The resource creation or modification is rejected if it violates the constraints (see Figure 7-6).

---

[10]Additional information about creating LimitRange: https://docs.openshift.com/container-platform/3.11/admin_guide/limits.html#creating-a-limit-range

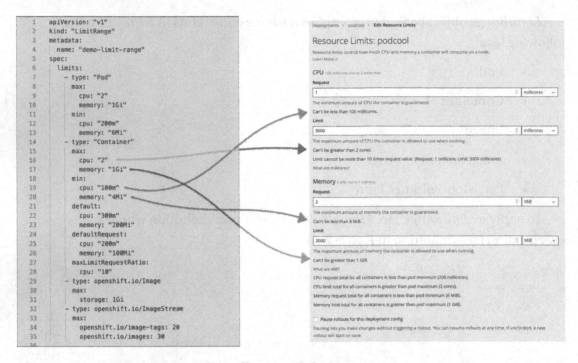

Figure 7-6. *LimitRange and its effect on Pod requests*

The *ResourceQuota* object is used to set up *Project*-level *Quota* to limit the number of objects in a *Project* or the total *Limits* for a *Project*. Figure 7-7 shows an example defining and verifying the creation of a *ResourceQuota*.

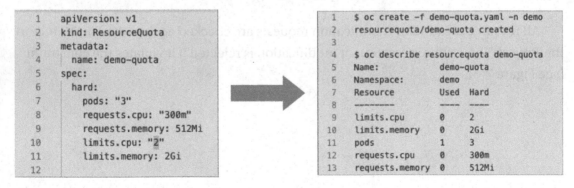

Figure 7-7. *Definition and creation of ResourceQuota*

When a particular request for creation or modification of a resource violates a Quota, the system will prevent the creation or modification of the resource (see Figure 7-8).

```
3m        3m         1        podcool.159a121288cda012         DeploymentConfig                              Normal      ReplicationControllerScaled    deploymentconfig-cont
oller     Scaled replication controller "podcool-1" from 1 to 4
3m        3m         1        podcool-1-mhkmj.159a1212dcb8966f  Pod                                           Normal      Scheduled                      default-scheduler
          Successfully assigned demo/podcool-1-mhkmj to ocp-n3.shift.zone
3m        3m         1        podcool-1.159a1212a65f02d2        ReplicationController                         Normal      SuccessfulCreate               replication-controller
          Created pod: podcool-1-mhkmj
3m        3m         1        podcool-1.159a1212bb2ca6b7        ReplicationController                         Warning     FailedCreate                   replication-controlle
          Error creating: pods "podcool-1-f882k" is forbidden: exceeded quota: demo-quota, requested: requests.cpu=200m, used: requests.cpu=200m, limited: requests.cpu=300m
3m        3m         1        podcool-1.159a1212cc93dabab       ReplicationController                         Warning     FailedCreate                   replication-controller
          Error creating: pods "podcool-1-942b4" is forbidden: exceeded quota: demo-quota, requested: requests.cpu=200m, used: requests.cpu=200m, limited: requests.cpu=300m
3m        3m         1        podcool-1.159a1212dabca1d4        ReplicationController                         Warning     FailedCreate                   replication-controller
          Error creating: pods "podcool-1-26s7r" is forbidden: exceeded quota: demo-quota, requested: requests.cpu=200m, used: requests.cpu=200m, limited: requests.cpu=300m
```

Figure 7-8. Example of quota enforcement

OpenShift Service Catalogs

OpenShift includes a *Service Catalog* which implements the Open Service API[11] (OSP API) for Kubernetes. This capability allows users to connect applications deployed in OpenShift to services instantiated through service brokers.

A user with cluster-admin privileges registers one or more *Service Brokers* with *OpenShift* cluster. Each Service Broker defines a set of *Cluster Service Classes* and *Service Plans* available to users.

Users request to provision or deprovision a resource provided by a *Service Class*. When provisioning a new resource, the *Users bind* the *service instance* with their local application *Pods*.

OpenShift provides two Service Brokers with the Service Catalog:

- **Template Service Broker (TSB)** gives the visibility into the *Instant App* and *Quickstart Templates*[12] that are shipped with *OpenShift*. In addition, the TSB makes available as a service any services defined as an *OpenShift Template*.

- **OpenShift Ansible Broker (OAB)**[13] is an implementation of the *OSB API* that manages application defined by *Ansible Playbook Bundles (APBs)*.

---

[11]Details about the Open Service Broker API are available at the project home page: www.openservicebrokerapi.org

[12]Additional information on using Instant App and Quickstart Templates is available at https://docs.openshift.com/container-platform/3.11/dev_guide/templates. html#using-the-instantapp-templates

[13]Additional details about the Ansible Service Broker is available at https://docs.openshift.com/container-platform/3.11/architecture/service_catalog/ansible_service_broker. html#arch-ansible-service-broker

OpenShift Templates

OpenShift Templates provide a way to parameterize the creation of any OpenShift and Kubernetes objects. A template can be processed to create anything the user executing the Template has the permission to create within a Project (i.e., Services, BuildConfig, Deployments, Routes, etc.).

Templates are one of the mechanisms used to provide self-service capabilities with OpenShift. They provide a way for developers to deploy, on self-serve style, applications or backend stacks, when needed, while administrators retain full control on how a particular application or backend stack is implemented.

A Template can be executed from CLI or using the web console if the Template has been uploaded to the Project or Global Template library. Installing a Template can be done over GUI or CLI (see Figure 7-9).

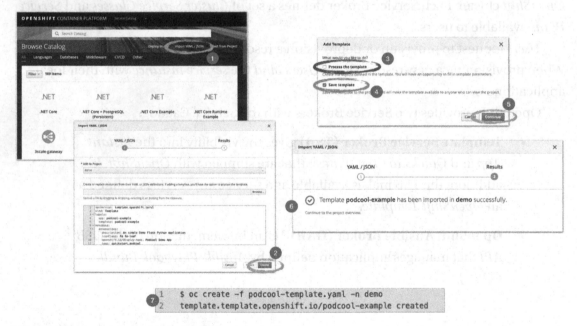

Figure 7-9. *Installing OpenShift Template*

When using the *GUI* to install an *OpenShift Template,* there are two options: an option to immediately process the *Template* (#3 on Figure 7-9) and another option to save the template to the service catalog (#4 on Figure 7-9).

Note   When installing a *Template,* it needs to be associated to a namespace. To make the *Template* available cluster-wide, it should be installed into the *openshift Project.*

An example of an OpenShift Template is shown in Listing 7-9.

Listing 7-9. OpenShift Template example

```
apiVersion: template.openshift.io/v1
kind: Template
labels:
  app: podcool-example
  template: podcool-example
metadata:
  annotations:
    description: An simple Demo Flask Python application
    iconClass: fa fa-leaf
    openshift.io/display-name: Podcool Demo App
    tags: quickstart,podcool
  name: podcool-example
objects:
- apiVersion: v1
  kind: Service
  metadata:
    annotations:
      description: Exposes and load balances the application pods
    name: podcool-example
  spec:
    ports:
    - name: web
      port: 8080
      targetPort: 8080
    selector:
      name: podcool-example
- apiVersion: v1
```

```
  kind: ImageStream
  metadata:
    annotations:
      description: Keeps track of changes in the application image
    name: podcool-example
- apiVersion: v1
  kind: BuildConfig
  metadata:
    annotations:
      description: Defines how to build the application
    name: podcool-example
  spec:
    output:
      to:
        kind: ImageStreamTag
        name: podcool-example:latest
    source:
      contextDir: ${CONTEXT_DIR}
      git:
        ref: ${SOURCE_REPOSITORY_REF}
        uri: ${SOURCE_REPOSITORY_URL}
      type: Git
    strategy:
      sourceStrategy:
        from:
          kind: ImageStreamTag
          name: python:3.6
          namespace: openshift
      type: Source
    triggers:
    - type: ConfigChange
    - github:
        secret: ${GITHUB_WEBHOOK_SECRET}
      type: GitHub
```

```
- apiVersion: v1
  kind: DeploymentConfig
  metadata:
    annotations:
      description: Defines how to deploy the application server
    name: podcool-example
  spec:
    replicas: 1
    selector:
      name: podcool-example
    strategy:
      type: Rolling
    template:
      metadata:
        labels:
          name: podcool-example
        name: podcool-example
      spec:
        containers:
        - image: podcool-example
          name: podcool-example
          ports:
          - containerPort: 8080
          env:
          - name: APP_VERSION
            value: v1
          - name: APP_MESSAGE
            value: Deployment from Template
    triggers:
    - imageChangeParams:
        automatic: true
        containerNames:
        - podcool-example
```

```
      from:
        kind: ImageStreamTag
        name: podcool-example:latest
    type: ImageChange
  - type: ConfigChange
parameters:
- description: The URL of the repository with your application source code
  name: SOURCE_REPOSITORY_URL
  value: https://github.com/williamcaban/podcool.git
- description: Set this to a branch name, tag or other ref of your
repository if you
    are not using the default branch
  name: SOURCE_REPOSITORY_REF
- description: Set this to the relative path to your project if it is not
in the root
    of your repository
  name: CONTEXT_DIR
- description: Github trigger secret.  A difficult to guess string encoded
as part
    of the webhook URL.  Not encrypted.
  from: '[a-zA-Z0-9]{40}'
  generate: expression
  name: GITHUB_WEBHOOK_SECRET
```

An *OpenShift Template*[14] can use or create any *OpenShift* and *Kubernetes* object the user executing it has privileges to create in a *Project*. That is a wide range of options and possible objects to create with a *Template*. As such, the process of writing *OpenShift Templates* is beyond the scope of this book.

---

[14]Additional information about writing OpenShift Templates: https://docs.openshift.com/ container-platform/3.11/dev_guide/templates.html

Summary

This chapter focused on the main tasks of user management, security, quotas, and Templates. With respect to user management, this chapter covered basic user management, groups, virtual users, and service accounts. The security topics covered setting secure profiles, quotas, and limits. Finally, this chapter described using OpenShift Templates with the service catalog as a mechanism to provide self-service capabilities to the users.

The administration of OpenShift Clusters involves much more than what is covered in the chapter, and the reader should explore additional topics that will enhance the experience for the users while facilitating sustainable operations of the platform.

One of the OpenShift features designed to enhance the developer experience is the native capability to support CI/CD pipelines. The OpenShift Pipelines are covered in Chapter 8.

CHAPTER 8

Architecting OpenShift Jenkins Pipelines

The OpenShift platform provides multiple features to enhance the developer experience. These features are enabled and managed using the same RBAC and SCC options seen in Chapter 7. This chapter focuses on the OpenShift Jenkins Pipelines capabilities.

The *OpenShift Jenkins Pipelines* capabilities in *OpenShift Container Platform (OCP)* provide the ability to create advanced CI/CD pipelines that can be used to create new CI/CD processes, or to integrate with existing organizations CI/CD processes.

OpenShift Jenkins Pipelines provide support for using CI/CD pipelines to build, deploy, and promote applications on OpenShift. These Pipelines can use a combination of the *Jenkins Pipeline Build Strategy*, *Jenkinsfiles,* and the *OpenShift Jenkins Client Plugin.*

This chapter describes the basic configurations to start using the capabilities provided by the *OpenShift CI/CD* feature.

CI/CD Pipelines As a Service with OpenShift

When using the *Jenkins Pipeline Build Strategy* or using a *Jenkinsfile*, *OpenShift* CI/CD capabilities autoprovision a *Jenkins Master* for the *Project* and the *Jenkins Slaves* required to complete the stages.

This *Jenkins Master* will be used to execute all the *Jenkins Pipelines* defined at the *Project.*

By default, the *Jenkins Master* server uses the *OpenShift Jenkins-ephemeral* template to instantiate the server. To deploy a Jenkins server with persistent storage for the data and configuration stored in /var/lib/jenkins, the Project admin can manually deploy a Jenkins Master using the Jenkins-persistent template from the self-service catalog.

195

© William Caban 2019
W. Caban, *Architecting and Operating OpenShift Clusters*, https://doi.org/10.1007/978-1-4842-4985-7_8

To change the default Jenkins template, a cluster-admin can modify the *Master Nodes* configuration[1] to set up the Jenkins-persistent template as the default template to use when autoprovisioning a Jenkins server (see Listing 8-1).

Listing 8-1. Jenkins-persistent as default template for autoprovisioning of Jenkins servers

```
# Update /etc/origin/master/master-config.yaml to include
jenkinsPipelineConfig:
  autoProvisionEnabled: true
  templateNamespace: openshift
  templateName: jenkins-persistent
  serviceName: jenkins-persistent-svc
```

During the instantiation of the Jenkins Master, the process

- Deploys *Jenkins* into the *Project* using the official *OpenShift Jenkins* image

  - The Jenkins deployment can be done using ephemeral or persistent storage.

- Creates *Service* and *Route* resources for the *Jenkins Master*

- Creates a *jenkins Service Account (SA)* in the *Project*

  - Grant *Project*-level *edit* access to the new *jenkins Service Account*

When using an *OpenShift Pipeline* across *Projects*, the *jenkins* SA on the project hosting the *Jenkins Master* requires *edit* access level on the *Projects* it will manage.

Listing 8-2. Grant 'edit' access to 'jenkins' Service Account

```
# Option 1: Grant 'edit' access to 'jenkins' Service Account on specific
Projects
oc policy add-role-to-user edit system:serviceaccount:<cicd-
project>:jenkins -n <target-project>
```

---

[1]Using Jenkins-persistent template: https://docs.openshift.com/container-platform/3.11/install_config/configuring_pipeline_execution.html

```
# Option 2: Grant 'edit' access to 'jenkins' Service Account on all
Projects
oc adm policy add-cluster-role-to-user edit system:serviceaccount:<cicd-
project>:jenkins
```

Jenkins Pipeline Build Strategy

OpenShift has the notion of *build configurations* or *BuildConfigs*. A *BuildConfig* is a configuration describing a single build definition. This includes information like the triggers that will provoke a new *build* and the *build strategy* to use. The *build strategy* determines the process to be used to execute a *build*. One of the build strategies is the *Pipeline Build Strategy.*[2]

The *Pipeline Build Strategy* is an *OpenShift Build*[3] type that enables developers to define *Jenkins* pipeline workflows which are executed inside the *OpenShift* platform.

To use this *Build Strategy*, the *Jenkins Pipeline* is defined in a *Jenkinsfile*. This can be embedded directly in the *BuildConfig* (see #3 on Figure 8-1) or provided on a *Git* repository (see #2 on Figure 8-2) referenced by the *BuildConfig* (see #3 on Figure 8-2).

---

[2]*OpenShift Pipeline Build Strategy* https://docs.openshift.com/container-platform/3.11/
dev_guide/builds/build_strategies.html#pipeline-strategy-options

[3]OpenShift *Build* process https://docs.openshift.com/container-platform/3.11/
architecture/core_concepts/builds_and_image_streams.html#builds

```
1     kind: "BuildConfig"
2     apiVersion: "v1"                                    1
3     metadata:
4       name: "sample-pipeline"
5     spec:
6       strategy:                            2
7         jenkinsPipelineStrategy:
8           env:
9           - name: "MY_STRATEGY_VAR"
10            value: "Demo Env Var from Pipeline Strategy"
11          type: JenkinsPipeline
12          jenkinsfile: |-              3
13            pipeline {
14              agent any
15
16              options {
17                // set a timeout of 5 minutes for this pipeline
18                timeout(time: 5, unit: 'MINUTES')
19              } //options
20
21              environment {
22                MY_PIPELINE_VAR = "Demo Env Var from Pipeline"
23              }
24
25              stages {
26                  stage('Build') {
27                      steps {
28                          echo "Sample Build stage with variable from pipeline startegy >> ${MY_STRATEGY_VAR}"
29                      }
30                  } //stage
31
32                  stage('Test') {
33                      steps {
34                          echo "Sample Test stage with variable from Jenkinsfile >> ${MY_PIPELINE_VAR}"
35                      }
36                  } //stage
37
38                  stage('Promote') {
39                      steps {
40                          echo "Sample Promote stage with OpenShift Client Plugin DSL"
41                          script {
42                              openshift.withCluster() {
43                                  openshift.withProject() {
44                                      echo "Using project: ${openshift.project()}"
45                                  }
46                              }
47                          } // script
48                      } //steps
49                  } //stage
50
51              } // stages
52          } // pipeline
53
```

Figure 8-1. *OpenShift Pipeline Build Strategy with embedded Jenkinsfile definition*

The *BuildConfig* with the embedded Jenkins pipeline definition is a YAML formatted configuration file specifying the *Jenkins Pipeline Strategy* (see #2 on Figure 8-1). The content of the *Jenkinsfile* is included as a multiline string block (see #3 on Figure 8-1) in the definition.

```
1    kind: "BuildConfig"
2    apiVersion: "v1"                    1
3    metadata:
4      name: "sample-pipeline-2"
5    spec:
6      source:          2
7        git:
8          uri: "https://git.example.com/demo/myapp"
9      strategy:
10       jenkinsPipelineStrategy:
11         env:
12         - name: "MY_STRATEGY_VAR"
13           value: "Demo Env Var from Pipeline Strategy"
14    3   jenkinsfilePath: path/to/jenkinsfile/filename
15
16
```

Figure 8-2. *OpenShift Pipeline Build Strategy with Git Jenkinsfile definition*

The other option for the Pipeline Strategy is the *BuildConfig* referencing a Jenkinsfile (see #3 on Figure 8-2) on a Git repository (see #2 on Figure 8-2). In this particular case, the Jenkinsfile can be in any directory of the referenced Git repository and can have any name as long as the full path and filename are specified in the corresponding *Jenkinsfile Path* variable. If this variable is not defined, it will retrieve a file named *Jenkinsfile* from the root directory of the Git repo.

Creating the Pipeline BuildConfig

The BuildConfig on Figure 8-1 is for a sample pipeline that defines environment variables at the pipeline strategy level (line 8 on Figure 8-1) and at the *Jenkinsfile* level (line 21 on Figure 8-1). The embedded *Jenkinsfile* defines a Jenkins Pipeline (line 13 on Figure 8-1) with some sample stages (line 25 on Figure 8-1). For the purpose of this example, there are three stages. To maintain a minimal structure to illustrate the use of the pipeline, in this example, each stage simply displays a message.

The YAML configuration for the *BuildConfig sample-pipeline* from Figure 8-1 is shown in Listing 8-3.

Listing 8-3. Sample Pipeline BuildConfig with embedded Jenkinsfile

```
kind: "BuildConfig"
apiVersion: "v1"
metadata:
  name: "sample-pipeline"
spec:
  strategy:
    jenkinsPipelineStrategy:
      env:
      - name: "MY_STRATEGY_VAR"
        value: "Demo Env Var from Pipeline Strategy"
      type: JenkinsPipeline
      jenkinsfile: |-
        pipeline {
          agent any

          options {
            // set a timeout of 5 minutes for this pipeline
            timeout(time: 5, unit: 'MINUTES')
          } //options

          environment {
            MY_PIPELINE_VAR = "Demo Env Var from Pipeline"
          }

          stages {
              stage('Build') {
                  steps {
                      echo "Sample Build stage with variable from
                      pipeline startegy >> ${MY_STRATEGY_VAR}"
                  }
              } //stage

              stage('Test') {
```

```
            steps {
                echo "Sample Test stage with variable from
                Jenkinsfile >> ${MY_PIPELINE_VAR}"
            }
        } //stage

        stage('Promote') {
            steps {
                echo "Sample Promote stage with OpenShift Client
                Plugin DSL"
                script {
                    openshift.withCluster() {
                        openshift.withProject() {
                            echo "Using project: ${openshift.
                            project()}"
                        }
                    }
                } // script
            } //steps
        } //stage

    } // stages
} // pipeline
```

The YAML configuration for the *BuildConfig sample-pipeline-2* from Figure 8-2 is shown in Listing 8-4.

Listing 8-4. Sample Pipeline BuildConfig with Git referenced Jenkinsfile

```
kind: "BuildConfig"
apiVersion: "v1"
metadata:
  name: "sample-pipeline-2"
spec:
  source:
    git:
      uri: "https://git.example.com/demo/myapp"
```

```
strategy:
  jenkinsPipelineStrategy:
    env:
    - name: "MY_STRATEGY_VAR"
      value: "Demo Env Var from Pipeline Strategy"
    jenkinsfilePath: path/to/jenkinsfile/filename
```

Deploying the Pipeline BuildConfig

The BuildConfig is created at a Project level. It is up to the user to use a dedicated Project for the Pipeline and another for the application or use the same Project for the Pipeline and application.

From the OpenShift Application Console, import the YAML for the BuildConfig (see #1 on Figure 8-3).

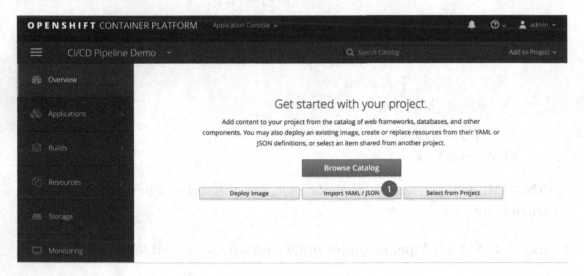

Figure 8-3. *Import BuildConfig YAML definition*

The *Import YAML* window allows for uploading a YAML file from the local machine or for the copy and paste of the *BuildConfig* at the editor window (see #1 on Figure 8-4). On the successful upload or definition of the *BuildConfig,* a new Pipeline is created.

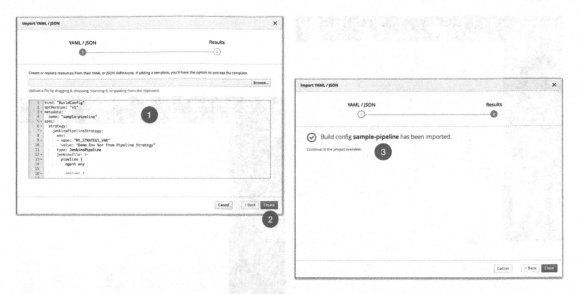

Figure 8-4. *Importing the BuildConfig and creating the Pipeline*

The first time a *Pipeline* strategy is defined for a *Project, OpenShift* instantiates a *Jenkins Master* server in that *Project* (see Figure 8-5). This Jenkins server is used to execute the Pipeline definition from the BuildConfig.

Note   Additional *Pipeline Build* configurations or *BuildConfigs*, in the same project, will share the same Jenkins server.

Figure 8-5. *Instantiation of an embedded Jenkins server*

Note   The instantiation of the initial Jenkins server takes some time to complete. After about 10 minutes after the instantiation, the system will be ready to receive triggers to execute the Pipeline.

The *Pipeline* can be triggered by a *Webhook, Image Change, Configuration Change, or Manually*. To execute a manual trigger from GUI, at the *Application Console,* go to *Builds ➤ Pipelines* (see #1 and #2 on Figure 8-6) or from CLI (see #3 on Figure 8-6).

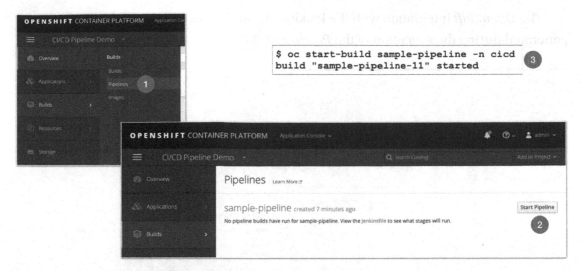

Figure 8-6. *Executing the Pipeline Build Strategy*

A visual representation of the pipeline will be highlighting the step that is executing (see #2 on Figure 8-7). As stages are successful, the stage representation will be colored green.

After several execution of the Pipeline, the *History* tab of the Pipeline pane will show a histogram of the time it took to complete an execution and a color-coded view showing failed and successful attempts (see #3 on Figure 8-7).

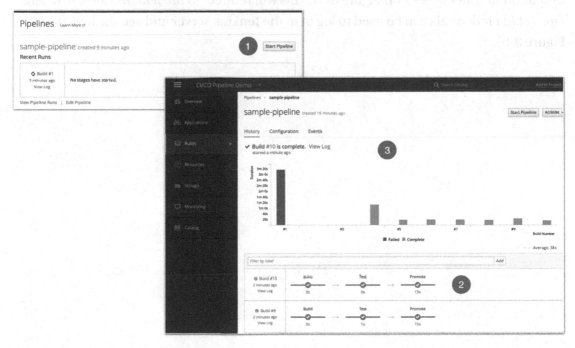

Figure 8-7. *Pipeline Build History*

The *OpenShift* integration with the Jenkins instance allows access to the logs generated during the execution of the *Pipeline Build*.

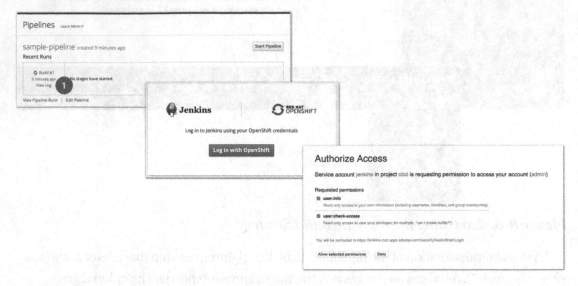

Figure 8-8. *View Logs from Jenkins Console*

To access the Logs for a particular *Build* execution, select the *View Log* link under the execution number (see #1 on Figure 8-8). This will redirect to the *Jenkins Console* where *OpenShift* credentials can be used to log in to the Jenkins server and see the logs (see Figure 8-9).

Figure 8-9. *Build Logs at Jenkins Console*

The logs for a particular *Pipeline* will include the actions and output from those actions (see #2, #3, #4, and #5 on Figure 8-9), for each one of the *Pipeline Stages* defined by the *Jenkinsfile*.

Note   The Jenkins server must be manually deleted by the user. It will not be automatically removed, even after deleting all Pipeline build configurations.

Jenkinsfile with Source Code

When using this option, the *Jenkinsfile* must be included with the application source code at the root of the repository or at the root of the *contextDir* of the repository. When deploying an application and referencing a repository containing a *Jenkinsfile*

- If there is not an existing Jenkins instance in the Project, *OpenShift* creates a *DeploymentConfig* and deploys a Jenkins instance.

- OpenShift creates a *BuildConfig* (see #1 on Figure 8-10) with

  - A *jenkinsPipelineStrategy* (see #5 on Figure 8-10) referring the *Jenkinsfile* in the Git repository (see #5 on Figure 8-10)

  - A set of Webhook triggers: GitHub and Generic (see #6 and #7 on Figure 8-10)

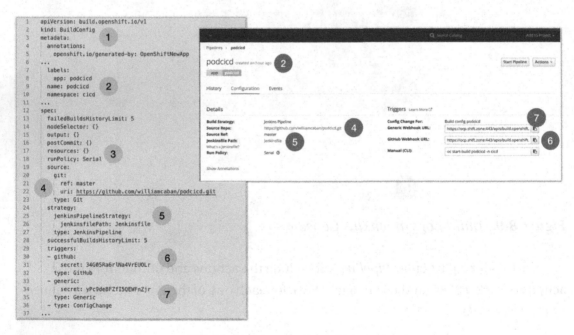

Figure 8-10. *Pipeline BuildConfig from Jenkinsfile on Git repository*

The URL for the Webhook triggers will follow the format:

`https://`**`<ocp-cluster-fqdn>`**`/apis/build.openshift.io/v1/namespaces/`**`<name-of-project>`**`/buildconfigs/`**`<name-of-buildconfig>`**`/webhooks/`**`<trigger-token>`**`/`**`<trigger-type>`**

These Webhook triggers[4] enable external tools to initiate a new pipeline execution. Figure 8-11 shows a Webhook call (#1 on Figure 8-11) triggering a new Build for the pipeline (#3 on Figure 8-11). #4 on Figure 8-11 clearly shows the CI/CD pipeline was triggered by a *Generic Webhook* call.

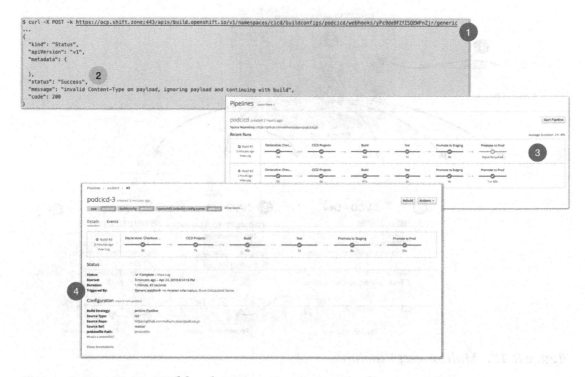

Figure 8-11. *Using Webhook triggers to start a Pipeline execution*

---

[4]Additional information on using Webhooks to trigger builds is available from the official documentation: `https://docs.openshift.com/container-platform/3.11/dev_guide/builds/triggering_builds.html`

Multiproject Pipelines

When using an OpenShift Jenkins Pipelines to promote an application build across multiple projects, the *jenkins* Service Account must have *edit* access privileges on each of the target Projects as shown in Listing 8-2.

The implementation of a *CI/CD Pipeline* like the one shown in Figure 8-12 involves four different projects. In this example, the *Jenkins Master* is instantiated in the "cicd" project (#2 on Figure 8-12) where it may be used by multiple Pipelines in the same Project.

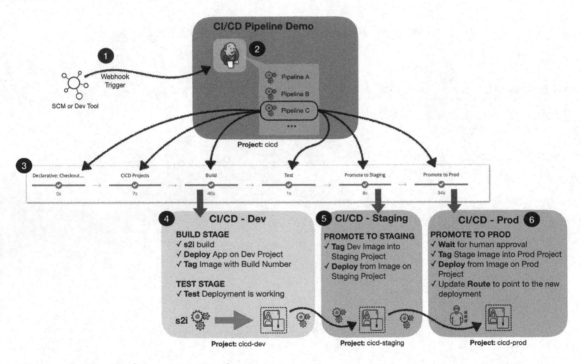

Figure 8-12. *Multiproject Pipeline*

In this case, "Pipeline C" (#3 on Figure 8-12) has multiple stages across three Projects. A reference Jenkinsfile implementing this type of Pipeline is shown in Listing 8-5.

Listing 8-5. Jenkinsfile—Multiproject Pipeline

```
pipeline {
    agent any
    options {
        // set a timeout of 20 minutes for this pipeline
        timeout(time: 20, unit: 'MINUTES')
    } //options

    environment {
        APP_NAME     = "podcicd"
        GIT_REPO     = "https://github.com/williamcaban/podcicd.git"
        GIT_BRANCH   = "master"
        CONTEXT_DIR  = "myapp"

        CICD_PRJ     = "cicd"
        CICD_DEV     = "${CICD_PRJ}"+"-dev"
        CICD_PROD    = "${CICD_PRJ}"+"-prod"
        CICD_STAGE   = "${CICD_PRJ}"+"-staging"
        SVC_PORT     = 8080
    }
    stages {
            stage('CICD Projects'){
                steps {
                    echo "Making sure CI/CD projects exist"
                    script {
                        openshift.withCluster() {
                            echo "Current Pipeline environment"
                            sh 'env | sort'
                            echo "Making sure required CI/CD projects
                            exist"
                            try {
                                openshift.selector("projects",CICD_DEV).
                                exists()
                                echo "Good! Project ${CICD_DEV} exist"
                            } catch (e) {
```

```
                        error "Missing ${CICD_DEV} Project or RBAC
                        policy to work with Project"
                    }
                    try {
                        openshift.selector("projects",CICD_STAGE).
                        exists().
                        echo "Good! Project ${CICD_STAGE} exist"
                    } catch (e) {
                        error "Missing ${CICD_STAGE} Project or
                        RBAC policy to work with Project"
                    }
                    try {
                        openshift.selector("projects",CICD_PROD).
                        exists()
                        echo "Good! Project ${CICD_PROD} exist"
                    } catch (e) {
                        error "Missing ${CICD_PROD} Project or RBAC
                        policy to work with Project"
                    }
                } // cluster
            } // script
        } //steps
    } // stage - projects

    stage('Build') {
        steps {
            echo "Sample Build stage using project ${CICD_DEV}"
            script {
                openshift.withCluster() {
                    openshift.withProject("${CICD_DEV}")
                    {
                        if (openshift.selector("bc",APP_NAME).
                        exists()) {
                            echo "Using existing BuildConfig.
                            Running new Build"
```

```
        def bc = openshift.startBuild(APP_NAME)
        openshift.set("env dc/${APP_NAME}
        BUILD_NUMBER=${BUILD_NUMBER}")
        // output build logs to the Jenkins
        conosole
        echo "Logs from build"
        def result = bc.logs('-f')
        // actions that took place
        echo "The logs operation require
        ${result.actions.size()} 'oc'
        interactions"
        // see exactly what oc command was
        executed.
        echo "Logs executed: ${result.
        actions[0].cmd}"
    } else {
        echo "No proevious BuildConfig.
        Creating new BuildConfig."
        def myNewApp = openshift.newApp (
        "${GIT_REPO}#${GIT_BRANCH}",
        "--name=${APP_NAME}",
        "--context-dir=${CONTEXT_DIR}",
        "-e BUILD_NUMBER=${BUILD_NUMBER}",
        "-e BUILD_ENV=${openshift.
        project()}"
        )
        echo "new-app myNewApp ${myNewApp.
        count()} objects named: ${myNewApp.
        names()}"
        myNewApp.describe()
        // selects the build config
        def bc = myNewApp.narrow('bc')
        // output build logs to the Jenkins
        conosole
        echo "Logs from build"
```

```
                            def result = bc.logs('-f')
                            // actions that took place
                            echo "The logs operation require
                            ${result.actions.size()} 'oc'
                            interactions"
                            // see exactly what oc command was
                            executed.
                            echo "Logs executed: ${result.
                            actions[0].cmd}"
                        } //else

                        echo "Tag Container image with 'build
                        number' as version"
                        openshift.tag("${APP_NAME}:latest",
                        "${APP_NAME}:v${BUILD_NUMBER}")

                        echo "Validating Route for Service exist,
                        if Not create Route"
                        if (!openshift.selector("route",APP_NAME).
                        exists()) {
                            openshift.selector("svc",APP_NAME).
                            expose()
                        }

                    } // project
                } // cluster
            } // script
        } // steps
    } //stage-build
    stage('Test') {

        steps {
            echo "Testing if 'Service' resource is operational and
            responding"
            script {
                openshift.withCluster() {
                    openshift.withProject() {
```

```
                    echo sh (script: "curl -I ${APP_
                    NAME}.${CICD_DEV}.svc:${SVC_PORT}/
                    healthz", returnStdout: true)
                } // withProject
            } // withCluster
        } // script
    } // steps
} //stage

stage('Promote to Staging') {
    steps {
        echo "Setup for Staging"
        script {
            openshift.withCluster() {
                openshift.withProject("${CICD_STAGE}") {
                    echo "Tag new image for staging"

                    openshift.tag("${CICD_DEV}/${APP_
                    NAME}:v${BUILD_NUMBER}", "${CICD_
                    STAGE}/${APP_NAME}:v${BUILD_NUMBER}")

                    //openshift.tag("${CICD_STAGE}/${APP_
                    NAME}:v${BUILD_NUMBER}", "${CICD_
                    STAGE}/${APP_NAME}:latest")
                    echo "Deploying to project: ${openshift.
                    project()}"
                    def myStagingApp = openshift.newApp(
                        "${APP_NAME}:v${BUILD_NUMBER}",
                        "--name=${APP_NAME}-v${BUILD_NUMBER}",
                        "-e BUILD_NUMBER=${BUILD_NUMBER}",
                        "-e BUILD_ENV=${openshift.project()}"
                    )
                    myStagingApp.narrow("svc").expose()
                }
            }
        } // script
    } //steps
} //stage
```

```
stage('Promote to Prod'){
    steps {
        echo "Promote to production? Waiting for human input"
        timeout(time:10, unit:'MINUTES'){
            input message: "Promote to Production?", ok:
            "Promote"
        }
        script {
            openshift.withCluster() {
                openshift.withProject("${CICD_PROD}") {
                    echo "Tag Staging Image for Production"
                    openshift.tag("${CICD_STAGE}/${APP_
                    NAME}:v${BUILD_NUMBER}", "${CICD_
                    PROD}/${APP_NAME}:v${BUILD_NUMBER}")

                    echo "Deploying to project: ${openshift.
                    project()}"
                    def myProdApp = openshift.newApp(
                        "${APP_NAME}:v${BUILD_NUMBER}",
                        "--name=${APP_NAME}-v${BUILD_NUMBER}",
                        "-e BUILD_NUMBER=${BUILD_NUMBER}",
                        "-e BUILD_ENV=${openshift.project()}"
                    )

                    if (openshift.selector("route",APP_NAME).
                    exists()){
                        echo "Sending the traffic the the
                        latest version"
                        openshift.set("route-backends",APP_
                        NAME,"${APP_NAME}-v${BUILD_
                        NUMBER}=100%")
                    } else {
                        echo "Creating new Route"
                        myProdApp.narrow("svc").expose("--
                        name=${APP_NAME}")
                    }
```

```
            } // project
        }
      } // script
    } // steps
  } //stage

  } // stages
} // pipeline
```

For the successful completion of the Pipeline shown in Figure 8-12 and documented in Listing 8-5, the *jenkins Service Account* in the "cicd" Project must have *edit* privileges in the "cicd-dev," "cicd-staging," and "cicd-prod" Projects (see Listing 8-6).

Listing 8-6. Deploying a Multiproject Pipeline

Step 1: Create the CI/CD Project in the OpenShift cluster
```
oc new-project cicd --description="CI/CD Pipeline Demo"
oc new-project cicd-dev --description="CI/CD - Dev"
oc new-project cicd-prod --description="CI/CD - Prod"
oc new-project cicd-staging --description="CI/CD - Staging"
```
Step 2: Give jenkins Service Account edit access to the other Projects
```
oc policy add-role-to-user edit system:serviceaccount:cicd:jenkins -n cicd-dev
oc policy add-role-to-user edit system:serviceaccount:cicd:jenkins -n cicd-prod
oc policy add-role-to-user edit system:serviceaccount:cicd:jenkins -n
cicd-staging
```
Step 3: Deploy the OpenShift Pipeline from a Git repository containing the Jenkinsfile
```
oc new-app https://github.com/williamcaban/podcicd.git -n cicd
```

Deploying the example in the listing once the Jenkins Master is running and the Pipeline BuildConfig is ready, executing a manual trigger or simulating a Webhook trigger should yield results similar to the ones shown in Figure 8-11.

To start a new pipeline build from GUI, go to "Application Console" ➤ Project "cicd" ➤ Builds ➤ Pipelines and click the "Start Pipeline" button. To start a new pipeline build from CLI, execute oc start-build podcicd -n cicd. The Pipeline logs and progress are visible at the "Application Console."

OpenShift Client Plugin

The *OpenShift Client Plugin*[5] or the OpenShift Jenkins Pipeline (DSL) Plugin is a Jenkins Plugin that provides comprehensive *Fluent-style* syntax for use in Jenkins Pipelines interacting with OpenShift clusters. The plugin leverages the *OpenShift "oc"* client binary and integrates with Jenkins credentials and cluster.

The OpenShift Client Plugin exposes any option available with "oc" to the Jenkins Pipeline.

Note   The *OpenShift Client Plugin for Jenkins* supersedes the previous *OpenShift V3 Plugin for Jenkins* which is now deprecated.[6]

Custom Jenkins Images

The *Jenkins Images* can be customized by using the traditional *Docker* layering capabilities with a *Dockerfile* or by using the *OpenShift* native *Source-to-Image* capabilities.

To use the Source-to-Image capabilities, create a Git repository following the structure shown in Figure 8-13.

```
# Git repository structure for Custom Jenkins Image with s2i:
plugins.txt                 <-- List of plugins to install in the format "pluginID:pluginVersion"
plugins/                    <-- binary Jenkins plugins to copy into the Jenkins image
configuration/              <-- The content of this directory will be copied into the /var/lib/jenkins/

# Examples on using the configuration/ folder:
configuration/jobs/         <-- Jenkins job definitions to copy into /var/lib/jenkins/jobs/
configuration/config.xml    <-- Custom Jenkins configuration to copy into /var/lib/jenkins/config.xml
configuration/credentials.xml <-- Credentials configuration to copy into /var/lib/jenkins/credentials.xml
```

Figure 8-13. *Git repository structure for custom Jenkins Image with s2i*

---

[5]For the latest documentation and features of the OpenShift Client Plugin, refer to
https://github.com/openshift/jenkins-client-plugin

[6]For reference to the legacy OpenShift Jenkins Plugin, visit the Git repository:
https://github.com/openshift/jenkins-plugin

For the creation of the custom Jenkins Image from the structure defined in a Git repository, create a BuildConfig similar to Listing 8-7.

Listing 8-7. BuildConfig for creating custom Jenkins Images

```
# BuildConfig to customize the Jenkins Image
apiVersion: v1
kind: BuildConfig
metadata:
  name: custom-jenkins-build
spec:
  source:
    git:
      uri: https://github.com/williamcaban/openshift-custom-jenkins.git
    type: Git
  strategy:
    sourceStrategy:
      from:
        kind: ImageStreamTag
        name: jenkins:latest
        namespace: openshift
    type: Source
  output:
    to:
      kind: ImageStreamTag
      name: custom-jenkins:latest
```

Integrating External CI/CD Pipelines

External Jenkins instances can be integrated with OpenShift in one of the following ways:

- Using the *Jenkins Kubernetes Plugin*[7] which provides the ability for Jenkins agents to be dynamically provisioned[8] on multiple Pods

- Using the *OpenShift Client Plugin*[9] and the *OpenShift Sync Plugin*[10]

The level of integration provided by the *OpenShift Client Plugin* (i.e., embedding pipeline status in the GUI) currently is only available with Jenkins, and it is maintained by Red Hat. Other popular CI/CD tools like GitLab CI, Spinnaker, Bamboo, TeamCity, and so on provide support for OpenShift Container Platform with a vendor-provided plugin for OpenShift or by using their Kubernetes plugin.

Summary

The OpenShift Jenkins Pipelines capabilities enable development teams to continue the adoption of modern development paradigms by providing CI/CD as a first-class service into the platform. When using *Jenkins Pipeline Build Strategy*, or by having a *Jenkinsfile* with the source code, or by using the *OpenShift Jenkins Plugin*, the OpenShift Jenkins Pipelines ease the learning curve for using CI/CD and simplify the management and operation of the Jenkins CI/CD Pipelines.

Beyond knowing how to do the initial administrative tasks or manage value-added features like the CI/CD Pipelines, a cluster administrator should be aware of Day-2 operations and maintenance tasks for maintaining an optimized cluster. Some of these Day-2 tasks are covered in Chapter 9.

---

[7]For details about the Jenkins Kubernetes Plugin, refer to `https://wiki.jenkins-ci.org/display/JENKINS/Kubernetes+Plugin`

[8]For configuration details, refer to the OpenShift documentation at `https://docs.openshift.com/container-platform/3.11/using_images/other_images/jenkins.html#configuring-the-jenkins-kubernetes-plug-in`

[9]OpenShift Client Plugin `https://docs.openshift.com/container-platform/3.11/using_images/other_images/jenkins.html#client-plug-in`

[10]OpenShift Sync Plugin `https://docs.openshift.com/container-platform/3.11/using_images/other_images/jenkins.html#sync-plug-in`

CHAPTER 9

Day-2 Operations

As seen in the previous chapter, OpenShift provides features or capabilities to enhance developer experience like the CI/CD Pipelines covered in Chapter 8 and the self-service Templates in Chapter 7. The day-to-day work of developers may leave a high number of objects behind. In very active development environments, the garbage collection processes might need tuning. For example, when executing CI/CD Pipelines or building Containers using features like source to image (s2i), there might be intermediate Containers or Image layers that get created and left behind, consuming the Node ephemeral storage and increasing the size of the etcd database. To work with this, once the OpenShift cluster is in operation, there are certain tasks required for the proper maintenance, operations, and fine-tuning of the cluster. This chapter covers some of these common tasks.

Managing Leftover Objects

During the normal operation and utilization of the cluster and cluster services, objects created in OpenShift can accumulate. Maintaining all previous versions of all the objects may end up consuming significant amount of storage which may have an impact on the performance of elements of the platform. For example:

- High storage consumption of the *etcd data store* may add additional pressure on *etcd* response time which leads to higher latency per request.

Note The upstream OSS *etcd* project provides the *benchmark*[1] tool that can be used to measure etcd performance.

---

[1]Measuring performance of *etcd*, refer to the documentation at https://github.com/etcd-io/etcd/blob/master/Documentation/op-guide/performance.md

© William Caban 2019
W. Caban, *Architecting and Operating OpenShift Clusters*, https://doi.org/10.1007/978-1-4842-4985-7_9

- Depending on the storage backend used by the internal Container Registry, high storage consumption of the backend storage may yield to slower upload (push) time for new images being build or onboard into the platform.

Tip   Using object storage as the storage backend for the internal Container Registry regularly is the most resilient and cost-effective storage backend for this job.

- High storage utilization of /var/lib/containers which is used by the Container Runtime to cached Container Images and for the Container ephemeral storage will have an impact on the ability to instantiate new Containers in the node or the ability to download new Images.

Tip   Use a dedicated disk or partition to map to the /var/lib/containers directory to avoid saturating the *root* disk of the *Node*.

The high storage consumptions can be the result of normal cluster operations by users of the platform. This is particularly relevant when using objects like *Deployments*, *Builds*, manipulating *Images* (i.e., tagging and keeping multiple releases, etc.), groups, *CronJobs*, and others.

The *OpenShift* client CLI provides a mechanism for cluster administrator to prune[2] older versions of some of this resource (see Figure 9-1).

```
1    $ oc adm prune
2    Remove older versions of resources from the server
3
4     The commands here allow administrators to manage the older versions of resources on the system by removing them.
5
6    Usage:
7      oc adm prune [flags]
8
9    Available Commands:
10     auth        Removes references to the specified roles, clusterroles, users, and groups.
11     builds      Remove old completed and failed builds
12     deployments Remove old completed and failed deployments
13     groups      Remove old OpenShift groups referencing missing records on an external provider
14     images      Remove unreferenced images
15
```

Figure 9-1.   *Removing older version of resources*

---

[2]Additional details on pruning object are available at the online documentation: https://docs. openshift.com/container-platform/3.11/admin_guide/pruning_resources.html

The execution of the prune command will perform a *dry run* by default (see line #2 on Figure 9-2). During the run it identifies the resources of the particular time that will be removed (see line #4 on Figure 9-2) during the actual process.

```
1    $ oc adm prune images ①
2    Dry run enabled – no modifications will be made. Add --confirm to remove images
3    Deleting istags openshift-sdn/node: v3.11                          ③
4    Deleting istags cicd-staging/podcicd-v4: v4
5    Deleting istags openshift-node/node: v3.11
6    Deleting istags cicd-staging/podcicd-v3: v3
7    Deleting istags cicd-staging/podcicd-v1: v1  ④
8    Deleting istags cicd-staging/podcicd-v5: v5
9    Deleting istags cicd-prod/podcicd-v6: v6
10   Deleting istags cicd-prod/podcicd-v1: v1
11   Deleting istags cicd-staging/podcicd-v6: v6
12   Deleting istags cicd-prod/podcicd-v5: v5
13   Deleting istags cicd-staging/podcicd-v2: v2
14   Deleted 11 objects. ⑤
```

Figure 9-2. *Command to prune Images*

The "confirm" flag must be appended to the *prune* command for the actual process to be executed (see line #2 on Figure 9-3). Additional flags are available to provide higher control and granularity of which objects should be removed or maintained (see lines #4 and #7 on Figure 9-3).

```
1    # To execute the actual prune operation the "confirm" flag must be appended
2    $ oc adm prune images --keep-tag-revisions=3 --keep-younger-than=2h --confirm
3
4    --keep-tag-revisions=3  Specify the number of image revisions for a tag in an image
5                            stream that will be preserved
6
7    --keep-younger-than=3h  Specify the minimum age of an image and its referrers for it
8                            to be considered a candidate for pruning.
9
```

Figure 9-3. *Confirming the prune command*

Note   The optional flags for the oc adm prune commands are object specific. Refer to the CLI command help for details.

Garbage Collection

There are two types of garbage collection[3] performed by the *OpenShift Nodes*:

- **Container garbage collection**: Removes terminated containers. This is enabled by default and it is executed automatically.

- **Image garbage collection**: Removes Images no longer referenced by any running Pods. It relies on disk usage as reported by cAdvisor on the Node to choose which Images to remove from the Node.

When the garbage collection is executed, the oldest images get deleted first until the stopping threshold is met. Both of these garbage collection types are configurable by modifying the *Kubelet* argument settings at the *Node ConfigMap* (see Figure 9-4).

```
1    # oc edit cm -n openshift-node node-config-compute
2    apiVersion: v1
3    kind: ConfigMap                    1
4    data:
5      node-config.yaml: |
6        apiVersion: v1
7    ...
8        kind: NodeConfig
9        kubeletArguments:
10         minimum-container-ttl-duration:      # Minimum age that a container is eligible for garbage collection    2
11         - "10s"
12         maximum-dead-containers-per-container: # Number of instances to retain per pod container
13         - "2"
14         maximum-dead-containers:             # Maximum number of total dead containers in the node
15         - "240"
16         image-gc-high-threshold:             # Percent of disk usage which triggers image garbage collection
17         - "85"
18         image-gc-low-threshold:              # Percent of disk usage to which image garbage collection attempts to free
19         - "80"
20         bootstrap-kubeconfig:
21         - /etc/origin/node/bootstrap.kubeconfig
22         cert-dir:
23         - /etc/origin/node/certificates
24         enable-controller-attach-detach:
25         - 'true'
26         feature-gates:
27         - RotateKubeletClientCertificate=true,RotateKubeletServerCertificate=true
28         node-labels:
29         - node-role.kubernetes.io/compute=true
30         pod-manifest-path:
31         - /etc/origin/node/pods
32         rotate-certificates:
33         - 'true'
34    ...
35
```

Figure 9-4.   Garbage collection settings in the Node ConfigMap

---

[3]Additional details are available in the documentation at https://docs.openshift.com/ container-platform/3.11/admin_guide/garbage_collection.html

Node Optimizations

There are multiple ways to optimize *Nodes* to deliver the performance required for the workloads and the experience required by an organization. The specific settings to modify to achieve certain optimization are tied to the specifications of the *Hosts* and the characteristics of the workload that will be running in those *Nodes*.

OpenShift provides many settings to tune the performance of the Platform. The following subtopics are some of the common settings available for cluster administrators to configure to achieve desired *Node* optimizations.

Node Resource Allocation

OpenShift provides configuration[4] parameters to allocate per *Node* resources to maintain reliable scheduling of workloads to a Node while minimizing overcommitting compute and memory resources. There are two types of resource allocations:

- **kube-reserved**: Allocation of resources reserved for Node components (i.e., kubelet, kube-proxy, Container Runtime, etc.). The default is None.

- **system-reserved**: Allocation of resources reserved for Host system components (i.e., sshd, NetworkManager, etc.). The default is None.

Both of these resource reservation types are configurable by modifying the *Kubelet* argument settings at the *Node ConfigMap* (see Figure 9-5).

---

[4]Additional information about configuring Node resources is available at the online documentation: https://docs.openshift.com/container-platform/3.11/admin_guide/allocating_node_resources.html

```
1    # oc edit cm -n openshift-node node-config-compute
2    apiVersion: v1
3    kind: ConfigMap
4    data:
5      node-config.yaml: |
6        apiVersion: v1
7    ...
8      kind: NodeConfig
9      kubeletArguments:
10       kube-reserved:              # Resources reserved for node components.
11       - "cpu=200m,memory=512Mi"
12       system-reserved:            # Resources reserved for the remaining system components.
13       - "cpu=200m,memory=512Mi"
14   ...
```

Figure 9-5. *Node resource reservation*

Setting Max Pods Per Node

OpenShift provides two *Kubelet* configuration setting to control the maximum number of Pods that can be scheduled into a Node:

- **pods-per-core**: Configures the maximum number of Pods the Node can run per core on the Node. When using this parameter, the maximum number of Pods allowed in the Node will be <pods-per-core> x <number-of-cores-in-node>

Note   To disable this limit, set *pods-per-core* to 0.

- **max-pods**: Configures a fixed number as the maximum number of Pods that can run on the Node. The default value is 250.

Note   When both of these settings are configured, the lower of the two is used.

These settings are configurable by modifying the *Kubelet* arguments at the *Node ConfigMap* (see Figure 9-6).

```
1   # oc edit cm -n openshift-node node-config-compute
2   apiVersion: v1
3   kind: ConfigMap
4   data:
5     node-config.yaml: |
6       apiVersion: v1
7   ...
8       kind: NodeConfig
9       kubeletArguments:
10        pods-per-core: # <max. number of running Pods> =  <pods-per-core> * <num. cores on Node>
11        - "10"
12        max-pods:       # explicit max. number of Pods running on Node
13        - "250"
14  ...
```

Figure 9-6. *Maximum number of running Pods per Node*

Using the Tuned Profile

Tuned[5] is a daemon that monitors devices connected to the Host and statically and dynamically tunes system settings based on a selected Profile.

During the deployment of *OpenShift*, the installer configures the *Nodes* with *Tuned* profiles[6] for *OpenShift* (see Figure 9-7) and assigns them to the *Nodes* based on their role.

```
1   [root@ocp ~]# tuned-adm active                                                    ①
2   Current active profile: openshift-control-plane
3
4   [root@ocp ~]# tuned-adm list  ②
5   Available profiles:
6   - balanced                  - General non-specialized tuned profile
7   - desktop                   - Optimize for the desktop use-case
8   - latency-performance       - Optimize for deterministic performance at the cost of increased power consumption
9   - network-latency           - Optimize for deterministic performance at the cost of increased power consumption, focused on low latency network performance
10  - network-throughput        - Optimize for streaming network throughput, generally only necessary on older CPUs or 40G+ networks
11  - openshift                 - Optimize systems running OpenShift (parent profile)
12  - openshift-control-plane   - Optimize systems running OpenShift control plane
13  - openshift-node            - Optimize systems running OpenShift nodes
14  - powersave                 - Optimize for low power consumption
15  - throughput-performance    - Broadly applicable tuning that provides excellent performance across a variety of common server workloads
16  - virtual-guest             - Optimize for running inside a virtual guest
17  - virtual-host              - Optimize for running KVM guests
18  Current active profile: openshift-control-plane
19
```

Figure 9-7. *The tuned profiles for OpenShift*

---

[5]Additional information about Tuned is available at the RHEL documentation (requires a valid RHN subscription): `https://access.redhat.com/documentation/en-us/red_hat_enterprise_linux/7/html-single/performance_tuning_guide/index#chap-Red_Hat_Enterprise_Linux-Performance_Tuning_Guide-Tuned`

[6]Additional information about the OpenShift Tuned profiles is available at the scaling and performance documentation (Requires a valid RHN subscription) `https://access.redhat.com/documentation/en-us/openshift_container_platform/3.11/html-single/scaling_and_performance_guide/index#scaling-performance-capacity-tuned-profile`

Eviction Policy

The *Eviction Policy*[7] enables the *Node* to reclaim needed resources by failing one or more *Pods* when the *Node* is running low on available resources. OpenShift supports two types of eviction policy:

- **hard**: The *Node* takes immediate action to reclaim resources from a Pod that exceeds predefined thresholds (see #1 Figure 9-8).

- **soft**: The *Node* waits for a grace period (see #3 Figure 9-8) before reclaiming resources from a Pod exceeding the thresholds (see #2 Figure 9-8).

```
1   # oc edit cm -n openshift-node node-config-compute
2   apiVersion: v1
3   kind: ConfigMap
4   data:
5     node-config.yaml: |
6       apiVersion: v1
7   ...
8       kind: NodeConfig
9       kubeletArguments:
10        eviction-hard:   1
11        - memory.available<100Mi
12        - nodefs.available<10%
13        - nodefs.inodesFree<5%
14        - imagefs.available<15%
15  ...
```

```
1   # oc edit cm -n openshift-node node-config-compute
2   apiVersion: v1
3   kind: ConfigMap
4   data:
5     node-config.yaml: |
6       apiVersion: v1
7   ...
8       kind: NodeConfig
9       kubeletArguments:
10        eviction-soft:   2
11        - memory.available<500Mi
12        - nodefs.available<500Mi
13        - nodefs.inodesFree<100Mi
14        - imagefs.available<100Mi
15        - imagefs.inodesFree<100Mi
16        eviction-soft-grace-period:  3
17        - memory.available=1m30s
18        - nodefs.available=1m30s
19        - nodefs.inodesFree=1m30s
20        - imagefs.available=1m30s
21        - imagefs.inodesFree=1m30s
22  ...
```

Figure 9-8. *Eviction Policies*

The *Eviction Policy* settings are configurable by modifying the *Kubelet* arguments at the *Node ConfigMap* (see Figure 9-8).

---

[7]Additional information on OpenShift Eviction Policies is available online at
`https://docs.openshift.com/container-platform/3.11/admin_guide/out_of_resource_handling.html#out-of-resource-eviction-policy`

Pod Scheduling

OpenShift Pod Scheduler[8] is an internal process responsible for determining the placement of new *Pods* onto *Nodes*. It does this by identifying a *Node* that can provide the *Pod's* requirements while complying with configured policies.

The available *Nodes* are filtered by rules known as *Predicates*. The resulting list is sorted by rules that rank *Nodes* according to preferences and determine a *Priority*.

The configuration for the default scheduler policy containing the default *Predicates* and *Priorities* is on the *Master Nodes* at /etc/origin/master/scheduler.json.

In addition to the default scheduler, there are several ways to invoke advanced scheduling of Pods using

- **Pod Affinity and Anti-affinity**[9]: Pods specify affinity or anti-affinity toward a group of *Pods* (e.g., for an application's latency requirement) using labels on *Nodes* and label selectors on *Pods* to control where a *Pod* can be placed.

- **Node Affinity**[10]: Pods specify affinity or anti-affinity toward a group of Nodes using labels on *Nodes* and label selectors on *Pods* to control where a *Pod* can be placed.

- **Node Selectors**[11]: Use labels on *Nodes* and label selectors on *Pods* to control the scheduling on where a *Pod* can be placed.

- **Taints and Tolerations**[12]: *Taints* are labels on a *Node* to refuse Pods to be scheduled onto the *Node* unless the *Pod* has a matching *Toleration*. *Tolerations* are labels on a *Pod*. The *Taints* and *Tolerations* labels on the *Node* and on the *Pod* must match in order to be able to schedule the *Pod* onto the *Node*.

---

[8]The OpenShift default scheduler is described in more detail in the online documentation: https://docs.openshift.com/container-platform/3.11/admin_guide/scheduling/scheduler.html

[9]Advanced Scheduling using Pod Affinity and Anti-Affinity: https://docs.openshift.com/container-platform/3.11/admin_guide/scheduling/pod_affinity.html#admin-guide-sched-pod-affinity

[10]Advanced Scheduling using Node Affinity: https://docs.openshift.com/container-platform/3.11/admin_guide/scheduling/node_affinity.html#admin-guide-sched-affinity

[11]Advanced Scheduling using Node Selector: https://docs.openshift.com/container-platform/3.11/admin_guide/scheduling/node_selector.html#admin-guide-sched-selector

[12]Advanced Scheduling using Taints and Tolerations: https://docs.openshift.com/container-platform/3.11/admin_guide/scheduling/taints_tolerations.html#admin-guide-taints

Pod Priority

Pod Priority[13] is used to indicate the relative importance of a *Pod* compared to other *Pods*. The *Scheduler* orders *Pods* in queues by their *Priority* with higher *priority Pods* ahead of other lower *priority Pods*.

The *PriorityClass* are cluster-level (non-namespaced) objects defining a mapping between a *name* and an integer representing the *Priority* of the class. The higher the number, the higher the *priority*.

The *priority* number is any 32-bit integer with a value smaller than or equal to 1,000,000,000 (one billion). Higher values are reserved for critical *Pods* that should not be preempted or evicted.

OpenShift has two reserved *PriorityClasses* for critical system *Pods* as seen in Table 9-1.

Table 9-1.   OpenShift Reserved PriorityClasses

PriorityClass Name	Priority Value	Description
system-node-critical	2,000,001,000	Used for all Pods that should never be evicted from a Node. This includes Pods like sdn-ovs, sdn, and others.
system-cluster-critical	2,000,000,000	Used with Pods that are important for the normal operations of the cluster. Pods with this priority include fluentd, descheduler, and others.

The *PriorityClass name* field is used by the *Priority Admission Controller* to identify the integer value of the *priority*. If the named *PriorityClass* is not found, the *Pod* is rejected. An example of the definition and utilization of a *PriorityClass* can be seen in Figure 9-9.

---

[13]Additional information about Pod Priority is available at the online documentation: https://docs.openshift.com/container-platform/3.11/admin_guide/scheduling/priority_preemption.html#priority-priority-about_priority-preemption

```
1   apiVersion: scheduling.k8s.io/v1beta1
2   kind: PriorityClass (1)
3   metadata:
4     name: demo-high-priority (2) # name of the PriorityClass object
5   value: 1000000              # priority actual value
6   globalDefault: false        # default for Pods not specifying a PriorityClass name?
7   description: "This is a demo priority class."
```

```
1    apiVersion: v1
2    kind: Pod (3)
3    metadata:
4      name: my-demo-app
5    spec:
6      containers:
7      - name: myy-demo-app
8        image: my-demo-app
9        imagePullPolicy: IfNotPresent
10     priorityClassName: demo-high-priority (4)
```

Figure 9-9. *Defining and using a PriorityClass*

When a high-priority *Pod* disrupts the *Node resource budget*, the scheduler attempts to preempt *Pods,* starting with lower-priority *Pods,* avoiding violating the *Pod disruption budget.*

When the scheduling of a new high-priority Pod requires the eviction of a lower-priority *Pod* that has a *Pod Affinity* rule with a high-priority *Pod* running in the *Node*, the scheduler attempts to identify a different *Node* to schedule the new high-priority *Pod*.

Summary

This chapter documents some of the Day-2 operations tasks for the maintenance and operation of OpenShift clusters. In addition, the chapter presents some of the settings a cluster administrator can use to allocate resources for system or platform critical tasks.

There are many more settings available for the reader to discover from the official OpenShift documentation. The settings covered in this chapter are applicable for the most common scenarios.

The OpenShift platform provides sensible defaults optimized for what is sometimes referred to as general Cloud-native workloads, meaning the workloads for which Kubernetes has been designed which were expected to be TCP-based, web-enabled, and entirely agnostic to the underlying hardware infrastructure. With the adoption of Kubernetes outside the web-based application, there is the need to support hardware acceleration (i.e., GPUs, FPGAs, etc.) or multiple NICs per Container, and much more. Chapter 10 explores how some of these advanced compute and networking capabilities are supported in OpenShift.

CHAPTER 10

Advanced Network Operations

The OpenShift platform provides defaults optimized for Cloud-native workloads. These have been covered throughout this book. As with many successful Open Source project, Kubernetes is being used in setups for which it was never designed. With the adoption of Kubernetes outside the web-based application, there is the need to support specialized hardware acceleration (i.e., GPUs, FPGAs, etc.), multiple NICs per Container, and much more. This chapter focuses on advanced networking features or capabilities for increasing network performance and for the onboarding of applications or microservices using nontraditional web protocols into *OpenShift*.

Network Optimizations

OpenShift SDN uses *OpenvSwitch*, *VXLAN* tunnels, *OpenFlow* rules, and *iptables* or *firewalld* rules. Some possible optimizations to this overlay network are based on best practices for fine-tuning a system in a high-performance environment.

Jumbo Frames and VXLAN Acceleration

The standard Ethernet Maximum Transmission Unit (MTU) is 1500 Bytes. A regular IP UDP packet will consume 20 Bytes for the IP header (see #2 in Figure 10-1) and 8 Bytes for the UDP header (see #3 in Figure 10-1), and the remaining 1472 Bytes are available for payload (see #4 to #8 in Figure 10-1).

Note   The outer Ethernet header (14 Bytes) (see #1 in Figure 10-1) is not counted as part of the MTU.

© William Caban 2019
W. Caban, *Architecting and Operating OpenShift Clusters*, https://doi.org/10.1007/978-1-4842-4985-7_10

In SDN networks using the VXLAN protocol, the whole Ethernet frame of traffic from *Pods* in one *Node* destined to *Pods* in another *Node* is encapsulated as IP UDP packets and forwarded to the *Node* running the destination *Pods*. For this, the VXLAN header (see #4 in Figure 10-1) is added to the original Layer 2 Ethernet frame (see #5 in Figure 10-1), minus its FCS, and all this content becomes the payload of the outer IP UDP packets (see #2 and #3 in Figure 10-1) and is sent to the remote *Node*.

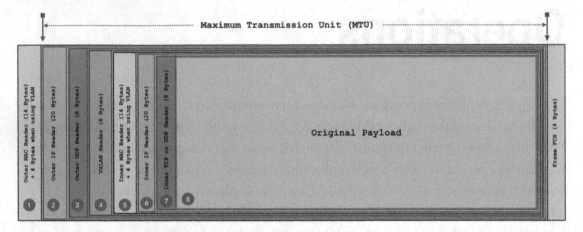

Figure 10-1. *Format of a VXLAN packet*

From the diagram in Figure 10-1, the effective MTU for payload (see #8) is 1422 Bytes. When working with environments with large streams of data to transfer among Pods on different Nodes, those streams of data need to be broken into very small chunks of 1422 Bytes or less. Each one of these packets undergoes an encapsulation process. Under high network utilization or high network throughput, this may lead to high CPU utilization and high latency.

To reduce the CPU utilization and latency under such circumstances, the recommendations are

- Use Jumbo frames (i.e., MTU 9000 or more) to be able to send more data per packet and reduce the number of packets and overhead required to move the data from one Node to the other.

- Use NIC cards supporting VXLAN acceleration so the encapsulation process is offloaded to hardware and CPU.

Caution   Not all the VXLAN-accelerated NICs support Jumbo frames. Consult the technical specification of your NIC provider. In those cases where VXLAN acceleration is not supported with Jumbo frames, the cluster administrators should avoid Jumbo frames as the NIC driver will determine the final behavior which may have a negative impact in performance.

Tuning Network Devices

Advanced Linux system administrator with deep understanding of the Linux networking stack and the available tuning options for high-performance computing may use similar techniques with OpenShift clusters.

Caution   Some of the following optimizations have limited availability or configuration options in some NIC drivers. Consult your hardware and driver technical information.

Some of the optimizations that may be considered are

- **Adjusting the number and size of RX and TX queues**: Improved throughput, latency, and multi-queue techniques can be used to distribute the processing of queues across multiple CPUs.

- **Interrupt coalescing**: Prevents interrupt storms and increases throughput or latency.

- **Adaptive RX and TX coalescing**: Interrupt delivery is optimized to improve latency or throughput based on packet rate.

- **Hardware-accelerated Receive Flow Steering (RFS)**: When supported by the NIC's driver, the NIC and the Kernel work together to determine which flows to send to which CPU for processing.

- **Adjusting IRQ affinity**: Optimizes for data locality for interrupts generated by the NIC.

- **Adjusting UDP receive queue size**: Increases throughput.

- **Generic Receive Offloading (GRO) and Large Receive Offloading (LRO)**

- **Receive Packet Steering (RPS) and Receive Side Scaling (RSS)**

Some of the Linux commands used for these optimizations are *sysctl* and *ethtool*.

These levels of optimizations are unique to each hardware and driver combination. As such, this book highlights the existence of these capabilities but leaves it to the reader to explore and test the ones suitable for their environment.

Routing Optimizations

The *OpenShift Router* can handle the *Routes* for multiple applications. This can be anywhere from one to thousands of applications. The actual number of Routes an OpenShift Router can handle is determined by the technology in use by the applications behind the *Routes*.

As seen in previous chapters, the OpenShift Router is based on HAProxy. One of the tunable parameters for HAProxy is the *maxconn* parameter which is configurable by using the *ROUTER_MAX_CONNECTION*[1] environment variable of the *OpenShift Router DeploymentConfig*. This parameter sets the per-process maximum number of concurrent connections.

Note   When configuring the *maxconn* parameter, consider *HAProxy* counts of the *frontend* connection and *backend* connection as two different connections. Because of this, a connection from an external client to an application load balanced by HAProxy counts as two.

Additional parameters[2] for the optimization of the OpenShift Router are

- CPU and interrupt affinity

- Increasing number of threads

- Setting up connection timeouts

---

[1]Additional information about configuring the maximum number of connection is available at the online documentation: https://docs.openshift.com/container-platform/3.11/scaling_performance/routing_optimization.html#scaling-performance-optimizing-router-haproxy-maxconn

[2]OpenShift HAProxy optimization parameters: https://docs.openshift.com/container-platform/3.11/scaling_performance/routing_optimization.html#scaling-performance-optimizing-router-haproxy

> **Note**   *OpenShift Routers*, by default, listen on ports 80 (HTTP) and 443 (HTTPS), but they can be configured to listen for HTTP and HTTPS traffic on other ports. This option is configured using the environment variable `ROUTER_SERVICE_HTTP_PORT` and the environment variable `ROUTER_SERVICE_HTTPS_PORT`.

Route-Specific Optimizations Annotations

In addition to the global configuration parameters of the HAProxy, OpenShift provides the ability to modify certain behavior on per-Route basis. This is done by using Route Annotations (see Table 10-1).

Table 10-1. *OpenShift Route Annotations*[3]

Variable	Description
haproxy.router.openshift.io/balance	Load balancing algorithm: *source*, *roundrobin*, or *leastconn*
haproxy.router.openshift.io/disable_cookies	Disables the use of *cookies* to track *related* connections
router.openshift.io/cookie_name	Optional *cookie* to use for *Route*
haproxy.router.openshift.io/pod-concurrent-connections	Sets the maximum number of connections allowed for each backing *Pod* from a specific *Router*
haproxy.router.openshift.io/rate-limit-connections.concurrent-tcp	Limits the number of concurrent TCP connections by an IP address
haproxy.router.openshift.io/rate-limit-connections.rate-http	Limits the rate at which an IP address can make HTTP requests
haproxy.router.openshift.io/rate-limit-connections.rate-tcp	Limits the rate at which an IP address can make TCP connections

(continued)

---

[3]Additional information and the updated list of possible Route Annotations are available from the online documentation: `https://docs.openshift.com/container-platform/3.11/architecture/networking/routes.html#route-specific-annotations`

Table 10-1. (*continued*)

Variable	Description
haproxy.router.openshift.io/timeout	Sets a server-side timeout for the *Route*
router.openshift.io/haproxy.health.check.interval	Sets interval for the backend health checks
haproxy.router.openshift.io/ip_whitelist	(See "*IP Whitelists*" section)
haproxy.router.openshift.io/hsts_header	Sets a Strict-Transport-Security header for the terminated or re-encrypt *Route*

IP Whitelists

OpenShift supports the use of special annotations to restrict which source IP address or network can access a specific *Route*. The *ip_whitelist* annotation (see Figure 10-2) is a space-separated list of whitelisted source IP addresses and CIDRs that are allowed to access the particular *Route*.

```
1   ...
2   metadata:
3     annotations:
4       haproxy.router.openshift.io/ip_whitelist: 209.132.183.105 192.168.1.0/24 10.5.25.0/24
5   ...
```

Figure 10-2. *IP Whitelist annotations for a Route*

OpenShift Router Sharding

To horizontally scale the routing layer, *OpenShift* provides the capability to define and use *Router Shards*. In this case, the *Routes* are shared among a group of *Routers* based on a *selection expression* defining the *Shard*. There are two levels of Route sharding:

- Cluster administrators configure and manage sharding at cluster-wide level.

- Users can configure sharding for namespaces where they have admin privileges.

When using sharding, each *Router* in the group handles a portion of the traffic based on the assigned *Shard*.

Note   Based on the *selection expression*, the *Router Shards* can be unique, in which case a *Route* belongs to only one *Shard*, or there can be overlapping in which case some *Routes* can belong to more than one *Shard*.

When using *Router Sharding*, the first *Route* matching a particular *Shard* reserves the right to exist on that *Shard* permanently and even across restarts. Figure 10-3 illustrates both ways of configuring *Router Sharding*.

```
USING  NAMESPACE LABELS                                    USING  ROUTE LABELS
1    # Create new router (no replicas)           1    # Create new router (no replicas)
2    oc adm router router-dev --replicas=0       2    oc adm router router-shard-2 --replicas=0
3                                                 3
4    # Set the NAMESPACE selection expression    4    # Set the Shard selection expression
5    oc set env dc/router-dev NAMESPACE_LABELS="router=dev"   5    oc set env  dc/router-shard-2 ROUTE_LABELS="bizunit=prod"
6                                                 6
7    # Run one replica of the router             7    # Run one replica of the router
8    oc scale dc/router-ns-dev --replicas=1      8    oc scale dc/router-shard-2 --replicas=3
9                                                 9
10   # Label a NAMESPACE to be matched by selection expression   10   # Label a ROUTE to be matched by selection expression
11   oc label namespace myproject "router=dev"   11   oc label route myroute "bizunit=prod"
```

Figure 10-3. *Router Sharding using Namespace or Route labels*

Note   When using the *Namespace* labels, the *Service Account* assigned to the *Router* must have *cluster-reader* permission to access the labels in the *Namespaces*.

Supporting Non-HTTP/HTTPS/TLS Applications

There is a wide range of applications that cannot be classified as HTTP-, HTTPS-, or TLS-based applications. For example:

- Applications using specialized TCP protocols (i.e., database protocols)

- UDP-based applications

- Applications requiring direct access to the Pods IP

For these applications, OpenShift provides various mechanisms:

- Using IngressIP or ExternalIP

- Using NodePorts or HostPorts

Using IngressIP and ExternalIP

When using an ingressIP and externalIP, OpenShift uses Kube-Proxy to configure all Nodes into accepting traffic destined to the particular IP address. When traffic destined for a particular ExternalIP arrives to a Node, it forwards the traffic internally to the Pods associated to the Service (see #2 and #5 on Figure 10-4).

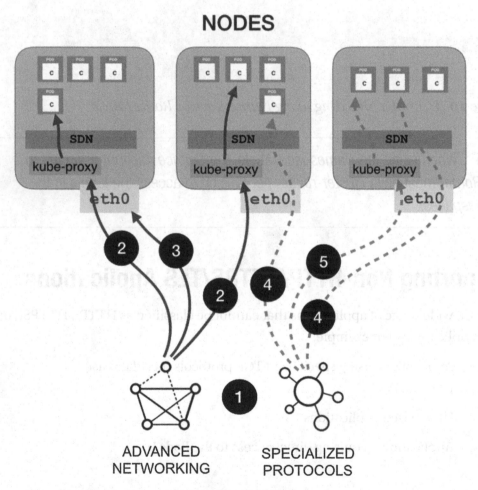

Figure 10-4. Traffic flow for non-http/https traffic

At first sight, both of these objects behave similarly but have a different default or intended purpose.

- **IngressIP**: This IP address is allocated from the *ingressIPNetworkCIDR* (default to 172.29.0.0/16 when not defined) for *Service* type *LoadBalancer*. This *CIDR* should not overlap with other IP ranges used in the Cluster.

- **ExternalIP**: This IP is allocated from a *CIDR* defined by the *externalIPNetworkCIDRs* variable in the `master-config.yaml` (see Figure 10-5). This can be a public IP address range or an organization-level visible and unique network CIDR.

Note   IP Addresses from the *externalIP* CIDR are not managed by *OpenShift*. It is up to the network administrator to make sure the traffic destined to these IP arrives to the *Nodes*.

```
1    vi /etc/origin/master/master-config.yaml
2    ...
3    networkConfig:
4      externalIPNetworkCIDRs:
5      - 198.18.100.0/23
6      - <network_2>/<cidr>
7      - ...
8
9
10   # Restart Master service for changes to get into effect
11   $ master-restart api
12   $ master-restart controllers
```

Figure 10-5. *Defining an externalIPNetworkCIDR*

Creating a service type *LoadBalancer* (see Listing 10-1) gets an ingressIP by default (see Figure 10-6).

Listing 10-1. Creating a Service type LoadBalancer

```
apiVersion: v1
kind: Service
metadata:
  name: pgsql-lb
spec:
  ports:
  - name: pgsql
    port: 5432
  type: LoadBalancer
  selector:
    name: pgsql
```

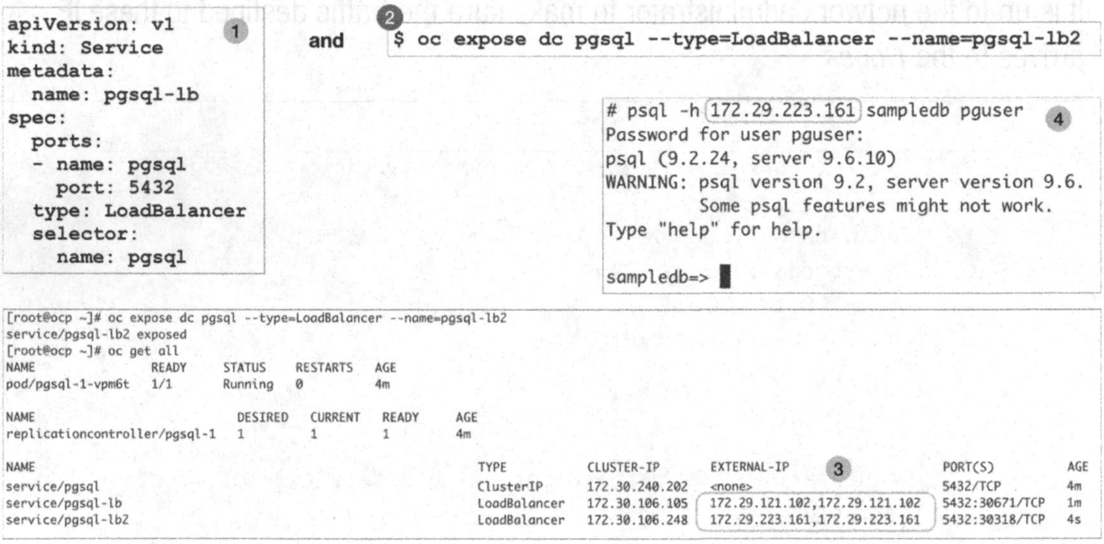

Figure 10-6. *LoadBalancer Service, IngressIP, and ExternalIP*

The *LoadBalancer* resource can be created using a YAML file (see #1 in Figure 10-6) or using the OpenShift client command (see #2 in Figure 10-6). The resulting LoadBalancer object will be assigned an IP from the *ingressIPNetworkCIDR*.

Note   The *CIDR* for `ingressIPNetworkCIDR` can be modified on the `master-config.yaml`.

Assigning an externalIP to a service is achieved by adding it to the spec.externalIPs definitions of the services (see Figure 10-7).

```
[root@ocp ~]# oc get svc
NAME                                                        TYPE           CLUSTER-IP       EXTERNAL-IP                           PORT(S)           AGE
glusterfs-dynamic-22a6a050-7efe-11e9-b815-001a4a160101      ClusterIP      172.30.55.81     <none>                                1/TCP             32m
pgsql                                                       ClusterIP      172.30.240.202   <none>                                5432/TCP          32m
pgsql-lb                                                    LoadBalancer   172.30.106.105   172.29.121.102,172.29.121.102         5432:30671/TCP    30m
pgsql-lb2                                                   LoadBalancer   172.30.106.248   172.29.223.161,172.29.223.161  ①     432:30318/TCP     28m
[root@ocp ~]# oc patch svc pgsql-lb2 -p '{"spec":{"externalIPs":["198.18.101.200"]}}'
service/pgsql-lb2 patched                                                                                    ②
[root@ocp ~]# oc get svc
NAME                                                        TYPE           CLUSTER-IP       EXTERNAL-IP                                    PORT(S)           AGE
glusterfs-dynamic-22a6a050-7efe-11e9-b815-001a4a160101      ClusterIP      172.30.55.81     <none>                                         1/TCP             33m
pgsql                                                       ClusterIP      172.30.240.202   <none>                                         5432/TCP          34m
pgsql-lb                                                    LoadBalancer   172.30.106.105   172.29.121.102,172.29.121.102            ③    5432:30671/TCP    31m
pgsql-lb2                                                   LoadBalancer   172.30.106.248   172.29.223.161,198.18.101.200 172.29.223.161   5432:30318/TCP    30m
[root@ocp ~]# ▌
```

Figure 10-7. *Assigning externalIP to a Service*

Using NodePorts and HostPorts

Another way to bring traffic into the Pods is by using a NodePort or HostPort. These two objects are similar in their behavior with respect to allocating ports in the actual Nodes. The difference is how the Ports are allocated in all Nodes from a range or allocated on the Node where the Pod is running.

- **NodePort**: Will allocate a port from the range 30000–32767 in all Nodes. (Note: It is possible to request a specific port in this range). The NodePort can be allocated for a Service or a specific Pod (see Figure 10-8).

- **HostPort**: Will allocate the specified port in the Node where it is running (see Figure 10-9).

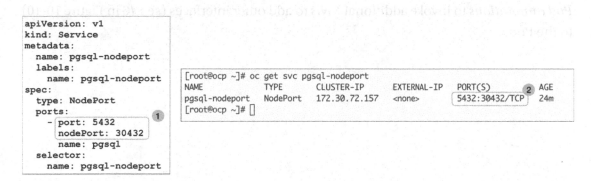

Figure 10-8. *Using NodePort*

```
apiVersion: v1
kind: Pod
metadata:
  name: podcool-hostport
  labels:
    name: podcool-hostport
spec:
  containers:
    - name: podcool-hostport
      image: podcool
      ports:
        - containerPort: 8080
          hostPort: 8080      (1)
```

```
[root@ocp ~]# oc get pod podcool-hostport -o wide
NAME                READY    STATUS    RESTARTS   AGE     IP            NODE                (2)  NOMINATED NODE
podcool-hostport    1/1      Running   0          9m      10.128.2.15   ocp-n3.shift.zone        <none>
[root@ocp ~]# curl ocp-n3.shift.zone:8080/hello  (3)
Hello from podcool-hostport v1-dockerfile
[root@ocp ~]# curl ocp-n2.shift.zone:8080/hello  (4)
curl: (7) Failed connect to ocp-n2.shift.zone:8080; No route to host
[root@ocp ~]# []
```

Figure 10-9. Using HostPort

Multiple NIC per POD

OpenShift 4.1 and later support the ability to provide multiple network interfaces to Pods. This capability is provided by the *Multus CNI*.[4]

Multus CNI is a meta plugin for Kubernetes which enables the creation of multiple network interfaces per *Pod*. Each interface can be using a different CNI plugin.

As seen in Figure 10-9, when *Multus CNI* receives the request for the creation of a new network interface for the *Pod*, it sends that request to the primary Kubernetes CNI (see #4 in Figure 10-10) for the creation of the eth0 interface. In addition, it interprets the *Pod annotations* to invoke additional *CNIs* to add other interfaces (see #6 in Figure 10-10) to the Pod.

---

[4]Additional information on providing multiple network interface to Pods can be found at the OCP 4.1 online documentation: https://docs.openshift.com/container-platform/4.1/ networking/managing-multinetworking.html

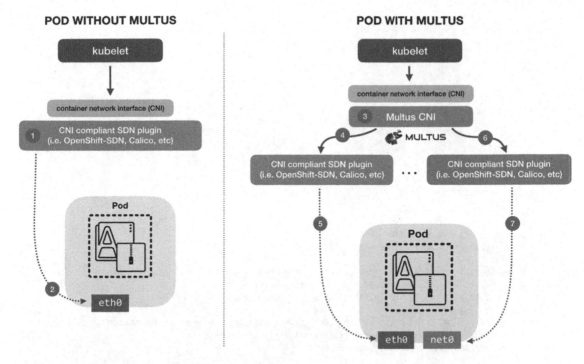

Figure 10-10. *Multus CNI logical diagram*

Multus requires the creation of a `NetworkAttachmentDefinition` defining the additional CNI (see #1 in Figure 10-11). The Pod must be annotated with the additional CNIs to use to provide additional interfaces (see #2 in Figure 10-11). At the Pod level, the new network interface is created (see #4 in Figure 10-11).

```
1   apiVersion: "k8s.cni.cncf.io/v1"
2   kind: NetworkAttachmentDefinition    1
3   metadata:
4     name: my-cni2-conf
5   spec:
6     config: '{
7           "cniVersion": "0.3.0",
8           "type": "macvlan",
9           "master": "eth0",
10          "mode": "bridge",
11          "ipam": {
12              "type": "host-local",
13              "subnet": "192.168.2.0/24",
14              "rangeStart": "192.168.2.10",
15              "rangeEnd": "192.168.2.200",
16              "routes": [
17                  { "dst": "0.0.0.0/0" }
18              ],
19              "gateway": "192.168.2.1"
20          }
21      }'
22
```

```
1   apiVersion: v1
2   kind: Pod
3   metadata:
4     name: podcool-multus
5     annotations:
6   2  k8s.v1.cni.cncf.io/networks: my-cni2-conf
7   spec:
8     containers:
9     - name: podcool-multus
10      image: podcool
11      ports:
12      - containerPort: 8080
13
```

```
1   $ oc exec -ti podcool-multus sh
2   /usr/src/app $ ip addr | grep -A2 "@"    3
3
4   3: eth0@if12: <BROADCAST,MULTICAST,UP,LOWER_UP,M-DOWN> mtu 1450 qdisc noqueue state UP
5       link/ether 0a:58:0a:80:02:0f brd ff:ff:ff:ff:ff:ff
6       inet 10.128.2.15/23 brd 10.128.3.255 scope global eth0
7                4
8   4: net0@if2: <BROADCAST,MULTICAST,UP,LOWER_UP> mtu 1500 qdisc noqueue state UNKNOWN group default
9       link/ether 00:1a:4a:16:01:01 brd ff:ff:ff:ff:ff:ff link-netnsid 0
10      inet 192.168.2.17/24 scope global net0
11
```

Figure 10-11.   Defining NetworkAttachmentDefinition and using Multus CNI

OpenShift ServiceMesh

The OpenShift ServiceMesh is based on the upstream project Maistra.[5] Some of the components of OpenShift ServiceMesh are

- **Istio:** Based on the Istio[6] project; enables the intelligent control of the flow of traffic; enables the authentication, authorization, and encryption of communication between microservices; enforces policies; and enables observability of the communication among the microservices of an application

- **Envoy:** Service proxy used by Istio and based on Envoy Proxy[7] project

---

[5]For more details of the Maistra project, refer to the online documentation at `https://maistra.io/docs/`

[6]Upstream Istio project is available at `https://istio.io`

[7]Upstream Envoy Proxy project is available at `www.envoyproxy.io`

- **Jaeger**: Distributed tracing capability based on the Jaeger[8] project (see #2 in Figure 10-12)

- **Kiali**[9]: Graphical interface integrating the components of OpenShift ServiceMesh (see #1 in Figure 10-12)

- **Grafana**: Used for the Istio mesh dashboards (see #3 and #4 in Figure 10-12)

- **Prometheus**: Used to collect Istio mesh metrics

- **Elasticsearch**: Used as the backend storage for the Istio metrics

---

Note   At the time of this writing, installing OpenShift ServiceMesh[10] in OCP 3.11.x is still considered a *Technology Preview* capability.

Some of the OpenShift ServiceMesh consoles are shown in Figure 10-12.

Figure 10-12. *OpenShift ServiceMesh*

---

[8]Upstream Jaeger project is available at www.jaegertracing.io

[9]Upstream Kiali project is available at www.kiali.io

[10]The instructions for the installation and configuration of the OpenShift Service Mesh are available at the online documentation: https://docs.openshift.com/container-platform/3.11/servicemesh-install/servicemesh-install.html#installing-service-mesh

The main functionality of the OpenShift ServiceMesh requires injecting the Istio sidecar, the Envoy proxy, into the Pod. This requires the proper annotation of the *Deployment* configuration (see #1 in Figure 10-13).

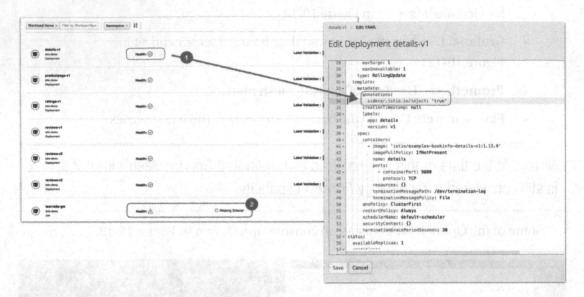

Figure 10-13. *OpenShift ServiceMesh annotations for Istio sidecar*

Once the Istio proxy sidecar is injected into the Pod (see #5 in Figure 10-14), all traffic incoming or outgoing to that Pod goes over the Istio-proxy sidecar container.

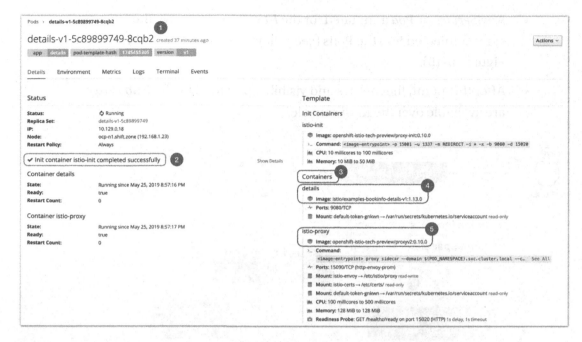

Figure 10-14. *OpenShift ServiceMesh Istio-Proxy sidecar injection*

From the *OpenShift ServiceMesh* perspective, when using *OpenShift Routes* in conjunction with the *Istio Gateway* resources, the traffic flow will be as follows:

- External traffic arrives to the Route (see #1 in Figure 10-15) which points to a *LoadBalancer* type *Service* (see #2 in Figure 10-15).

    - A *LoadBalancer* resource gets allocated an IngressIP and the cluster administrator could also assign an ExternalIP.

- Traffic is then delivered to the *Istio Gateway* on the destination *Project* or *Namespace* as seen in #3 on Figure 10-15.

    - The *Istio Gateway* is considered the edge of the *Mesh* for incoming and outgoing connections. It describes the ports and protocol (HTTP/HTTPS/TCP) it will accept traffic for.

- Traffic accepted at the *Istio Gateway* is forwarded based on the *VirtualService* definition (see #5 on Figure 10-15).

    - The *VirtualService* defines one or more destinations where the traffic should go inside the *ServiceMesh* to reach the actual destination (i.e., a *Service* or *Pod*).

- Any *Service* or *Pod* annotated for the *Istio Proxy* will have the Istio sidecar injected into the Pods (see yellow pentagon shapes in Figure 10-15).

- After this point, the metrics and visibility provided by the *Istio Proxy* are available over the *Kiali* console.

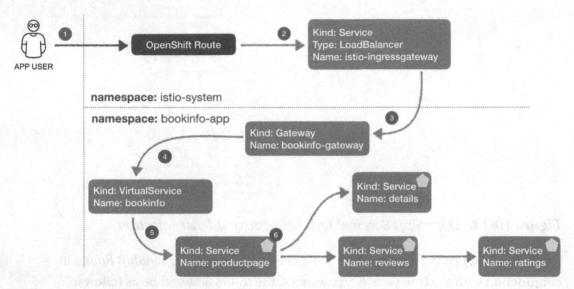

Figure 10-15. *Traffic flow with OpenShift ServiceMesh*

Caution   At the moment of this writing, the Istio-Proxy (Envoy) has limited support for non-TCP traffic. Applications relying on non-TCP protocols should investigate the impact of these limitations to avoid service disruption.

Summary

This chapter covers some of the advanced network optimizations available in the OpenShift Container Platform (OCP). Some of these optimizations, like hardware acceleration, are dependent on the availability of underlying infrastructure supporting the capability. Other optimizations are more in the fine-tuning of configuration attributes to increase performance and scalability of the capability, like the optimizations available for the *OpenShift Routers*.

In addition to the optimization, this chapter describes the use of IngressIP, ExternalIPs, NodePorts, and HostPorts to bring specialized IP protocols to Services and Pods running on the platform.

Finally, the chapter explored advanced functionalities provided by OpenShift Multi-Network capabilities with Multus and the OpenShift ServiceMesh with Istio, Jaeger, and other upstream projects.

Some of the optimizations described in this chapter are intended for OpenShift bare-metal deployments. Chapter 11 provides a glimpse of the installation of OpenShift 4.1 using the User Provisioned Infrastructure (UPI) deployment option. This new OpenShift version provides the support for advanced networking capabilities like the multiple network for Containers using Multus, OpenShift ServiceMesh, and many others.

CHAPTER 11

OCP 4.1 UPI Mode Bare-Metal with PXE Boot Deployment

Some of the advanced networking optimizations discussed in Chapter 10 are intended to be used with bare-metal deployments of OpenShift. Furthermore, some of the capabilities are now included in OpenShift 4.1.[1] This chapter provides supplementary information that goes into the details of an installation of OpenShift 4.1 in bare-metal deployment using the User Provisioned Infrastructure (UPI) mode that was discussed in Chapter 6.

Note   At the time of this writing, the UPI mode is still in beta, but it has been validated to work with bare-metal deployments.

UPI Mode

With the Installer Provisioned Infrastructure (IPI) mode, covered in Chapter 6, the *openshift-installer* takes care of configuring ancillary services like internal and external load balancers, DNS records, and the provisioning of the base Operating System (OS); with the UPI mode, all those ancillary configurations need to be in place before starting the deployment.

---

[1]During the development of this book, Red Hat decided to keep OpenShift 4.0 as a Developer Preview release and instead did the release of OpenShift 4.1 as the first General Availability (GA) release of the 4.x major version.

© William Caban 2019
W. Caban, *Architecting and Operating OpenShift Clusters*, https://doi.org/10.1007/978-1-4842-4985-7_11

The installation of OCP 4.1 with UPI mode varies based on the infrastructure target. For example, using UPI mode in a VMware environment, vs. an AWS environment, vs. Bare-Metal, has different steps. The core prerequisites are the same but the infrastructure-specific requirements will vary.

Bare-Metal with PXE Boot Example

This chapter covers UPI mode for Bare-Metal using PXE Boot for provisioning the OS during the installation. The diagram for the documented deployment is as shown in Figure 11-1.

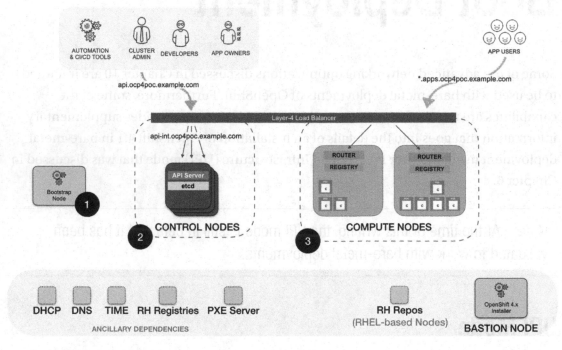

Figure 11-1. *OCP 4.1 UPI standard deployment*

The basic deployment for OCP 4.x is a high availability (HA) configuration with three *Master* or *Control Nodes* and at least two *Workers* or *Compute Nodes*. The Bootstrap Node is only used during the initial deployment of the *Master* or *Control Nodes*. See Table 11-1 for details on the reference environment.

Note   The reference configuration uses `ocp4poc` as the cluster name and `example.com` as the base domain, hence the use of `ocp4poc.example.com` as the domain for the cluster.

Table 11-1. *Reference Environment*

Node Name	IP Address	Mac Address
bootstrap	192.168.1.10	02:01:01:01:01:01
master-0	192.168.1.11	02:00:00:00:01:01
master-1	192.168.1.12	02:00:00:00:01:02
master-2	192.168.1.13	02:00:00:00:01:03
worker-0	192.168.1.15	02:00:00:00:02:01
worker-1	192.168.1.16	02:00:00:00:02:02

UPI Bare-Metal with PXE Boot

There are two ways to install the Red Hat Enterprise Linux CoreOS (RHCOS). One is using an ISO image which then requires manual entry of parameters to load the Ignition configuration files, and the other option is using the PXE Boot install in which case all the Ignition parameters are passed using the PXE APPEND configuration fields.

Prerequisites

The deployment of OpenShift 4.1 using UPI mode with PXE Boot bare-metal has the following prerequisites:

- Designate a cluster name (i.e., cluster name = `ocp4poc`).

- Designate a base domain (i.e., base domain = `example.com`) for the subdomain dedicated to the cluster.

  - The cluster subdomain will be composed of <cluster-name>.<based-domain>.

    - That is, `ocp4poc.example.com`

- Fully resolvable FQDN forward and reverse DNS entries for all the Nodes (including the Bootstrap node).

  - Special *etcd* service entries are required.

  - Special *Kubernetes API* internal and external entries.

- Set up a Load Balancer in pass-through mode for Kubernetes API (tcp/6443), Machine Server Config (tcp/22623), and OpenShift Routers HTTP and HTTPS (tcp/80, tcp/443).

Note   At the moment of this writing, when using UPI mode in bare-metal with PXE Boot, the Red Hat Enterprise Linux CoreOS (RHCOS) uses reverse DNS resolution for assigning the hostname to the Nodes.

DNS Configuration (Example)

Following the reference information from Table 11-1, the corresponding DNS configuration must include the entry layout in Table 11-2.

Table 11-2. *Reference DNS Configuration*

Role	FQDN	
bootstrap	bootstrap.\<cluster_name>.\<base_domain>	192.168.1.10
master-0	master-0.\<cluster_name>.\<base_domain>	192.168.1.11
master-1	master-1.\<cluster_name>.\<base_domain>	192.168.1.12
master-2	master-2.\<cluster_name>.\<base_domain>	192.168.1.13
worker-0	worker-0.\<cluster_name>.\<base_domain>	192.168.1.15
worker-1	worker-1.\<cluster_name>.\<base_domain>	192.168.1.16
Kubernetes API (tcp/6443)	api.\<cluster_name>.\<base_domain>	External Load Balancer for Master Nodes
	api-int.\<cluster_name>.\<base_domain>	Internal Load Balancer for Master Nodes
etcd	etcd-0.\<cluster_name>.\<base_domain>	192.168.1.11

(continued)

Table 11-2. (*continued*)

Role	FQDN	
	etcd-1.<cluster_name>.<base_domain>	192.168.1.12
	etcd-2.<cluster_name>.<base_domain>	192.168.1.13
etcd SRV	etcd-server-ssl._tcp.<cluster_name>.<base_domain>	
	For each Master Node, OpenShift requires a SRV DNS record for etcd server on that machine with priority 0, weight 10, and port 2380.	
Wildcard Subdomain for Apps	*.apps.<cluster_name>.<base_domain>	192.168.1.15, 192.168.1.16

The reference configurations in Listings 11-1 and 11-2 are for the *Bind DNS* server. When using other DNS servers, a similar configuration is required.

Listing 11-1. Forward DNS Record

```
; /var/named/ocp4poc.example.com
$TTL 1D
@   IN SOA   bastion.ocp4poc.example.com.   root.ocp4poc.example.com. (
             2019052001  ; serial
             1D          ; refresh
             2H          ; retry
             1W          ; expiry
             2D )        ; minimum
@             IN NS      bastion.ocp4poc.example.com.
@             IN A       192.168.1.1

; Ancillary services
lb            IN A       192.168.1.200
lb-ex         IN A       10.10.10.10

; Bastion or Jumphost
bastion       IN A       192.168.1.1

; OCP Cluster
bootstrap     IN A       192.168.1.10
```

```
master-0    IN A      192.168.1.11
master-1    IN A      192.168.1.12
master-2    IN A      192.168.1.13

worker-0    IN A      192.168.1.15
worker-1    IN A      192.168.1.16

etcd-0      IN A      192.168.1.11
etcd-1      IN A      192.168.1.12
etcd-2      IN A      192.168.1.13

_etcd-server-ssl._tcp.ocp4poc.example.com.  IN SRV  0   0   2380    etcd-0.
ocp4poc.example.com.

                                             IN SRV  0   0   2380    etcd-1.
ocp4poc.example.com.

                                             IN SRV  0   0   2380    etcd-2.
ocp4poc.example.com.

api         IN CNAME   lb-ext  ; external LB interface
api-int     IN CNAME   lb      ; internal LB interface

apps        IN CNAME   lb-ext
*.apps      IN CNAME   lb-ext
```

Note   The configuration of the etcd server records is required for the OpenShift installation. The api (external VIP pointing to the Control Nodes) and api-int (internal VIP pointing to the Control Nodes) records must exist pointing to the correct VIP.

Listing 11-2. Reverse DNS Record

```
;   /var/named/1.168.192.in-addr.arpa
$TTL 1h
$ORIGIN 1.168.192.IN-ADDR.ARPA.

@   1h  IN SOA  bastion.ocp4poc.example.com.  root.ocp4poc.example.com. (
            2019052901  ; serial
            2H          ; refresh
```

```
15          ; retry
1W          ; expiry
2H )        ; minimum

    IN NS       bastion.ocp4poc.example.com.
```

1	IN PTR	bastion.ocp4poc.example.com.
10	IN PTR	bootstrap.ocp4poc.example.com.
11	IN PTR	master-0.ocp4poc.example.com.
12	IN PTR	master-1.ocp4poc.example.com.
13	IN PTR	master-2.ocp4poc.example.com.
15	IN PTR	worker-0.ocp4poc.example.com.
16	IN PTR	worker-1.ocp4poc.example.com.
100	IN PTR	lb.ocp4poc.example.com.

Load Balancer Configuration (Examples)

The load balancer configuration is divided into external-facing configuration and cluster-facing configuration. The external-facing configuration should resolve to the external IP of the load balancer. The cluster-facing configuration should resolve to the internal IP of the load balancer. All the ports must be configured in pass-through mode. The ports required by OpenShift and that should be configured in the load balancer are listed in Table 11-3.

Table 11-3. Reference Load Balancer Configuration

Service VIP	Backend	Port
Kubernetes API	bootstrap.ocp4poc.example.com:6443	6443
	master-0.ocp4poc.example.com:6443	The entry for the Bootstrap Node should
	master-1.ocp4poc.example.com:6443	be removed after the cluster bootstrap
	master-2.ocp4poc.example.com:6443	installation process is completed
Machine Server	bootstrap.ocp4poc.example.com:22623	22623
	master-0.ocp4poc.example.com:22623	The entry for the Bootstrap Node should
	master-1.ocp4poc.example.com:22623	be removed after the cluster bootstrap
	master-2.ocp4poc.example.com:22623	installation process is completed

(continued)

Table 11-3. (*continued*)

Service VIP	Backend	Port
Ingres HTTP	worker-0.ocp4poc.example.com:80	80
	worker-1.ocp4poc.example.com:80	
	worker-1.ocp4poc.example.com:80	
Ingress HTTPS	worker-0.ocp4poc.example.com:443	443
	worker-1.ocp4poc.example.com:443	
	api-int.<cluster_name>.<base_domain>	Internal Load Balancer for Master Nodes

NGINX and HAProxy are Open Source projects commonly used as load balancers. A reference load balancer configuration using NGINX is presented in Listing 11-3.

Listing 11-3. Load Balancer with NGINX (Example)

```
# ngnix.conf
user nginx;
worker_processes auto;
error_log /var/log/nginx/error.log;
pid /run/nginx.pid;

events {
    worker_connections 1024;
}

# Pass-through
stream {
    upstream ocp4poc-k8s-api {
        # Kubernetes API
        server bootstrap.ocp4poc.example.com:6443;

        server master-0.ocp4poc.example.com:6443;
        server master-1.ocp4poc.example.com:6443;
        server master-2.ocp4poc.example.com:6443;
    }
```

```
upstream ocp4poc-machine-config {
    # Machine-Config
    server bootstrap.ocp4poc.example.com:22623;

    server master-0.ocp4poc.example.com:22623;
    server master-1.ocp4poc.example.com:22623;
    server master-2.ocp4poc.example.com:22623;
}

server {
    listen 6443;
    proxy_pass ocp4poc-k8s-api;
}

server {
    listen 22623 ;
    proxy_pass ocp4poc-machine-config;

}


# Passthrough required for the routers
upstream ocp4poc-http {
    # Worker Nodes running OCP Router
    server worker-0.ocp4poc.example.com:80;
    server worker-1.ocp4poc.example.com:80;
}
upstream ocp4poc-https {
    # Worker Nodes running OCP Router
    server worker-0.ocp4poc.example.com:443;
    server worker-1.ocp4poc.example.com:443;
}
server {
    listen 443;
    proxy_pass ocp4poc-http;
}
```

```
    server {
        listen 80 ;
        proxy_pass ocp4poc-https;

    }
}
```

A reference load balancer configuration using HAProxy is presented in Listing 11-4.

Listing 11-4. Load Balancer with HAProxy (Example)

```
# haproxy.cfg
defaults
    mode                    http
    log                     global
    option                  httplog
    option                  dontlognull
    option forwardfor       except 127.0.0.0/8
    option                  redispatch
    retries                 3
    timeout http-request    10s
    timeout queue           1m
    timeout connect         10s
    timeout client          300s
    timeout server          300s
    timeout http-keep-alive 10s
    timeout check           10s
    maxconn                 20000

frontend openshift-api-server
    bind *:6443
    default_backend openshift-api-server
    mode tcp
    option tcplog
backend openshift-api-server
    balance source
    mode tcp
```

```
      server bootstrap 192.168.1.10:6443 check
      server master-0 192.168.1.11:6443 check
      server master-1 192.168.1.12:6443 check
      server master-2 192.168.1.13:6443 check

frontend machine-config-server
    bind *:22623
    default_backend machine-config-server
    mode tcp
    option tcplog

backend machine-config-server
    balance source
    mode tcp
    server bootstrap 192.168.1.10:22623 check
    server master-0 192.168.1.11:22623 check
    server master-1 192.168.1.12:22623 check
    server master-2 192.168.1.13:22623 check

frontend ingress-http
    bind *:8080
    default_backend ingress-http
    mode tcp
    option tcplog

backend ingress-http
    balance source
    mode tcp
    server worker-0 192.168.1.15:80 check
    server worker-1 192.168.1.15:80 check

frontend ingress-https
    bind *:8443
    default_backend ingress-https
    mode tcp
    option tcplog
```

```
backend ingress-https
    balance source
    mode tcp
    server worker-0 192.168.1.15:443 check
    server worker-1 192.168.1.15:443 check
```

DHCP with PXE Boot Configuration (Example)

Listing 11-5 is a reference configuration of DHCP using *DNSmasq*, sending the PXE Boot server information to the Nodes.

Listing 11-5. DHCP for PXE Boot with DNSmasq

```
# OCP4 PXE BOOT Lab
### dnsmasq configurations
# disable DNS /etc/dnsmasq.conf set port=0
#
no-dhcp-interface=eth0
interface=eth1

#domain=ocp4poc.example.com

#### DHCP (dnsmasq --help dhcp)
dhcp-range=eth1,192.168.1.10,192.168.1.200,24h
dhcp-option=option:netmask,255.255.255.0
dhcp-option=option:router,192.168.1.1
dhcp-option=option:dns-server,192.168.1.1
dhcp-option=option:ntp-server,204.11.201.10

# Bootstrap
dhcp-host=02:01:01:01:01:01,192.168.1.10

# master-0, master-1, master-2
dhcp-host=02:00:00:00:01:01,192.168.1.11
dhcp-host=02:00:00:00:01:02,192.168.1.12
dhcp-host=02:00:00:00:01:03,192.168.1.13

# worker-0, worker-1
dhcp-host=02:00:00:00:02:01,192.168.1.15
dhcp-host=02:00:00:00:02:01,192.168.1.16
```

```
#### PXE
enable-tftp
tftp-root=/var/lib/tftpboot,eth1
dhcp-boot=pxelinux.0
```

PXE Boot Configuration (Example)

Listing 11-6 is a reference configuration of using DNSmasq as the PXE Boot server.

Listing 11-6. DNSmasq as PXE Boot Server

```
UI vesamenu.c32
DEFAULT LOCAL
PROMPT 0
TIMEOUT 200
ONTIMEOUT LOCAL

MENU TITLE PXE BOOT MENU

LABEL WORKER-BIOS
  MENU LABEL ^1 WORKER (BIOS)
  KERNEL rhcos/rhcos-kernel
  APPEND rd.neednet=1 initrd=rhcos/rhcos-initramfs.img console=tty0
coreos.inst=yes coreos.inst.install_dev=sda coreos.inst.
ignition_url=http://192.168.1.1:8000/worker.ign coreos.inst.image_
url=http://192.168.1.1:8000/metal/rhcos-410.8.20190516.0-metal-bios.raw.gz
ip=eth1:dhcp

LABEL MASTER-BIOS
  MENU LABEL ^2 MASTER (BIOS)
  KERNEL rhcos/rhcos-kernel
  APPEND rd.neednet=1 initrd=rhcos/rhcos-initramfs.img console=tty0
coreos.inst=yes coreos.inst.install_dev=sda coreos.inst.
ignition_url=http://192.168.1.1:8000/master.ign coreos.inst.image_
url=http://192.168.1.1:8000/metal/rhcos-410.8.20190516.0-metal-bios.raw.gz
ip=eth1:dhcp
```

```
LABEL BOOTSTRAP-BIOS
  MENU LABEL ^3 BOOTSTRAP (BIOS)
  KERNEL rhcos/rhcos-kernel
  APPEND rd.neednet=1 initrd=rhcos/rhcos-initramfs.img console=tty0
coreos.inst=yes coreos.inst.install_dev=sda coreos.inst.ignition_
url=http://192.168.1.1:8000/bootstrap.ign coreos.inst.image_
url=http://192.168.1.1:8000/metal/rhcos-410.8.20190516.0-metal-bios.raw.gz
ip=eth1:dhcp

LABEL LOCAL
  MENU LABEL ^7 Boot from Local Disk
  MENU DEFAULT
  LOCALBOOT 0

LABEL RECOVERY1
  MENU LABEL ^8 Recovery (initqueue)
  KERNEL rhcos/rhcos-kernel
  APPEND rd.break=initqueue  rd.neednet=1 initrd=rhcos/rhcos-initramfs.img
console=tty0 ip=eth1:dhcp

LABEL RECOVERY2
  MENU LABEL ^9 Recovery (pre-mount)
  KERNEL rhcos/rhcos-kernel
  APPEND rd.break=pre-mount  rd.neednet=1 initrd=rhcos/rhcos-initramfs.img
console=tty0 ip=eth1:dhcp
```

Preparing the Installation

The bare-metal deployment of OpenShift 4.1 using UPI mode with PXE Boot requires special attention to the hardware configuration in use, especially the BIOS configuration and NIC interface configured for the PXE Boot.

Note   The examples in this chapter use a Bastion Node in the same network as the Cluster Nodes, but this is not strictly necessary. They can be on different networks as long as the reachability exists.

Considerations with UPI Mode with PXE Boot

At the time of this writing, there are several considerations to have when using UPI Mode with PXE Boot:

- When using a physical server with multiple NICs

    - The PXE APPEND command **must specify** the exact NIC to use during the PXE boot. For example, use a syntax similar to ip=eth2:dhcp and NOT a generic DHCP entry like ip=dhcp.

    - If the PXE APPEND uses the ip=dhcp, the DNS information from the **last** NIC to come up will be used as the entry for /etc/resolv.conf.

    - If the **last** NIC to come up has a self-assigned IP and does not receive a DNS, the resulting /etc/resolv.conf will be empty. When this happens, the *Node* will attempt to use the localhost [::1] as the DNS and the installation will fail. To work around this, during the installation

        - When possible, avoid having NICs with active link that are not receiving valid IPs.

        - Pass the nameserver=<nameserver_ip> with the PXE APPEND command.

    - When the server has many NICs, it is possible for the NetworkManager-wait-online.service to time out before the DHCP request over each NIC timeout. When this happens, a cascaded failure may be triggered. To avoid this situation, a recommended patch is to increase the timeout of this *NetworkManager* service and avoid the situation.

- At the time of this writing, using the PXE APPEND to disable IPv6 using the ipv6.disable is not supported.

- When customizing Ignition files to write custom files or configurations in the Node, the permissions must be specified in OCTAL mode (i.e., 384), NOT in DECIMAL mode (i.e., 600).

- If there is no valid reverse DNS resolution during the installation, the Masters (and all the Nodes) will register as `localhost.localdomain` into the *Kubernetes etcd*. When this happens, *Kubernetes* will fail to identify the existence of multiple masters and the installation process will fail.

Downloading RHCOS and Installation Binaries

The installation requires the download of the Red Hat Enterprise Linux CoreOS (RHCOS) corresponding to the 4.1 version, the OpenShift 4.1 client, and the OCP 4.1 openshift-installer. These are available from the corresponding mirror repositories:

- Obtain the latest RHCOS images from `https://mirror.openshift.com/pub/openshift-v4/dependencies/rhcos/4.1/latest/`

- Obtain the latest OpenShift client and installer binaries from `https://mirror.openshift.com/pub/openshift-v4/clients/ocp/`

For the UPI mode using PXE Boot, the required images are as shown in Figure 11-2 (the specific subrelease and release will be different after GA).

```
images/
├── openshift-client-linux-4.1.0-rc.7.tar.gz
├── openshift-install-linux-4.1.0-rc.7.tar.gz
├── rhcos-410.8.20190516.0-installer-initramfs.img
├── rhcos-410.8.20190516.0-installer-kernel
├── rhcos-410.8.20190516.0-metal-bios.raw.gz
└── rhcos-410.8.20190516.0-metal-uefi.raw.gz
```

Figure 11-2. RHCOS and OCP 4.1 installation binaries (example)

Preparing the PXE Boot Images

Copy the RHCOS PXE Boot images to the PXE server similar to #1 on Figure 11-3. Copy the RHCOS Operating System Images to the web server to be used by the PXE installation similar to #2 on Figure 11-3.

```
# RHCOS PXE Boot Images    1
mkdir /var/lib/tftpboot/rhcos
cp ./images/rhcos-410.8.20190516.0-installer-initramfs.img /var/lib/tftpboot/rhcos/rhcos-initramfs.img
cp ./images/rhcos-410.8.20190516.0-installer-kernel /var/lib/tftpboot/rhcos/rhcos-kernel

# RHCOS OS Images    2
mkdir /usr/share/nginx/html/metal/
cp -f ./images/rhcos-410.8.20190516.0-metal-bios.raw.gz /usr/share/nginx/html/metal/
cp -f ./images/rhcos-410.8.20190516.0-metal-uefi.raw.gz /usr/share/nginx/html/metal/
```

Figure 11-3. *Installing RHCOS PXE Boot and OS Images*

Installation

At high level, the installation process consists of creating the *install-config.yaml* configuration, generating the Ignition files, and using those Ignition configurations to bootstrap the cluster.

Any customization required for the initial installation of the cluster must be done to those Ignition files. There are three initial Ignition files:

- **bootstrap.ign**: This Ignition file contains all the information the Bootstrap Node will use to render the cluster configuration and generate the *MachineConfig* configuration files for the Master Nodes.

- **master.ign**: This is the Ignition file the Master Nodes will use to install the RHCOS image into the bare-metal server. It also contains the information on how to obtain the Master Node configuration from the Bootstrap Node.

- **worker.ign**: This is the Ignition file the Worker Nodes will use to install the RHCOS image into the bare-metal server. It also contains the information on how to obtain the Worker Node configuration from the Master Nodes.

The discovery of the Kubernetes API to retrieve the state of the deployment process, the discovery of the API to retrieve the configuration for the Nodes, the discovery of the etcd database, and other access required by the Ignition process are highly dependent on the existence of the specific DNS entries discussed previously in this chapter.

Creating the Configuration

The OpenShift 4.1 installer UPI mode requires the creation of the install-config.yaml file which will be used to generate the Ignition files (Listing 11-7).

Listing 11-7. Sample install-config.yaml

```
apiVersion: v1
baseDomain: example.com
compute:
- hyperthreading: Enabled
  name: worker
  replicas: 0
controlPlane:
  hyperthreading: Enabled
  name: master
  replicas: 3
metadata:
  name: ocp4poc
networking:
  clusterNetworks:
  - cidr: 10.128.0.0/14
    hostPrefix: 23
  networkType: OpenShiftSDN
  serviceNetwork:
  - 172.30.0.0/16
platform:
  none: {}
pullSecret: '{"auths": ...}'
sshKey: 'ssh-ed25519 AAAA...'
```

The pullSecret must be obtained from https://try.openshift.com. The SSH key is the public SSH key from the key pair that is going to be used by the administration during the installation.

Generating the Ignition Files

Create a folder for the installation, copy the `install-config.yaml` file into it, and proceed to generate the Ignition files, as shown in Figure 11-4.

```
# Creating installation folder
mkdir ocp4poc

# Copy installation configuration
cp ./install-config.yaml ocp4poc

# Generating Ignition files
./openshift-install create ignition-configs --dir=ocp4poc
```

Figure 11-4. *Generating Ignition files*

When using UPI PXE Boot with a system with multiple NIC, it is recommended to increase the timeout of the `NetworkManager-wait-online.service` (see Listing 11-8).

Listing 11-8. Increase Network Manager timeout patch

```
{
"systemd": {
    "units": [
    {
      "name": "NetworkManager-wait-online.service",
      "dropins": [{
        "name": "timeout.conf",
        "contents": "[Service]\nExecStart=\nExecStart=/usr/bin/nm-online -s
        -q --timeout=300"
      }]
    }
    ]
  }
}
```

By default, OCP 4.1 UPI only creates a local user in the Bootstrap Node. There is no local user in Master and Worker Nodes. To create a local user, follow Listing 11-9.

Listing 11-9. Adding local user

```
{
 "passwd": {
    "users": [
      {
        "name": "core",
        "sshAuthorizedKeys": [
          "ssh-rsa ...."
        ]
      }
    ]
  }
}
```

The patches from Listings 11-8 and 11-9 must be merged with the original Ignition file of the corresponding Node.

Note   At the moment of this writing, OpenShift does not provide a tool to edit the Ignition files and apply customization. Currently the administrator must rely on third-party tools to edit and merge the corresponding JSON files.

Copy the resulting Ignition files to the web server that will be used by the PXE Boot process—for example, `cp -f ./ocp4poc/*.ign /usr/share/nginx/html/`

Bootstrap and Master Nodes

The first Node to be installed is the Bootstrap Node. When using the PXE configuration from Listing 11-6, the PXE Boot menu will be similar to Figure 11-5.

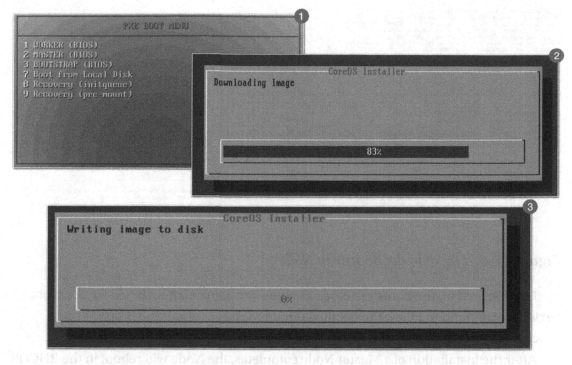

Figure 11-5. *PXE Boot menu (example)*

Select the Bootstrap from the menu and it will proceed with the installation of RHCOS.

Once the RHCOS installation of Bootstrap Node completes, it will reboot. After the Bootstrap is running, proceed to install RHCOS in the three Masters.

It is possible to use the ./openshift-install wait-for bootstrap-complete --dir=ocp4poc --log-level debug command to have a high-level overview of the progress of the Bootstrap process of the Master Nodes. For more granular view of the progress, log in to the Bootstrap Node using the "core" user and the SSH key provided in the install-config.yaml (see #1 on Figure 11-6).

```
[root@jumphost ocp4]# slogin core@192.168.1.10
The authenticity of host '192.168.1.10 (192.168.1.10)' can't be established.
ECDSA key fingerprint is SHA256:In5yVHSmjg1mIMUhJvHJ7sN5EWHod4Umr08Zmn3DYsM.
ECDSA key fingerprint is MD5:61:2c:fd:b7:d9:ed:39:71:e1:dd:10:d1:8a:d6:1c:87.
Are you sure you want to continue connecting (yes/no)? yes
Warning: Permanently added '192.168.1.10' (ECDSA) to the list of known hosts.
Red Hat Enterprise Linux CoreOS 410.8.20190516.0
WARNING: Direct SSH access to machines is not recommended.
This node has been annotated with machineconfiguration.openshift.io/ssh=accessed

---
This is the bootstrap node; it will be destroyed when the master is fully up.

The primary service is "bootkube.service". To watch its status, run e.g.

   journalctl -b -f -u bootkube.service
[core@bootstrap ~]$ journalctl -b -f -u bootkube.service                                                     ②
-- Logs begin at Fri 2019-05-31 18:25:23 UTC. --
May 31 18:27:49 bootstrap.ocp4poc.example.com bootkube.sh[3617]: I0531 18:27:49.498303    1 bootstrap.go:86] Version: 4.1.0-201905191700-dirty (a3a9a27ddff494b5735992a564b238ccae7564e2)
May 31 18:27:49 bootstrap.ocp4poc.example.com bootkube.sh[3617]: I0531 18:27:49.500290    1 bootstrap.go:141] manifests/machineconfigcontroller/controllerconfig.yaml
May 31 18:27:49 bootstrap.ocp4poc.example.com bootkube.sh[3617]: I0531 18:27:49.502203    1 bootstrap.go:141] manifests/master.machineconfigpool.yaml
May 31 18:27:49 bootstrap.ocp4poc.example.com bootkube.sh[3617]: I0531 18:27:49.502412    1 bootstrap.go:141] manifests/worker.machineconfigpool.yaml
May 31 18:27:49 bootstrap.ocp4poc.example.com bootkube.sh[3617]: I0531 18:27:49.502584    1 bootstrap.go:141] manifests/bootstrap-pod-v2.yaml
May 31 18:27:49 bootstrap.ocp4poc.example.com bootkube.sh[3617]: I0531 18:27:49.502900    1 bootstrap.go:141] manifests/machineconfigserver/csr-bootstrap-role-binding.yaml
May 31 18:27:49 bootstrap.ocp4poc.example.com bootkube.sh[3617]: I0531 18:27:49.503169    1 bootstrap.go:141] manifests/machineconfigserver/kube-apiserver-serving-ca-configmap.yaml
May 31 18:27:49 bootstrap.ocp4poc.example.com bootkube.sh[3617]: Starting etcd certificate signer...
May 31 18:27:52 bootstrap.ocp4poc.example.com bootkube.sh[3617]: 8b86e511eb863ae674423a40c0272b7aae2f307dc8ed291d46a100800afa5db1
May 31 18:27:52 bootstrap.ocp4poc.example.com bootkube.sh[3617]: Waiting for etcd cluster...
May 31 18:37:54 bootstrap.ocp4poc.example.com bootkube.sh[3617]: https://etcd-0.ocp4poc.example.com:2379 is unhealthy: failed to connect: dial tcp 192.168.1.11:2379: connect: no route to host
May 31 18:37:54 bootstrap.ocp4poc.example.com bootkube.sh[3617]: https://etcd-2.ocp4poc.example.com:2379 is unhealthy: failed to connect: context deadline exceeded
May 31 18:37:54 bootstrap.ocp4poc.example.com bootkube.sh[3617]: https://etcd-1.ocp4poc.example.com:2379 is unhealthy: failed to connect: dial tcp 192.168.1.12:2379: connect: no route to host
May 31 18:37:54 bootstrap.ocp4poc.example.com bootkube.sh[3617]: Error: unhealthy cluster
May 31 18:37:54 bootstrap.ocp4poc.example.com bootkube.sh[3617]: etcdctl failed. Retrying in 5 seconds...                                                                                    ③
```

***Figure 11-6.** Log in to the Bootstrap Node*

Once logged in, the Bootstrap Node executes the `journalctl -b -f -u bootkube.service` command to follow the detailed output messages about the progress of the process (see #2 and #3 in Figure 11-6).

After the installation of a Master Node completes, the Node will reboot in the RHCOS version used for the installation (see #1 on Figure 11-7). At this point, the Master requests the Machine Configuration rendered by the Cluster Version Operator running in the Bootstrap Node (see #2 on Figure 11-7). This will instruct the Node into downloading and applying the latest RHCOS (see #3 on Figure 11-7) and to start downloading and running the services corresponding to the Master Node.

Figure 11-7. *Master Node Boot and Upgrade*

Once the three Master Nodes are fully operational, the `openshift-install wait-for bootstrap` command will notify the Bootstrap Node has completed its job and it is time to shut down the Bootstrap Node (see #1 in Figure 11-8).

Note   At this point, it is safe to remove the Bootstrap Node from the Load Balancer configuration.

The log message from the Bootstrap Node will also indicate the Bootstrap process has been completed (see #2 on Figure 11-8).

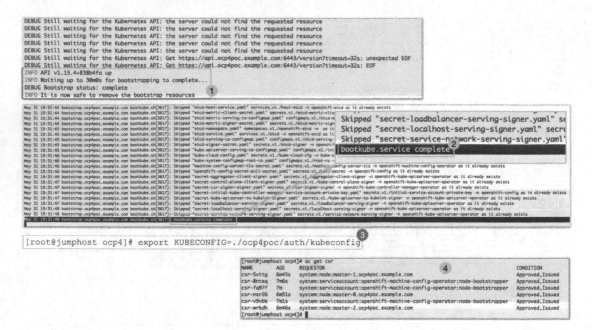

Figure 11-8. Bootstrap complete

During the bootstrap process, the *Bootstrap Node* takes care of signing the certificate requests from the *Masters* so they can become a single cluster (see #3 and #4 on Figure 11-8). After this point, adding workers or any other *Node* into the cluster requires for the cluster administrator to manually accept the *Certificate Signing Requests (CSR)* from the new *Nodes*.

After the *Bootstrap Node* has completed its purpose, the etcd and Kubernetes APIs are online, but the installation of the OpenShift Master Nodes is still in progress. To monitor this progress, use the command `./openshift-install wait-for install-complete --dir=ocp4poc --log-level debug`

Worker Nodes

Once the *Bootstrap Node* has been removed from the cluster, it is possible to install and onboard the *Worker Nodes*.

Note   Even when the installation of the *OpenShift Master Nodes* is still in progress, the successful completion of the OCP cluster installation requires at least two Worker Nodes to be online and be part of the cluster.

Boot and install RHCOS in the *Worker Nodes* using the same PXE Boot menu as before. This time, select the *Worker* option. The installation will be similar as with the Master Nodes. This time the Master Nodes are the ones providing the Machine Configuration to the Worker Nodes. For a Worker to start this process, it generates a Certificate Signing Request (CSR) for a node-bootstrapper Service Account which needs to be accepted by the cluster administrator (see #1 and #2 on Figure 11-9). Then it generates a system Node account CSR which needs to be approved for the Worker to join the cluster (see #3 and #4 on Figure 11-9).

```
[root@jumphost ocp4]# oc get csr
NAME       AGE   REQUESTOR                                                                        CONDITION
csr-5vttg  15m   system:node:master-1.ocp4poc.example.com                                         Approved,Issued
csr-8ntsq  15m   system:serviceaccount:openshift-machine-config-operator:node-bootstrapper        Approved,Issued
csr-fq97f  15m   system:serviceaccount:openshift-machine-config-operator:node-bootstrapper        Approved,Issued
csr-g5qqn  27s   system:serviceaccount:openshift-machine-config-operator:node-bootstrapper        Pending  1
csr-nzr26  15m   system:node:master-0.ocp4poc.example.com                                         Approved,Issued
csr-v9vbk  15m   system:serviceaccount:openshift-machine-config-operator:node-bootstrapper        Approved,Issued
csr-wrkdh  15m   system:node:master-2.ocp4poc.example.com                                         Approved,Issued
csr-zk9vr  22s   system:serviceaccount:openshift-machine-config-operator:node-bootstrapper        Pending  1
[root@jumphost ocp4]# oc adm certificate approve csr-g5qqn csr-zk9vr
certificatesigningrequest.certificates.k8s.io/csr-g5qqn approved
certificatesigningrequest.certificates.k8s.io/csr-zk9vr approved  2
[root@jumphost ocp4]#
```

```
[root@jumphost ocp4]# oc get csr
NAME       AGE    REQUESTOR                                                                        CONDITION
csr-5vttg  16m    system:node:master-1.ocp4poc.example.com                                         Approved,Issued
csr-8ntsq  16m    system:serviceaccount:openshift-machine-config-operator:node-bootstrapper        Approved,Issued
csr-bbd5g  8s     system:node:worker-0.ocp4poc.example.com                                         Pending  3
csr-fq97f  16m    system:serviceaccount:openshift-machine-config-operator:node-bootstrapper        Approved,Issued
csr-g5qqn  115s   system:serviceaccount:openshift-machine-config-operator:node-bootstrapper        Approved,Issued
csr-nzr26  16m    system:node:master-0.ocp4poc.example.com                                         Approved,Issued
csr-tbc7w  4s     system:node:worker-1.ocp4poc.example.com                                         Pending  3
csr-v9vbk  16m    system:serviceaccount:openshift-machine-config-operator:node-bootstrapper        Approved,Issued
csr-wrkdh  16m    system:node:master-2.ocp4poc.example.com                                         Approved,Issued
csr-zk9vr  110s   system:serviceaccount:openshift-machine-config-operator:node-bootstrapper        Approved,Issued
[root@jumphost ocp4]# oc adm certificate approve csr-bbd5g csr-tbc7w
certificatesigningrequest.certificates.k8s.io/csr-bbd5g approved
certificatesigningrequest.certificates.k8s.io/csr-tbc7w approved  4
[root@jumphost ocp4]#
```

Figure 11-9. *OCP CSR signing*

During this process, the Worker Nodes go over a RHCOS upgrade process and receive information on which containers to download and which services to bring online.

With all the Master and Worker Nodes online (see #1 on Figure 11-10), the installation will continue but will not complete to 100% until persistent storage is assigned to the Image Registry (see #3 on Figure 11-10).

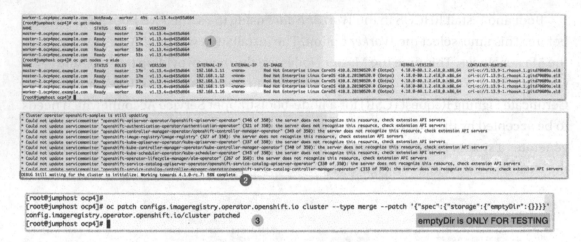

Figure 11-10. Installation progress and Image Registry

Note   Persistent storage for the *Image Registry* should NOT be ephemeral in nature (like *emptyDir*) as images may be lost during a reboot of the Node hosting the registry. This type of ephemeral storage may only be used during testing or in nonproduction environments.

Once the installation is successfully completed, all the Cluster Operators should be shown as available (see Figure 11-11).

```
[root@jumphost ocp4]# oc get co
NAME                                    VERSION      AVAILABLE  PROGRESSING  DEGRADED  SINCE
authentication                          4.1.0-rc.7   True       False        False     40m
cloud-credential                        4.1.0-rc.7   True       False        False     63m
cluster-autoscaler                      4.1.0-rc.7   True       False        False     64m
console                                 4.1.0-rc.7   True       False        False     43m
dns                                     4.1.0-rc.7   True       False        False     63m
image-registry                          4.1.0-rc.7   True       False        False     22s
ingress                                 4.1.0-rc.7   True       False        False     47m
kube-apiserver                          4.1.0-rc.7   True       True         False     61m
kube-controller-manager                 4.1.0-rc.7   True       False        False     61m
kube-scheduler                          4.1.0-rc.7   True       False        False     61m
machine-api                             4.1.0-rc.7   True       False        False     63m
machine-config                          4.1.0-rc.7   True       False        False     63m
marketplace                             4.1.0-rc.7   True       False        False     58m
monitoring                              4.1.0-rc.7   True       False        False     45m
network                                 4.1.0-rc.7   True       False        False     64m
node-tuning                             4.1.0-rc.7   True       False        False     60m
openshift-apiserver                     4.1.0-rc.7   True       False        False     59m
openshift-controller-manager            4.1.0-rc.7   True       False        False     61m
openshift-samples                       4.1.0-rc.7   True       False        False     47m
operator-lifecycle-manager              4.1.0-rc.7   True       False        False     63m
operator-lifecycle-manager-catalog      4.1.0-rc.7   True       False        False     63m
service-ca                              4.1.0-rc.7   True       False        False     64m
service-catalog-apiserver               4.1.0-rc.7   True       False        False     60m
service-catalog-controller-manager      4.1.0-rc.7   True       False        False     60m
storage                                 4.1.0-rc.7   True       False        False     58m
[root@jumphost ocp4]#
```

Figure 11-11. *Cluster Operators running after successful installation*

The OpenShift console (see Figure 11-12) for the new environment will be available at `https://console-openshift-console.apps.<cluster-name>.<base-domain>`.

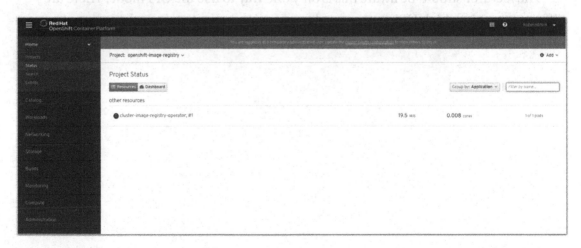

Figure 11-12. *The OpenShift 4.1 Console*

After the installation is completed, the system will have created the following Routes:

- `https://console-openshift-console.apps.ocp4poc.example.com`—default URL for the OpenShift console

- `https://oauth-openshift.apps.ocp4poc.example.com`

- `https://downloads-openshift-console.apps.ocp4poc.example.com`

- `https://alertmanager-main-openshift-monitoring.apps.ocp4poc.example.com`

- `https://grafana-openshift-monitoring.apps.ocp4poc.example.com`

- `https://prometheus-k8s-openshift-monitoring.apps.ocp4poc.example.com`

Summary

As seen in this chapter, the use of OpenShift User Provisioned Infrastructure (UPI) mode for Bare-Metal deployment may provide a way for organizations looking to retain control of the physical infrastructure while benefiting of a modern platform capable of auto-upgrade itself to the latest code.

The lecturer should be aware this is only one way to use the UPI mode. There are different ways in which UPI may be used to provision bare-metal or other types of infrastructures.

Index

A

Ansible service broker (ASB), 128

Application nodes/Pods, 100

B

BuildConfig, 197
  creation
    Jenkinsfile, Git, 199, 201
    sample Jenkinsfile, 200, 201
  deployment
    access logs, 206
    Jenkins Console, 206, 207
    Jenkins Master, 203, 204
    manual trigger, 204, 205
    new pipeline, 202, 203
    pipeline history, 205
    YAML, import, 202

C

Certificate signing request (CSR), 276, 277
CI/CD pipelines
  external integration, 220
  grant edit access, 196, 197
  Jenkins Master, 195
  Jenkins-persistent template, 196
Cluster Monitoring, 125
Container network interface (CNI), 7, 72
Container runtime, 77

Container runtime interface (CRI), 8

Containers, 77

Container storage interface (CSI), 7, 84,
    87, 88

D

Day-2 operations
  garbage collection, 224
  leftover objects
    cluster administrator, 222
    prune command, 223
    storage, consume, 221, 222
Default cluster roles, 173
DriveScale composable platform, 95

E

East-west traffic
  Calico SDN CN, 71–73
  Openshift SDN
    cluster network subnet
      allocation, 58
    flannel, 69, 70
    node, 59
    ovs-multitenant plugin, 63, 64
    ovs-networkpolicy plugin, 65–68
    ovs-subnet plugin, 62, 63
    routes, 61
    tun0 interface, 60

© William Caban 2019
W. Caban, *Architecting and Operating OpenShift Clusters*, https://doi.org/10.1007/978-1-4842-4985-7

Printed in the United States
By Bookmasters

Printed in the United States
By Bookmasters